John Cowper Powys
Old Earth-Man

H. P. COLLINS

John Cowper Powys

Old Earth-Man

Ex Umbris et Imaginibus
in Veritatem

166

BARRIE AND ROCKLIFF
LONDON

First published 1966 by
Barrie & Rockliff (Barrie Books Ltd.)
2 Clement's Inn, London, W.C.2.

Printed in Great Britain by
Northumberland Press Limited
Gateshead

TO
PHYLLIS JOY

CONTENTS

Preface

WHEN this book was put in hand John Cowper Powys was
alive and, with one exception, in a class of his own among our
more serious living novelists. He was also rather neglected—
the more surprisingly since the *Autobiography* is as fascinating
in its humours as it is great. But since his death interest has
quickened considerably. Though perhaps not the most shapely
of artists, he is probably the *largest* writer of our day; and
unsurpassed in integrity as in elemental poetry. He has maybe
suffered a little, as did Emily Brontë (that other great elemental) from being one of a famous family. I have tried to disentangle him. I feel that the good work has been greatly
advanced by Professor Wilson Knight's weighty analysis or
'chart', a little book (of a very different purpose) which has
just preceded this of mine.

I hope that nobody will be puzzled by the adoption of
Merezhkowsky's unforgettable characterisation of Tolstoy as
the sub-title of a book in which I attempt to draw, in non-
mystical terms, the essential John Cowper Powys. I can think
of no other sub-title so apposite and I feel sure that readers
will not find it belies the 'image' of John Cowper, at least as
I have understood him. At first blush it may indeed seem
that the two great creators of life have little in common save
a colossal brain and an uneasy conscience. But in pondering
their massive self-revelations I have become convinced—equally
of both of them—that the longer they strove to escape from
elemental things the more deeply they showed themselves to
be compounded of them.

I am indebted to the John Cowper Powys Estate and their
representative Laurence Pollinger Ltd and to Messrs Macdonald & Co. (Publishers) Ltd for so graciously allowing me to

quote from his works. I should like to express my warm acknowledgements to all who have given me kind assistance in various ways, especially Professor G. Wilson Knight, Mr. Harry Coombes, Mr. Gilbert Turner, Mr. Louis Wilkinson, Mr. Derek Langridge, Mr. Frances Powys and Mrs. June Mosdell.

For the life of John Cowper I have drawn chiefly on his *Autobiography*; C. Bragdon's *The Hidden Springs*; the autobiographical writings of Llewelyn Powys; *Welsh Ambassadors* by Louis Marlow (Wilkinson); the *Letters* of Llewelyn Powys and his *Life* by Malcolm Elwin; *The Joy of It* and *Still the Joy of It* by Littleton Powys; and the *Letters of John Cowper Powys to Louis Wilkinson*.

London, 1965.   H.P.C.

THE MORE IMPORTANT BOOKS OF
JOHN COWPER POWYS

Wood and Stone (Heinemann) 1917
Rodmoor (U.S.A. only) 1917
Ducdame (Richards) 1926
*Wolf Solent (Cape) 1929
The Meaning of Culture (Cape) 1930
*A Glastonbury Romance (Bodley Head) 1933
Autobiography (Bodley Head) 1934
*Jobber Skald, later Weymouth Sands (Bodley Head) 1935
*Maiden Castle (Cassell) 1937
The Pleasures of Literature (Cassell) 1938
Owen Glendower (Bodley Head) 1942
Dostoievsky (Bodley Head) 1947
Obstinate Cymric (Druid Press) 1947
Rabelais (Bodley Head) 1948
*Porius (Macdonald) 1951
*The Brazen Head (Macdonald) 1956
*Letters of J. C. Powys to Louis Wilkinson: 1935-1956 (Macdonald) 1958

The books marked with an asterisk are now published by Messrs. Macdonald. Among a number of translations, those in French of M. Cara-
vaggia of *Weymouth Sands* and *Autobiography* are specially notable.

'us Neanderthals'

'I have a great deal of the tramp in me'

On ne dict les aultres sinon pour d'autant
plus se dire—*Montaigne*

This is no man—this is some god or
devil—*Nurse at the State Infirmary in
Baltimore.*

CHAPTER I

The World of the Powyses

NOTHING is so dead as yesterday. It brings a reader of John Cowper Powys up with a jolt to recall from some chance date that this novelist grew up in the heyday of George Meredith. He himself has described vividly the excitement of buying *Tess of the D'Urbervilles* the day it came out. For John Cowper, unlike his coevals among those of our novelists whose being is centred far from the life of towns and town societies, is our own contemporary in sexual awareness and exploration of character and motive. More our contemporary, perhaps, than we are his.

It is not fantastic, despite John Cowper's absorption in post-Freudian psychology, to characterise him as an earth man. What does rapidly prove fantastic, and then impossible, is to account for either his work or his limitations in any other way. His urban culture is the only urban thing about this supremely clever intellectual. His genius for being John Cowper has always been much more evident than his genius for any kind of writing. It is considering the oddness of the writings without relating it fully to the oddness of the man that has defeated his less sympathetic critics. But whatever we may feel about his natural aptitudes as a novelist, we can only get him into a proper perspective against the background of the novel, and of the 'rural' novel at that. John Cowper has an inexhaustible and sometimes exhausting curiosity about many forms of human experience. But towards man's identification with the earth—and especially with his own $\gamma\hat{\eta}s$ $\dot{o}\mu\phi\alpha\lambda os$ of Wessex—he turns as the flower turns its face to the sun or the sparks fly upward.

In 1872 when John Cowper was born, the eldest of the now celebrated brood of changelings in a staidly clerical nest, Thackeray and Dickens were not so very long dead—Dickens only a twelvemonth. Henry James' first novel was published the year of John Cowper's birth as was also *Erewhon*, bringing back the allegorical vein of Bunyan and Swift with which his brother Theodore Powys was to be associated. Hardy had just given the world *Far From the Madding Crowd*, his first serious masterpiece. John Cowper may have humbly owned himself the disciple of Henry James and still more (and more truly, in one sense) of Hardy, but it is difficult to see how he could differ more than he does from both. His 'onlie begetter' in the novel is Dostoievsky.

During John Cowper's boyhood conscious intellectual aims were penetrating the English novel, while its old background the English countryside was rapidly losing its distinctiveness, its isolation. As the rustic was becoming conscious of the town the more sophisticated reader of fiction was becoming conscious of the artist. Meredith, whose 'pseudo-philosophic poppycock' has always been repugnant to John Cowper, was at the apex of a reputation no writer could wholly ignore. Meredith was—in no pejorative sense—a class novelist as his predecessors had never been. Despite *Love in the Valley* he inevitably tilted fiction towards the universities, the towns, the cultivated drawing-rooms. Lesser men, such as the debonair, popular, fascinating R.L.S., had much the same inclination to urbanity. It was not till long after John Cowper was a grown man that Hardy really came into his own. Though Hardy has a universal quality, his art has its marked limitations of time as well as of space. To extend the boundaries of old Wessex, as well as to liberate man from his social trammels, has been less an aim than an instinct with John Cowper all his life. It is his instinct, also, to escape from things by plunging deeper into them. Hence his purposive studies, his conventional marriage, his American professional adventures. He deals with the problems of modern consciousness much as with his duodenal ulcers, by exacerbating his own sufferings to the limit. This almost proved suicidal physically. He has done his best to commit slow suicide as an artist, too, and very nearly succeeded.

But though John Cowper grew up in a Meredithian world

he goes back far enough to remember a distinct rural England.
He grew up with Nature. His complicatedly un-complex father
knew intimately many aspects of botany, ornithology, zoology,
however he may have despised most other forms of knowledge.

> Of all men ever born into the world my father was the
> proudest, the most egoistic, and also the least interested in
> art, in literature, in philosophy! But with all this he was,
> as Hardy's Martie [*sic*] says of her Giles, 'a good man and
> one who did good things'.

John Cowper has called his revered Thomas Hardy a townsman, quite unaffectedly—indeed, he is incapable of any affectation except that of excessive humility. He has never seemed
quite able to face the fact that rural England is dead. There is
always tension as we approach this question; he slides awkwardly past it. One can instance his wilful archaisms or the
strange anachronisms in *A Glastonbury Romance*.

The passing of rural England and the decline, in varying
degrees, of the elemental in life elsewhere—bitterly as we may
deplore it—is less surprising than the vigorous attempts that
have been made to keep it alive in one semblance or another.
('Nature' is, of course, a far wider conception than rurality.)
To writers of fiction the temptation is irresistible, for it is
much easier to see man as a whole against a background of
lasting things, of all sentient and insentient life, than when too
conscious of his fellow-men.

In an island State often too prosperous, with a people not
below the average in intellectual activity, the change was inevitable from the Industrial Revolution and the coming of the
railways. Even the Reform Act of 1832 played its part; and
compulsory education from 1870 and the not gradual mechanisation of nearly all industry and life could only bring urban-
isation, soon declining into sub-topia. We shall have to consider how far John Cowper's attitude to these vital changes is
philosophical, or valid, and whether he has been master
enough of his art to portray them in convincing terms. That he
is an original interpreter of unexplored character and motive,
timeless and unlocalised, is far easier to concede.

The Powys family are above all a clan, often laughably so,
and frequently to the embarrassment of outsiders and 'in-laws'.
Great as are the differences between these formidable in-

dividualists, they are nothing compared with the differences between the Powys and the rest of mankind. And the clan are countrymen and countrywomen to the very bone. They appear to have no urban filiations and belong exclusively to the more modest squirearchy. They have produced several country parsons and an occasional talented member. John Cowper and his brothers and sisters apparently derive their sensitive and alert minds from their mother, who was collaterally descended from John Donne and William Cowper. Mrs. Powys, rather dimly outlined against a very dimming evangelical background, was of a repressed, not to say a masochistic temperament, and is too memorably described by her son Llewelyn in *Skin for Skin*. She was in love with 'the side of the moon that turns itself away from the earth'; and though it is credibly recorded that she loved John Cowper, 'her first-born, the best', her negativeness only rendered the social isolation of a well-to-do clerical family more isolated.

It is difficult to realise, in these easy-going days, how pronounced that isolation was in the 1880's. Those in the country not separated from the parson's family by a gulf of breeding and education were few in those days; and however approachable the Vicarage or Rectory might be, obvious wealth there could only make most neighbours more diffident. Mr. Powys inherited a fortune of some £40,000, worth eight or nine thousand a year untaxed in these days. His dogged simplicity did not necessarily make a bridge between him and his less sophisticated Somerset neighbours. Even the wilfully gregarious John must have found—as indeed his *Autobiography* confirms—intercourse with other children a little difficult. He grew up a Powys among Powyses; a petty aristocrat *malgré lui*. When his father gave him a football (of the round, plebeian variety) as a present on going to prep. school he was rapt in delighted expectation of a game by himself, solo football. Fortunately, the strong views of the other little boys prevailed.

John Cowper, even more than his brothers, had an introspective turn and a strong—though ego-centred—social conscience. The imaginative joys of his early childhood, the sense of nature's immensity, soon turned sour on him; but in addition to that he was impelled, as so many *good* people of our century have been impelled, to disapprove and repudiate whatever he loved. It is the puritanism and democracy in the air. John Cowper retreated not into aristocratic aloofness or a deliberate Jefferies-like absorption in nature—he was essentially too large, too sympathetic for either—but into a sort of time-lessness. This attitude his brothers Theodore and Llewelyn later partook of also, in their degrees and fashions. But the great difference that stands out between John Cowper and his more strikingly artistic brother Theodore is that *culturally* the elder belongs to the twentieth century. His awareness may be timeless, but his curiosity has never abated. Whereas Theodore has no real interest in his own age as such. It may be that John Cowper's exploratory greatness will give his work a more en-during fame than consummate art will give his brother's. But in one case as in the other, we must beware of identifying what is outside time and what is immune from decay. The writer who would give validity to timeless conceptions must always attain that *vrai style* which Remy de Gourmont so pertinently distinguishes from *le style abstrait*.

What makes John Cowper and Theodore Powys England's last real rural writers is their combination, despite all their differences, of the congenital Powys changelessness and iso-lation with an extreme sensitiveness to suffering and evil. Art is, of its nature, at once intensification and escape. The whole struggle of the true writer is both to realise life more deeply and to realise himself ideally. Now a common characteristic of the clan Powys is that they understand themselves a little better than they understand others. What John Cowper has distinguished as the egohood[1] is very strongly developed in them. With the exception of Theodore, whose fastidious dis-tastes almost amounted to a distaste for himself, they were at their happiest when writing autobiography. It is only when giving a description of his own life that John Cowper really stands above criticism: his *Autobiography* has no superior in the English language. Llewelyn's *Skin for Skin* and its suc-cessors will probably outlast his attractive essays and certainly outlast his fiction; while the conventional schoolmaster Little-ton, though he had no distinction of mind and little literary gift, produced two pleasant and eminently readable volumes in *The Joy of It* and *Still the Joy of It*. (And it is precisely where Littleton becomes recognisably Powys that he becomes recognisably salty.)

[1] *Aryan Path*, June 1934.

Though the Powys writers were fairly copious—John Cowper prodigally so—none of them, except in his later years the professional Llewelyn, wrote for a public. Probably few people have ever held vaguer ideas of what a public is, or indeed of what an ordinary person is like. What makes so piquant, fascinating and amusing the lifelong friendships of John Cowper and Llewelyn with Louis Wilkinson is the contrast between his keen insight as a man of the world and their insight of some other world of their own projection. The John Cowper—Louis Wilkinson correspondence becomes absorbing in its topsy-turveydom when, as in many discussions of the Second War, John Cowper's flash of super-psychology gets far nearer to the bone than does his friend's balanced observation. This super-psychology which undercuts all social knowledge and all sound psychology, and is a sense truer than accepted truth, appears at a deeper level at several vital crises of *Wolf Solent* and *A Glastonbury Romance*. (How often John Cowper's essentialised women reveal something unguessed at in the brilliant constructions of Meredith or the more sensitive creations of Henry James.)

Clan feeling and self-awareness are not the only innate Powys characteristics. As for the clan itself, John Cowper both humorously accepts its elementality—'us Neanderthals': 'the toughest family in England'—and cocks an eye at it: Alyse Gregory, the accomplished American writer, who found the temerity to marry into it, in paying a noble tribute to John Cowper refers aptly to 'the Powys family, whom he sees as belonging not to this world but to Grimm's fairy tales'. The idiosyncratic limitations, as also the homogeneity, of the Powyses derive from the simple, dominating personality of their father. He has so much of plain nature in him that, like nature, you can drive him out with a pitchfork and he will continually recur. A certain naïveté the sons could never escape: neither the experienced, hardened Llewelyn nor the vastly sophisticated John Cowper, who also had the innocent cunning of the vicar sitting on his strong-box in his solicitor's office. The sons had the evangelical parson's puritanism, spending much of their life in sloughing it off; and their want of real spirituality, which is significant in appraising their vision, was implicit in the Reverend Charles Francis' whole religious make-up.

Of the strange Powys ingenuousnesses we shall find countless instances in John Cowper. They are a part of his personality, almost a part of his force. Of satire he had no appreciation at all: he simply disliked it. He records, almost unbelievably, that the family 'reads Jane Austen for the romance' (surely there is no other intellectual family of whom this could be seriously said!). There is no wit in them, and John Cowper's insensitiveness to wit is astonishing: his remarks on Congreve are among his few misfires in all his widely sympathetic literary criticism. The Powys neither had nor acquired any ear for the common speech; and it is this remoteness of idiom which more than anything else gives an oddity and other-worldiness to so much of their writing, damning them as realists, for many readers. We shall find frequent examples of both the stilted and the *faux naïf* in John Cowper's novels. Another characteristic, which certainly does not come from the sturdy vicar, but which, if it does not touch John Cowper's novels, frequently impinges on his essay-books, is their far-fetched apprehensiveness. 'There was no suspicion, no worry, no superstition, no fantasy whatever, too grotesque to cast its anchor in the mind of either Theodore, Llewelyn or John,' writes Louis Wilkinson in *Swan's Milk*. 'Can you get typhoid from your own dung?' Llewelyn once asked him. The lack of everyday information was an equally peculiar mark of the family. 'What do you mean by sixty?' asked John Cowper indignantly, being quoted the temperature Fahrenheit; and Llewelyn believed Emile Zola to be Napoleon's mistress. John Cowper's letters are littered with references to 'Plush fours', 'Summer's sault', a 'Kawker' and 'Cow-towing'.

So far as it is possible to postulate an overriding temperament for the family—and it is important to recognise the common element—it might be called anti-Gallic. It is strange to recall that they had a French-Swiss grandmother, and on the paternal side at that. What makes so piquant the brothers' relations with Louis Wilkinson is the extreme contrast between their involuntary John-Bullishness and his marked Gallicism (his mother was French). But John Cowper is by no means content to be English, partly because 'What might be called extremely English persons have always puzzled me.'[1] This difficulty is, however, not uncommon among the poetic-

[1] *Autobiography.*

ally minded. John Cowper has lived nearly thirty years among the Welsh mountains, and has been since as long as 1902 deliberately cultivating the Celtic strain in his lineage. 'A Welsh "wave of the first water" seeking my aboriginal level' he calls himself in *Obstinate Cymric* and in the same book he writes 'I have a strong psychological affinity with the Welsh people'. He is actually eight generations removed from the last Powys to live in Wales and on his mother's side his forebears are plain English. He has Celtic affinities, but they are always affinities in difference.

It would be a fair generalisation on the Powys brothers that they are very English—quite obviously is Littleton so—and that they are exceptionally deficient in all those characteristics we vaguely associate with the French. Their want of social conformity and adaptability is quite extraordinary; and the most immediately striking thing about the characters in John Cowper's novels is their lack of defensive reserves. Indeed, they appear unconscious of the social pressures that condition existence in the everyday world. Wolf Solent, Johnnie Geard, Dud No-man behave as if they had no neighbours at all. In a sense they have not. Nor has John Cowper.

'Us cave-men Powyses' he calls the clan in one of his later letters. With all the curiosity in the world about what goes on outside, they have never quite left the cave. John Cowper, Theodore, Llewelyn, they share a certain affectionate hostility (less affectionate, perhaps, in Theodore) towards the human race. John Cowper owes his allegiance to nature more than to his fellow men. His life, below a certain depth, is something between himself and the primordial powers he worships. 'I derive an extraordinary satisfaction, not untouched by my curious "sacred malice"—in this case directed against the dogmatism of the Church as well as against the dogmatism of Science—from praying definitely to the Earth-spirit under her ancient names of Demeter and Cybelê,' is no isolated avowal. All this may imply, inevitably, that he is not fully equipped as a novelist insofar as the novel is a criticism of society *as* society. It also makes him rather terrifying as a critic of human nature from an outside point of vantage. It suggests largely why he stands with his brother Theodore—so different in equipment and methods—as the revitalizer of the novel of nature in England. Those who challenge his art can hardly deny his urgency.

Chesterton called John Henry Newman in a memorable phrase 'a naked man who carried a naked sword'. The complex son of heaven and the complex son of earth may seem to have almost laughably little in common save a genius for writing compellingly about themselves, an art of which both are undeniably masters. Yet when one ponders it more deeply, the vivid phrase seems to have a peculiar application to John Cowper in these days, an application which in fact it does not have to anybody else. The sword, differently forged from Newman's, is sharpened by psychology. John Cowper's purpose is even less destructive than John Henry's but he has cut deeper, here and there, than anybody before; and the starkness of his self-revelation itself calls for an unfashionable seriousness of response when the novel, increasingly 'minor' since Proust's day, inclines to break the surface at new points with new weapons rather than to delve further.

CHAPTER II

Boyhood, Dorset and Cambridge

IT is not at all surprising that the infant John Cowper's first
impression in life should have been one of nature's immensity.
This awoke in him an instinctive reverence (for all but the
conventional objects of reverence) which he has always striven
to preserve and enlarge and glorify. A 'power of finding the
infinitely great in the infinitely small'; the 'ecstasy of the unbounded', are lifelong characteristics which in his *Autobiography* he traces to earliest childhood.

The eldest of the eleven changelings, he was born in his
father's vicarage of Shirley, a village lying between Derby and
the part of Derbyshire which is known as Dovedale, on 8
October, 1872. His very different brother, Littleton, followed a
year later. The two were to be almost inseparable up to
Cambridge days. At the age of six, John Cowper mingled his
urine with his brother's in a 'rusty iron cauldron'. As the
family migrated in 1880 via Weymouth, to Dorchester, where
Powys *père* accepted a curacy, John Cowper is the only member of the family old enough to have been impressed by Derbyshire. Deeply impressed he was, especially by Mount Cloud
and the roaring, rushing, rock-flanked waters of the Dove. He
was equally awed, if more negatively impressed, by his father's
physical power and the confidence exuded from his large, mud-
defying country boots. He was a sensitive and assertive rather
than precocious child. One of the first incidents recorded of
him is that at the age of four he informed an astonished nurse-
maid 'I am the Lord of Hosts'. A little earlier he had nearly
hanged brother Littleton with a bell-rope fastened round his

throat: the future headmaster, when rescued, was black in the face. John Cowper developed an almost morbid conscience, deriving this tendency perhaps from an anxious mother and a puritanical father. He became early obsessed with the idea that he was a sadist, which inclination, or imagined inclination, it took him half-a-century to shake off. He records that in early childhood he derived a guilty thrill from a nursery picture of an eagle seizing upon a lamb. Soon after, he derived a mischievous amusement from transferring tadpoles from a pond to shallow rain pools. This was almost too much for the vicar's limited savoir-faire. An offspring whose being was unhappily divided between a conscience more sensitive than his own and an insuperable craving for 'sensual-mystic sensations' was, for better or worse, far outside his experience.

This conflict between puritan father and highly aesthetic son naturally recalls another gifted biographer, Edmund Gosse. Despite a more bigoted and intolerant, though also far more intelligent, father, Gosse apparently outgrew the experience entirely; but for this he could probably thank his less profound feeling. The parallel is interesting, especially to students of deep Victorianism. John Cowper never outgrew completely his father's dominance or his heavily moral influence; and the son's inverted snobbery has been partly a reaction from the vicar's unconscious pride and arrogance. (It shows also the mother's quasi-masochism.) But however little that was creative or positive in John Cowper derived from the parents, he did have a valuable taste and accomplishment confirmed in him by his begetter's anti-social love of the countryside. The amateur naturalist taught his son much in a factual way. John Cowper learned to recognise (especially later, in Wessex) the song of rare birds, the varieties of wild flowers and ferns, the formation of rocks and stones. His own more sensitive and intuitive love of naturalism achieved precision, which later was to give a needed tangibility and conviction to much of his descriptive writing in the novels. Whether his garrulity, which when transferred to literature became a weakness as much as a strength, is to be traced at all to reaction from his father's *boutonné* quality is another question. It is probably part and parcel of his exceptionally fluid nature.

The family's migration to Wessex stimulated John Cowper's notable alertness to impressions. He had already revelled in

holidays at the home of an elderly relative living in the beloved Weymouth of his *Jobber Skald*. (Weymouth is the
nearest approach to a hero in any of the novels!) He has told
us vividly in the *Autobiography* how the smell of the sea and
the seashore saturated his boyish imagination, and no reader of
Rodmoor, still less of *Jobber Skald*, can doubt this. But his
early susceptibility to nature was purely sensuous. Of what in
later years he called 'the enchantment with which the self can
fling itself upon the not-self in a spasm of mystic sensuality' the
dreamy child had scarcely a premonition in the Derbyshire
years. The most vivid early impressions of nature that remained with him were of a greenish tint in the Eastern sky at
morning, and of a widely spreading Pirus Japonica that clam-
bered up the front wall of Shirley vicarage. These, he insists,
were homely, physical satisfactions.

But in Dorset for a brief space before shades of the prison-
house closed, nature was mystery and romance and magic. 'An
ecstasy came to me, morning after morning, as I saw the sun
glittering on the sea.' The 'pale growths' of the cuckoo flowers,
redolent of their own wild poetry, evoked the waking Wordsworthianism of John Cowper, making the ruddy Pirus appear
blatant and the wild forget-me-nots that grew by the banks of
the Dove 'seem arrogant and even fashionable'.

The sense of being *abnormally* alive, touched with the curious maternal legacy of shame, which are always associated with
John Cowper, goes back to his early childhood. His infantile
assertiveness, his terror of the police, his refuge in the hymns of
Sankey and Moody, have already something of a phantasmal,
not to say a Dickensian, quality. In early Montacute days he
did literally act Hamlet, but before that he had begun to
evince his lifelong preference for acting at being an actor
rather than acting a part.

> I am a born actor, and why? Because I have no original
> self in me at all. I have always 'played' at life, 'played' at
> religion, 'played' at philosophy. I have always loved only
> sensations, especially the sensation of telling oneself a story,
> and in the story I become any one of all the characters, male
> or female.

And again:

> I *am* a born actor, but I am so self-conscious as to

cease to be self-conscious. I have indeed already acquired
a Jesus-child innocence.

This carefully nurtured capacity for self-deception lets
escape the sensationism which sets so wide a gap between John
Cowper as an intellectual and the few of his contemporaries
who can be called his peers. This sensationism remained the
signature tune of all his essays, giving them an exaggeratedly
earthly delimitation; but in his best writing he rapidly passed
beyond it into the realms of poetic psychology.

The child's passage from a helpless neurotic Johnnie to a
crafty neurotic John, as he disparagingly puts it, was a tormented one. The coming of imagination was the coming of
unhappiness. Born introspective, he became, as super sensitive
children do, self-conscious long before he could find escape in
expression; for even the most vocal of children cannot be truly
articulate.

> I sometimes feel as I survey my turbulent life that a
> human soul resembles a fountain whose nature spring is
> choked up by every kind of rubble and constantly invaded
> by a tidal estuary from the salt sea. Not until the fountain
> has banked itself up with great stones against this dead-sea
> invasion, not until it has pushed the sticks and gravel and
> leaves and roots and funguses and mud and cattle dung out
> of its way, can it draw upon the deep granite wells of its
> predestined floor. To look back to that Shirley childhood
> of mine is to look back to a convulsed mudpool of Chaos.
> In the midst of that Chaos a wavering human soul is grad-
> ually taking shape, gathering to itself curious and con-
> flicting signs and symbols and tokens of what its blind urge
> is driving us towards. From the beginning madness and
> fear beset us, vice enthrals us, humiliation benumbs us,
> pride intoxicates us. It may be hard to be a man; it is
> much harder to be a child.

'I was a born clown, a born zany,' he reiterates. 'The over-
whelmingly larger number of the things that come back to me
from those early years are shameful, destructive and grotesque.'
He has even suggested that his childhood was more miserable
than his school years; but if positive suffering is the implied
criterion this is against the tenor of his own reminiscences. At
Sherborne School between fourteen and seventeen he endured
things (to him) wretched and squalid; and except in 1917
when War and ulcers almost overwhelmed him, it is probable

he was never to suffer so much again. The acute malaise and disillusion of childhood are more subjective, after all, less difficult to outlive.

For all that which John Cowper was in the realms of fantasy, Littleton recalls him with admiration, an admiration typical of the clan and by no means uncommon outside, though the clan enhanced it with an affection less common among the profane. His virtuosity as a teller of original stories created a great impression, and at Sherborne he was to be a redoubtable raconteur after lights out in the dormitory. He had a sense of his responsibility, not to say his status, as the firstborn, and Littleton recalls him as by no means unwilling, even in those early days, to edify an audience. 'John who in a sermon of unusual length harangued his small brothers and sisters on the sufferings caused by sin.' We may be sure it was of unusual length. His father, of whom he gives a particularly memorable account in the *Autobiography*, hoped he would go into the Church (in sublime indifference to his unsuitability) and it is clear the idea of Ordination was purposively—one cannot say subtly—pressed on him. For some years he taught a class in Sunday School, and there is no doubt that all these things fostered an impressionability to puritanical notions, however uncongenial, of which he did not get really free for the best part of a lifetime.

'So sensitive, imaginative, introspective and so full of his own importance,' he appeared to brother Littleton. Full of his own un-importance would be nearer to the truth. His mother and his father were oddly at conflict within him. He was from the first defensive: a common enough state of things, but not so common among those as amiable as John Cowper. Indeed, human beings as amiable as John Cowper are far from plentiful. We shall from the beginning find ourselves confronted with this paradox of personality: the gregariousness of the solitary, the garrulity of the withdrawn. So in the adult writer we shall find never a truly integrated personality, but one shaped by tensions. Before he became a preparatory-school boy at Sherborne his craving for nature as against human nature had laid fatal hold on him.

> Deep in my nature—inherited directly from my father —was a longing to escape from organised society and find a temporary home for myself, a private, secret domain of

my own, where no one could intrude, where it was indeed almost impossible for anyone to intrude! This instinct—and I like to fancy it was an atavism going back to the times when our Welsh ancestors hid themselves in their mountain fastnesses—was composed of two kindred impulses, one to escape into the wilds, and the other to make a home of your own, a lair, a retreat, an embattled fortress, into which you could retire and defy society.... My dominant desire during the whole of my school life—whether in the Prep. or in the Big School—was to lead a double existence, and while just 'getting by' in the School Dimension, to find my real happiness in a secret subjective Dimension where I was 'monarch of all I surveyed'.

Even in childhood John Cowper was all too conscious of his own oddity, which indeed he has always overstressed. At Sherborne, to avoid intolerable persecution, he fell back upon feigning insanity as a natural ruse. He got away with it, as he was to get away with many things in life. About the real nature of 'insanity' he remains, with many other amateurs of psychology, very vague. From *The Inmates*, written at seventy, it is clear that he held fanciful ideas of mental estrangement. 'I am—all the while—never wholly sane' he declares, quite inaccurately, in the *Autobiography*. He was unfitted for boarding-school life, despite a certain toughness, by the seclusion and clannishness of his social background as well as by his guilty obsessions and his latent neurosis. (His neurosis does not appear ever to have been *acute*, and his prolonged and severe suffering from ulcers is very doubtfully traceable to mental causes.) His clumsiness, garrulity and unusual appearance must have made the school life still more difficult; and though all through life there has been much of the lovable and appealing child about John Cowper, this quality would not endear him to late Victorian schoolboys, with whom toughness and normality were universal cults. He was in marked contrast, of course, with Littleton, the most polished and conforming of all Powyses and the least imaginative.

'As a child he thought of himself as the king of the fairies,' Theodore told Llewelyn many years afterwards. It is no great reflection on the Loom of Youth, where after all Littleton and Llewelyn and John Cowper's own son were to be happy in their very differing fashions, that it should have ended any prospects of John Cowper's developing into a happy or natural boy. He needed not less understanding than he got at home, but more. It is not altogether fantastic to attribute to his entry at the Sherborne Preparatory School the beginning of John Cowper's lifelong exiled state of mind. It is impossible to say that this other genius of nature and the Wessex countryside would have in any circumstances developed a Hardy-like harmony of personality through all stresses; but it seems clear enough that from his first departure from home his was a being divided against itself. Artistic disharmony was implanted: he became evasive and indirect. The conception of himself as pitted against urban acceptances and dependence on craftiness to deceive others—and ultimately himself—begins early to colour his *Autobiography*. What saved Littleton was not insensitiveness but a far greater simplicity and directness; he was not tormented by an extreme sense of oddity nor by a hunger for illimitable intellectual experience. John Cowper writes:

> My physical and athletic disabilities at school must have made a dent on my mind from which I shall never recover. I got it thoroughly lodged in my brain that I was an awkward fool, a cowardly fool, an idiotic fool, an impossible fool, a pitiful fool, a graceless fool, a windy fool, a complete fool, an untidy fool, a master fool, an absent-minded fool, a vicious, sneaking, ungainly fool, a greedy-gut fool, an ugly-mug fool, a nondescript fool, a mad fool, an inexplicable fool ... why, at Wildman's my unpopularity grew and grew to such a pitch that it ended in what amounted to a Powys Ma. outlawing, a Powys Ma. baiting. They said that I ate my very food, in some gross sub-human, sub-animal way, chewing at it with my front teeth instead of with my grinders.[1]

Littleton confirms that in boyhood, as apart from manhood, John Cowper was disliked.

> I keep struggling to remember some occasion at the Prep. when my present-day cult of a life of sensation rather than of thought could be said to have originated. But in vain![2]

Wrapped in the mystery of himself, the tall, earnest, big-boned, wayward boy was continually bullied from the age of eight to seventeen. He made little mark either in Prep. school or at Sherborne itself. He occasionally exerted himself to outshine his younger brother in examinations, but usually he was in a

[1] *Autobiography*, p. 95.   [2] *Autobiography*, p. 102.

lower form. A duffer at games—as he recounts with great humour—he was noted only for eccentricity and powerful wrists, and his talents do not seem to have impressed the masters. School teachers of those days bothered a little about the morals and scholastic progress of their pupils, but hardly at all about them as individuals. 'Powys Ma.' lived only to escape into the countryside or to lose himself in a book. In 1886 his father moved to the roomy, rambling village of Montacute, so long the centre of the Powys legend, and it was not uncommon for the long-legged boy to run the nine miles each way for a breath of home on a Sunday afternoon.

Although John Cowper never came within a hundred miles of the natural life-loving paganism of his brother Llewelyn it is equally impossible to associate him with the religious beliefs of his home. That he humoured his father to a very great extent and quite uncynically is evident—he is of course by nature incapable of cynicism. But there is no real trace of orthodox belief to be found. Of the First Cause he has from boyhood had a sensitive horror. But he was, in his own words, a praying animal, 'tapping the altar stone of Stonehenge with my head'. His devotional instinct has in it more of humility and the need for reverence than it has of real worship. His animism, his fetichism, his craving for the occult were in early evidence; and the 'Wordsworthianism' he so emphatically claims as the essential of his awakening to nature has so little of the transcendental in it as barely to warrant the name. There is in Wordsworth a sense of immanent deity, closely bound up with a spirit of optimism and acceptance, that is quite alien to the earthy occultism of John Cowper.

We must be careful, of course, not to identify John Cowper's adult convictions with his boyish feelings. But it must be emphasised that much of his apparent wilfulness as an artist is traceable to early stress. With all his elemental, earth-seeking instincts he was always extremely amicable and sociable. Few men care as much for their fellows. But the world of school, of Victorian school, was a form of intensified gregariousness, a hive, an unnatural restraint of the imaginative character. It was also, for one of John Cowper's temperament and handicaps, a humiliation.

He was not only driven into an intense yearning for elemental things, but into an exaggerated distrust of society,

c

which he was at the same time too genial to admit. His reaction to modern society was really to remain different, to
remain Powysian, while amicably over-anxious to 'belong'. He
has always greatly underestimated the gap between himself,
the Powys in him, and conforming urban man. All John
Cowper's long lifetime Englishmen have been growing more
and more conformist, while his own individualism has strengthened. His error—and it shows up very clearly in the democratic
protestations that sit so oddly upon him—is in supposing that
you can be an unusual man at home and a usual one in society.
Most of those who live close to nature do not try to live close to
the man-in-the-street. There is, of course, a democratic sort of
natural man—perhaps one might glance at Walt Whitman—
but that is a special kind of genius remote from the rarefied
Powys. The trouble is that when a John Cowper insists on
being at one with the man-in-the-street, the man-in-the-street
hurriedly and without affection rejects him. A Wordsworth or
a Melville made few advances.

So the story of John Cowper at Sherborne is a pretty melancholy one, irrepressible though he remained. There is a comic
side to his deficiencies, suggested for instance in the drawing of
J.C.P. by J.C.P. recalled by Llewelyn's wife, Alyse Gregory,
many years later, 'running away from himself and talking as
fast as he could.' Littleton's account of him in *The Joy of It* is
naturally lacking in true candour; but the eighty pages of the
two chapters on 'Prep. School' and 'Sherborne' in the *Autobiography* are not far below John Cowper's best. His inwardness of course predominates but his account of his masters, of
the odd customs of a Victorian public school and of the ingenious devices of John Cowper to remain John Cowper, has a
consistent richness of quality.

His shadow of guilt, his self-accusation of sadistic leanings,
was now heavy on him. 'But meanwhile,' he says, 'my in-
durated sadistic vice was always seething in the background of
my nerves. I recollect wandering alone on more than one
occasion over hill and dale near Sherborne looking for something to tear to pieces ... I can only once—and that very
obscurely—remember really practising my sadism in those
days. Was it only my wicked wish on that occasion? No! I
believe I actually did offer up to my raging Demon a whole
nestful of unfledged little birds in one of those quarries on the

Bristol Road.' In those days he believed in 'a flaming Hell for wilful sensualists', and when his obsession with his 'sadic vice' left him it was at the same time as his Puritan guilt finally departed, after half-a-century of life. His 'sylpholepsy', his almost de-sensualised lust for slim, girlish, anonymous limbs, slowly developed during his schooldays. It seems to have been the only 'vice' he really enjoyed, but that enjoyment was later, after he left Cambridge. His sufferings at the hands of the bullies of Wildman's House were acute from the age of fourteen to seventeen. Finally his foes gathered one evening in the doorway of his study and a boot was thrown at his head. He was physically and psychologically incapable of showing fight. It was a deeply humiliating scene, but he soon rallied. 'I was unable to use my Derbyshire fists, why should I not use my Welsh tongue?' Lutyens, the runner, head of Wildman's House, consented to announce that Powys, Ma. 'had something to say' after chapel. He had, and did:

> beginning lamely enough, but quickly catching my cue, I poured forth a flood of tumultuous speech. Out of my foolishness it came, out of my humiliation, out of my inverted pride. It came literally *de profundis*. I had prayed in the Chapel: 'And take not the Holy Spirit from us', but whether this torrent of self-accusations, of self-incriminations, of wild self-mockery, proceeded from the Creator Spiritus, or from the Devil, I cannot tell. I dragged in every single detail they derided me for, I exposed my lacerations, my shames, my idiocies. 'Moony' was talking at last out of the madness of the mistress of his horoscope! I referred to the great dilapidated umbrella I took such stock in. I referred to my obscene fashion of chewing my food with my front teeth. I stripped myself naked before them. Taliessin himself could not have prophesied to such a tune when he celebrated the procession of his planetary metamorphoses. When I sat down, there was a moment's dead silence. I did not dare to look at Littleton. But I had not failed. A hullabaloo of applause, puzzled, stupefied, bewildered, confounded, rose up around me. Lutyens whispered something to Littleton before he made the sign for us to kneel down for the accustomed evening Collect. Next morning I was in the sickroom with an attack of my gastric trouble.

The scene of his torture knew him no more; but he was awarded the prize for the year's English poem. He always desired the fame of a poet which he has never achieved. He spent

an easy summer over Euripides' *Ion,* and at the end of it went
up to the family college, Corpus Christi, Cambridge, where old-
world Victorian dons let him alone to read, or not to read, this
new-fangled subject of English history.

An excellent account of Cambridge between 1891 and 1894
from the angle of an historian with philosophic-liberal leanings has recently appeared from the pen of G. P. Gooch in
his *Under Six Reigns.* Bertrand Russell's reminiscences of the
scene are also revealing. John Cowper differed by worlds from
either of these other remarkable men, though all three could
be called Liberal philosophers in their own kind. The learned
Dr. Gooch, by whom John Cowper was dazzled, is as essentially
of Cambridge as Newman or Matthew Arnold of Oxford; but
John Cowper is not of the stuff of which true *alumni* are made.
His responses to Cambridge were characteristic and revealing.
He describes his student years himself as years of 'unbalanced
and chaotic idealism'. He made friends, marvelled at many
things; and hero-worshipped abundantly, but to the academic
activities of Cambridge he was almost indifferent, and to her
antiquity and her architecture wholly indifferent. (It is difficult not to suspect here the trace of his father's old-fashioned
'manly' abhorrence of *objets d'art.*[1]) But he fell deeply in love
with the countryside. (The love, of course, was already there.)
He read a vast amount of poetry; and we must believe him
when he tells us he read little history, though with his reten-
tive and allusive mind he was to achieve second-class honours.
Not for many years yet was his passion for Welsh lore and
mythology to lead him to the almost over-elaborate researches
into the Dark Ages and mediaevalism which give *Owen Glendower* and *Porius* their massive impact. He developed while at
Cambridge a strong strain of asceticism (especially in the
matter of eating) that is surely a legacy of paternal puritanism,
for it does not seem related to anything in his physical or
temperamental make-up. In a fine vein of self-righteousness, he
denied himself in food and drink—though not in tobacco!—
and began to form those erratic feeding habits which did much
to aggravate, if they did not provoke, his ulcers. Running no
further risk of being bullied, he confronted such hearties as
invaded his rooms with a loaded revolver—a stratagem which
was adopted by his friend Louis Wilkinson at Oxford, with

---

[1] e.g. Jason Otter and his idol Mukalog in *Wolf Solent.*

equally good results, a decade later. In 1902 Llewelyn took possession of the same dim and delightful old room at Corpus, where he deciphered on a beam the scrawled words 'Pray for the Soul of John Cowper Powys'. Already, prayer was an established custom: at least daily the kneeling undergraduate invoked the protection of his ancestors.

As could only be expected, the attempt to come to terms with his father's religion proved helpless; and the vicar accepted the abandonment of all thought of Orders in characteristic silence. So far as the young man's loyalties can be called at this stage religious, they were divided between a very personal pantheism and a Catholic leaning that he later accepted as fetich-worship. The old umbrella of Sherborne days had yielded place to the first of a lifetime's succession of huge walking-sticks, often named 'Sacred', from which he was rarely separated, and which supported him through his endless peregrinations through the flat Cambridge countryside. His future brother-in-law, Henry Lyon, an Anglican convert who impinged largely on his Cambridge horizon, decided that 'Jack has no soul'.

It is small discredit to G. P. Gooch, and to a number of other very able people, that they were nonplussed by John Cowper's contradictions of character and came to odd conclusions about him. Shortly before his leaving Cambridge, according to his own (obviously delighted!) account, G. P. Gooch and an elder friend they had in common, Koelle, summed him up as 'a clever man, but lacking in all moral scruple'. One wonders if any human being has ever gone through a long life more tormented by scruples than John Cowper.[1] It is to this same Koelle, a travelled, quizzical divinity student, that we indirectly owe one of the most amusing and revealing stories of John Cowper's relations with his monolithic begetter.

in a vein of boastfulness, anxious to impress my father with my friend's knowledge of the world, I explained how Koelle had steered clear of those amorous relations with black women which was so lively a temptation ... my father remaining silent, I continued my discourse on the various

[1] One would have hated to disillusion Mr. Powys, but Dr. Gooch has assured me with emphasis that for his part he never entertained such a judgement and would certainly never have voiced it. Those who know the historian best say that such an *obiter dictum* would be quite out of character.

temptations of young men, hinting that there were other 'primrose paths' at a place like Cambridge, for all its lack of dark-skinned Houris, which might lead a person to the ever-lasting bonfire. The pleasure of boasting about the perils of the world became greater and greater to me at that moment, under those familiar trees, and I was surprised that my father continued silent.

Piqued a little at the small effect of my words, I was led on to indicate that although I had at present encountered few loose women near the gates of Corpus, there had been grave cases of alcoholism of late in his Alma Mater, and that I myself had more than once found the power of our famous college port insidiously attractive. My father continued silent. And under the weight of that silence, we advanced gloomily enough along the path by the edge of the Montacute House garden. I was racking my brains for further revelations and was just, like Lot's wife, looking towards the Cities of the Plain, when at last he broke the uncomfortable silence.

'John,' he remarked, 'I should be glad if you would read the Lessons for me tomorrow morning. It's a real help to me, my boy, during this season of long gospels!'

Corpus of the nineties was not the Corpus of today, and being largely peopled by athletes, seedy evangelicals and overgrown hearties she was not well qualified as the spiritual home of a John Cowper. His very fluidity and hospitality of mind tended to make him feel all the more a fish out of water. His humility, later to harden into inverted snobbery, had a slightly repelling effect upon many of the other men. His social *gaffes* were frequent and often painful, and were due of course not to lack of breeding but to intensive in-breeding. Some are painful to write down, and few but he would have had the candour and courage to record them, as with the incident of the dashing talker and the toothpick narrated in the *Autobiography*.[1]

There was just one outstanding occasion, late in his undergraduate days, when John Cowper's floating emotional experience crystallised. The Damascus Road of this revelation was hard by Trumpington Mill, and characteristically the occasion was his journeying, supported by the trusty Sacred, to meet his first novelist at a house not far from the university town:

Not far from Trumpington Mill—somewhere in the umbrageous purlieus to the rear of the Fitzwilliam Museum—there stands an ancient wall; and as I drifted

[1] Pp. 196-197.

along to meet my lively satirist, I observed, growing upon this wall, certain patches of grass and green moss and yellow stone-crop. Something about the look of these small growths, secluded there in a place seldom passed, and more seldom noticed, seized upon me and caught me up into a sort of Seventh Heaven.

This *beyond sensation*, which he cannot put into words, was constantly recurring to his mind forty years later, lying in the depths of his consciousness a sunken ship, full of fathom-deep treasure.

It has, however, whatever its fluctuating mystery may be, a power upon me that is like the power of a hidden Mass, celebrated by no human hands. It is impossible for me to describe it! And yet I never see the least patch of lichen, or moss, or grass, in the veinings of an ancient rock but something of the same feeling returns. Not, however, quite the same; for *that* impression, that vision of 'Living Bread', that mysterious meeting-point of animate with inanimate, had to do with some secret underlying world of rich magic and strange romance.

Illuminations of this order, striking auspiciously upon the sensuous being, are much more characteristic of the animist or occultist than of the mystic or the true Wordsworthian. The vision of Trumpington Mill was indeed the precursor of much deliberate nature-worship, a worship that is anxiously evoked by physical experience rather than spiritual experience, its objects explicitly the sea, the mountains, the earth, the sun, the moon, Homer, Shakespeare, Rabelais, Don Quixote, lichen growing upon tree stumps, moss growing upon stones, smoke rising from a cottage chimney.[1] He pursued the quest for nourishment on these sensations—for sensation was after all his *métier*—relentlessly and to the neglect of more orderly disciplines. Cambridgeshire temporarily disputed his territorial loyalty with Somerset, now the centre of the Powys tradition and eclipsing, if not supplanting, the more heady atmosphere and mythology of rural Dorset. Supplanting, no; for Thomas Hardy was now beginning to exercise his lifelong fascination and mastery over John Cowper's mind and Hardy is unmistakably a Dorset and not a Somerset man.

The Cambridge years loosened the hold of his sadic obsession and self-mistrust over John Cowper; and it is of relatively little significance that his sylpholeptic fantasies were develop-

[1] *Autobiography*, p. 206.

ing. The release from school and its restricting humiliations
naturally did something to mature and liberate him; and it is
not surprising to learn that with his ebullience he threw off his
fear of people and found himself able to speak with confidence
and freedom. (Only a cynic would say with too much freedom.)
He went down from Cambridge with the prospect of a small
allowance from his father but no idea in the world what he
could do, or wished to do, in the way of a calling. On an idle
impulse he wrote to W. T. Stead asking his advice and referring casually to journalism, and in reply received from that
fanatical devotee of Fleet Street a shattering quotation from
Mark Twain's 'Jumping Frog' series. He had much to learn of
this world.

Mr. Powys made his firstborn an allowance of sixty pounds a
year—worth about six pounds a week today—as he was to do
with all his sons, increasing it to a hundred pounds when they
should become married men. John Cowper's mood of acute
asceticism forbade him to live on this as a solitary in the beloved Somerset countryside, and as he has recalled with a wry
smile many years after, he did not think of going to Paris to
learn French properly: 'What would the pictures in *Ally
Sloper* have been to the much more provocative incitements
that I could thus have attained?' He did, however, pass a holiday in the Lake District with a friend, and there became deeply
immersed in botany. Essaying to climb Helvellyn alone, he was
seized with panic near the summit and stumbled down in head-
long flight, losing the current 'Sacred' on the way altogether.
There was small demand for the services of undistinguished
Oxford graduates in those days; and coming to London John
Cowper took his second-class degree to Messrs. Gabbitas &
Thring, the great scholastic agents, whose name had a Dickensian fascination for him.

CHAPTER III

The Lecturer, the Traveller, the Emigrant

'Why need I have laid upon my shifty,
Protean, unfrocked hedge-priest shoulders
the necessity of being dignified?'
——AUTOBIOGRAPHY

IT has been said that small fortunes are the ruin of great talents. The seven or eight years following John Cowper's departure from Cambridge with a second in history[1] and a failure for his prize-poem (the laurel being awarded that year to J. C. Masterman) were not outwardly productive for one so full of energy. He had no intention of drifting into the Limbo of an usher, and it is pleasant to record that on journeying to Brighton with an introduction from Gabbitas & Thring he at once secured a post as visiting lecturer in literature to a girls' school. He proceeded to several similar lectureships, all of which he contrived to fulfil on the same day of the week, to the detriment of his health but to the then useful tune of some five pounds. Wild, ecstatic dreams of sylph-hood filled his mind, fortunately unsuspected by the directors of the young ladies' schools: though he was to derive little pleasure from these pedagogic contacts.

For the truth is, what I am so intensely attracted to, what I worshipped in those days to a point of idolatrous aberration, are hardly of the feminine sex at all! It is as if I had been born into this world from another planet—

[1] Only two firsts in the second part of the Historical Tripos were given in 1894, one to G. P. Gooch, who was still under twenty-one.

certainly not Venus: Saturn possibly!—where there was a
different sex altogether from the masculine and feminine
that we know. It is of this sex, of this Saturnian sex, that
I must think when in the secret chambers of my mind
I utter the syllable 'girl'. I suppose women are more like
these elfin sylphs, these fleeting elementals, than most men
are; but I am not perfectly sure even about this! The
maternal instinct in women, so realistic, so formidable,
so wise, so indulgent, is more remote from, and destructive
of, the sylph-nature—the nature of those girls who are more
girlish than girls—than the spirit of Hercules himself. I
think that the inmost flame of my soul, the vital leap of
my life-force, must be as fragile and tenuous as it is formidable and fierce; and that it is this brittleness and fineness
in this interior flame which makes it flee, as if from cart-
loads of horned devils, at the faintest approach of any warm
maternal lovingness, as if such lovingness would bury it
under a thousand bushels, like the scriptural candle.

More satisfying than the fair learners were, in a remote way,
'the hundreds and hundreds of beautiful girls I stared at as
they bathed in the sea or as they lay prone for my delight upon
the beach!'

He has now launched on a long abandonment to what he
calls 'neurotic aberrations' which, with some relief at the time
of his marriage, lasted for nearly a decade. His friends, at any
rate, had many more misgivings about his sanity at that period
than before or since. But he knew himself best.

My nervous *power*, however, and the vitality of my constitution, were so terrific that I never had the remotest
danger of what is called a nervous breakdown. I have always
been the kind of person whose spirit is so defiant, whose
will so obstinate, whose pulse so steady, that he can *go
on carrying*, as a camel carries its load, a vast orb of
neurotic manias without any of them being able to break
the rational balance of my brain. If anyone asked me if I
had ever been mad I would answer, as Natalia did in
Wilhelm Meister when asked if she had ever loved: 'Never
or always'.

It was not until after Cambridge days that John Cowper first
heard of Pater or Wilde, both of whom were to fascinate him
so deeply if a little unaccountably. A year later he made the
acquaintance of Yeats, who fascinated him, though much less
than did Pater. He was also deep in French Literature, in
which he has always shown an amazing aptitude and catho-

licity of taste. A young intellectual at large, in fact, it was in the middle nineties that he acquired the breadth of culture which helped so much in making him a popular lecturer and would have equipped him, had he been orderly minded, as a rare professor of Comparative Literature. He had always what Joubert calls *l'âme et l'esprit hospitaliers.*

Existence was tense for him, living every day as his last, as he put it. He found himself a lodging, sea-weed scented and passing romantic, over a grocer's at Southwick. This was the period of certain terrors—how serious?—terror of travelling third-class on railways, terror of the feminine principle in life, terror of getting germs on his hands. It is interesting to conjecture what scope his rhetorical genius had already found in those lectures—were they much more than lessons?—directed at the daughters of gentlemen in Victorian Brighton and Eastbourne. The pupils can hardly have been responsive to Pater or Remy de Gourmont. Those were not yet the days when 'literary appreciation' is systematically fostered or blighted among children. Much reading in his twenties certainly incubated John Cowper's 'copy-cat' aptitudes. Through the influence of his cousin Ralph Shirley, Ryder and Company of London were persuaded to issue in 1896 a slim, elegant volume of verse called *Odes and Other Poems,* and bound in apple-and-gold. It is curious to read in the light of his mature achievement. For if his fiction is individualistic *à outrance* his verse has always been derivative to a fault. It is difficult to realise nowadays that he was one of the poets of the *fin de siècle.*

A first book is always a first book, and the zest of the occasion had not died when he wrote of it more than half a century later.[1]

In the year 1896, when I was twenty-two, [*sic*] a little book of my verse, beautifully bound in a pale green cover ornamented by shining golden flowers, was published by William Ryder & Co. in London. *The Bookseller*'s reviewer enquired 'How many poets has England today? Has she half-a-dozen? Into this small, exclusive circle Mr. Powys may perhaps one day come'. So, indeed, I thought myself! And how well I remember being seated under one of those massive, sea-breaking concrete groynes on the beach at Hove, West Brighton, now officially known as Hove in the county of Sussex, and reading, as only an author with

[1] 'Mark Twain Quarterly;' 1952 Winter.

his first work in print *can* read, quite alone and at an hour when the famous beach was practically deserted, and to no listener but the 'windy surges' the first galley-proofs of *any* book, not to speak of one of my own which I had ever seen. What things of marvel galley-proofs are! Were the pages which in the middle of the sixteenth century, Dolet and Rabelais read fresh from that German press of Sebastian Gryphius, in the French City of Lyons or Lugdunum 'ubi sedes est studiorum meorum', as the latter calls it, more akin to a galley-proof or to a page-proof? More akin than to either of these, I dare say, to a Papyrus or one of Periclean age!

But they were pretty good verses in their day, and could leave no doubt of his abilities. 'John the arch-imitator' he loved to call himself, and had he farmed a prize-poem, as did Kit Smart, he should have done it efficiently. Indeed, he might well have become the Shakespeare of prize-poets, despite his slight set-back at Cambridge. An influence less distinguished than Keats and Hardy on *Odes and other Poems* was Alfred de Kantzow, after whom John Cowper's only son was later named. His reminiscences of this patrician and picturesque, but very minor, ancient of literature are of more interest now for the light they shed on his own early—and unchanging—self than for their subject.

I was his disciple, his faithful lieutenant, his equerry, his man-at-arms, the bearer of his shield, the purveyor of his cap of maintenance. I tried for long to conceal from him the fact that I ever wrote poetry myself. I even suppressed *Odes and other Poems* as if it were some obscene or indecent publication.... I have never given to any work of my own the indomitable labour I lavished, day in and day out, on the polishing and revising of Mr. de Kantzow's poems. Two separate volumes of them I actually managed to get published before I had done. I journeyed to the country home of Mr. Fisher Unwin. I even carried Mr. de Kantzow himself up to London and in the studio of Mortimer Menpes, full of chat about Whistler, I compelled two count-esses and I don't know how many baronesses to acknow-ledge his genius.... Towards this old gentleman, indeed, I acted more like a devoted young woman than like a fellow-poet.

Well may he speak of 'my will so strong' which, though later, became a force in his own career.

Social ambition among the educated was, for better or worse, very much more common in those days than today, and of this John Cowper had no tinct. Indeed, his almost defiant indifference to public opinion was astonishing in one so humble. This was probably the legacy of the personal pride of his father, the 'proudest' of men, who wanted nothing. For he was filled with his 'childlike sense of the incredible romance of his own existence upon earth'. Of John Cowper, reared in his distinctive tradition, one always feels that he is the upper-class man who will not be an aristocrat but is too upper-class to be anything else.

It was in these years that his almost passionate intimacy with the growing boy Llewelyn began to take an important place in his complex life. The attractive child, so different, so Pagan, was equally devoted to 'daddy Jack' and with all the fascination of extreme contrast they became, in the elder's words, 'like spokes of the same wheel'. The child, himself never very studious, remembered daddy Jack as inexplicably concentrated, rapt in mysterious studies hour after hour, crouched ungainly over a desk, 'his long fingers stained with ink'. John Cowper's animist leanings were vividly recorded, many years later, in *Love and Death*. On a woodland walk the child ran on ahead and began to beat off the heads of campions with his hoop-stick, but Jown Cowper snatched him up, exclaiming 'Llewelyn, you must never, never do that again. Never in your whole life—for you must not forget that every tree, every leaf, every flower is alive *as we are alive* and it is only very stupid or very wicked people who can be indifferent to the destruction of their earth companions.' The closeness to Llewelyn is reflected in three novels, in all of which there is an acute study of a younger brother—in *Wood and Stone*, as Lexie Ashover in *Ducdame* and (with more arresting differences) as Jason Otter in *Wolf Solent*.

Lyon and 'the Catholic' John William Williams, a Thomist philosopher, were older influences whose religious preoccupations excited John Cowper but did not distract his earthy loyalties. Fears of sadism rarely ceased to trouble his conscience or ulcers his bodily serenity. His 'vice' of *voyeur* drew him as a magnet to Brighton beach. He hired the Town Hall at Hove and gave his first public lecture, characteristically covering 'three or four centuries of English literature'. It was hardly successful, being attended by three women and a child. It is

not recorded if the smallness of the audience damped even his
ebullience. In 1896, just before the marriage which he has
always allowed to remain something of a mystery, he acquired,
'not being able to find a small but very ancient Castle', a farm-
house lying in a fold of the Downs and dating back to Henry
III. It lay at Offham near Cooksbridge on the line from Lewes
to Haywards Heath. Here he took his bride, Margaret Alice
Lyon, a fair-haired girl of his own class and his friend's
sister.

For the honeymoon he made his first venture abroad, a trip
to Rome, showing himself a good sailor (in a non-manual
sense) if a muddled art-critic. A male friend accompanied the
couple. The marriage resulted in separation many years afterwards. John Cowper undoubtedly held the view of Magnus
Muir's father in *Jobber Skald* that 'the social fussiness of our
middle-class women destroys all the dignity and all the natural
enjoyment of life'. It is the belief of near friends that there was
never any violent break between the pair, who were friendly
until her death (as a Catholic convert) in 1947. Louis Wilkinson has a possibly revealing tale of the *ménage* in his *Welsh
Ambassadors*. The biblical Theodore, (this was 1907) 'held
firmly by the patriarchal doctrine of the submission of women'
(It is fair to remember here that John Cowper was deliberately
submissive). He would not visit his brother: 'I do not wish to
enter a house where a woman rules.' Louis Wilkinson advised
softening this by translating it into Latin, and Theodore,
being like Llewelyn no scholar, prevailed on his friend to do
this for him. John Cowper was hurt though not resentful, holding Wilkinson and not Theodore responsible.

Apparently in the first year of the new century—he himself
never helps with dates—John Cowper moved his household
from Court House, so shadowed by the Downs, to a more open
site at Burpham, near Arundel.

> If the Downs at Court House prevented the sunshine
> reaching us till the afternoon, all day long at Burpham
> there poured in upon us with the full flood of sunshine
> the voices of children, the bleating of sheep, the lowing
> of oxen, the ringing of bells, the stamping of horses, the
> tinkling of anvils, the sawing of timber, together with the
> most cheerful voices from the George & Dragon. We had
> so much sunshine, in fact, and such lively sounds in every
> direction that it seems strange that my proud and vicious

loneliness was not melted, humanised, precipitated, made into a sweet savour of humility.

Here he abandoned his 'huge, unprintable book', his largely fanciful avoidances of the human race, and—more suddenly if less lastingly—his Catholic leanings. One damp and depressing evening of 1902 in a neighbouring seaside town he got as far as the priest's doorstep and rang the bell. But the father happened to be out, and he accepted this as an omen. However, these Romish yearnings, stimulated by his anti-Evangelical recoil and his fetishism, have all the same recurred constantly through his later life, and as a very old man he had Pope John XXIII in the place of honour in the gallery of photos in his room.

A little time before this anti-crisis in his religious life, his son Littleton Alfred, the only child of his marriage, was born. Those who believe in the inheritance of temporary or acquired characteristics will not be surprised that Littleton the younger should abandon a popular and esteemed and successful life as a parish clergyman to enter the Roman priesthood and die (unhappily in early middle-life through a road accident) in that Faith. John Cowper's satyrish passion for 'anonymous ankles' did not leave him when he became a husband and father. Long into the new century he would journey eagerly from Burpham to Littlehampton or Brighton beach, drawn as by an irresistible magnet. What survived in him of the paternal conscience reproached him perpetually for this. There is no doubt that he strove to achieve sexual normality (for which he had an exaggerated admiration) both in marriage and in casual encounters, but he was singularly unsuccessful. As often as he understood women—and when he did it was with startling insight—he disliked them. When they remained as abstract hypostatisations of sylphhood, all slim ankles, he was lost in vague adoration. He persevered in his striving for intellectual communion:

> I came to find almost all women possessed of absorbing mental interest for me. They seemed, all of them, with the single exception of *society women*, whom I loathed from the bottom of my heart and whom I regarded as poisoners, perverters, spoilers, degraders, ruiners, destroyers, of all the dignity and poetry of human life, to be far more interested in the sort of generalisations about the universe that interested me than men *ever* were!

Some of those excluded from his *Autobiography* as being *society women* must have been almost as much gratified as surprised by the classification!

In 1902 John Cowper gave, by invitation of J. A. R. Marriott, his first University Extension lecture, at Cambridge, the subject being the Arthurian legend. In those early days of the movement, the lecturers were often viewed in the best circles as impostors, charlatans and cheapeners. He of course gloried in this. With his field preacher mannerisms he was never altogether in favour with the Establishment, but he was sufficiently successful to give up girls' schools and live by Extension and collateral work throughout the country. His omnivorous reading and his gift of inexhaustible discourse enabled him to cover a wide literary field. He was in fact launched on a way of life that—at whatever cost to his creative achievement—was to satisfy his energies for the best years of his life. He did indeed compose a chapter or so of a 'normal romance', and in the later Edwardian years a Life of Keats for Methuen over which he disagreed with the publishers, and which remains in manuscript to this day. He became the life and soul of a literary coterie of whose immortality he, but nobody else, was unshakeably convinced. This included his brother Theodore, 'the Catholic' Williams, the aged de Kantzow, Dr. Bernard O'Neill, Louis Wilkinson and a rakish, attractive Liverpool character named Tom Jones. Wilkinson, expelled from Pembroke College, Oxford on account of an anti-religion scandal, was up at Cambridge with Llewelyn, and published an undergraduate novel much less attractive than its author's personality. As he always played Devil's advocate to John Cowper, it may be interesting to quote his opinion in those early days.[1]

A god whose persuading intonations were loud and clear, a young god then, hard-fleshed, keen-boned, lean-bellied in his human manifestations; not beautiful, with his loose aberrant mouth, his Mousterian or simian forehead 'villainous low' or 'like a girl's'—he has called it both the one and the other—his beaked nose and the high-toned seemingly artificial colour of his 'Red Indian' cheeks. Yet he did give an effect of beauty, notably when he was lecturing, but not only then; and it was beauty of a transfiguring power for those who saw and heard him. He was, and is, full of life, full of beliefs, full of the power to

[1] *Welsh Ambassadors*, 1937.

communicate his abundance. When we first met I realised this was his greatest value.

It was to the delightfully named Tom Jones's amateur prostitutes that John Cowper would recite Milton and Wordsworth: and it was on his way to visit this friend at Liverpool that he was seized with his original fainting fit, on the platform of a Gloucestershire junction. It was the first of many, from which he did not gain release until he gave up violently itinerant lecturing.

The years before the First War might have been more lastingly fruitful had the form of expression he cherished, lyrical verse, achieved a closer relation with the life of nature that was his most deeply felt environment. But as a poet he remained bookish: Swinburnian and Hardyish in derivations, but not freshly renewing even the hopeful Hardy strain. *Poems*, issued by the same house of Ryder in 1899, was a mere repetition of the skilful, superficial 1896 volume. It is believed that *Lucifer* was first drafted about 1907, but with all its praiseworthy passages it is derivative and it did not appear till 1957. *The Death of God*, he had called it, and it is difficult not to suspect that it has been considerably revised. Littleton has preserved[1] some *Lines to a Green Woodpecker* written in the Burpham garden in 1903, and they are transcribed here as probably more worthy and more revealing than any of his other early verse.

To the Green Woodpecker, or Yaffle, or High Loe, or Hew-hole, or Wood-Spite, or Pick-a-tree; also Fain Fowl.

> Nature in her moods unites
> Waving shadows, warning lights,
> Giving partial scope to none
> Of her wide dominion.
> Gold from boughs that sunbeams smite,
> Green from leaves that shadows checker,
> Flits the Hew-hole, the Woodspite,
> Pick-a-tree, the Green Wood-pecker!
> Pluvial avis! You have seen
> Stranger things in forest green,
> Than the seagulls on the sea
> Or the swallows on the lea!
> You with mosses of the Wood,
> Must have staunched some wood-god's blood,
> So to wear upon your head
> Such a more than mortal red!

[1] *Still the Joy of It.*

D

Or you must have fixed your eyes
Through green leaves on sunset skies,
Till the splendour of their stain
Burnt itself into your brain!
Or, to suit your mocking call,
You an atheist Cardinal,
Must be spending impious glee
In a laughing Purgatory!
Where the wind-flower like a star,
Floats in mazes nebular,
And the primrose passion-pale
Sheds her fragrance on the gale,
Where the bird, whose bursting throat
Pours the immemorial note,
Cries aloud the Daulian dirge,
Over sanicle and spurge,
Flooding Sussex woodlands dim
With the wild Hellenic hymn;
Where the mosses soft as sleep
'Neath the whispering hazels heap
Beds of joy for lovers true
Shaded by the hyacinths blue,
God-wept grief-inscribed bells
Love's memorial sentinels:
Poets in such haunts as these
Sip a melancholy ease
And on sentiment's soft breast
Take a Honey-Lotus rest.
But the Mother brings to birth
From the spring-nooks of the Earth
From the bitter bark of trees,
And the wood's interstices
A strange sound that pricks him shrewd
Like a wasp's sting in the blood,
A strange sound that jibes and jeers
Like a demon in his ears!
Sound that gives ironic sense
To all life's inconsequence;
Sound that here and there is tost
Quickly heard and quickly lost,
An elfish sound, an impious laughter,
That draws you on and mocks you after.
All climes know it. Countries all
Know its mad and mocking call
'Yaffle! Yaffle! Yaffle! Yaffle!
Mortal wisdom I can baffle!
Ha-Ha! Ha-Ha! Ha-Ha! He!
Lord, what fools these mortals be!'
'Tis the voice of all that knows

Why the storm wind comes and goes
Why the rushes nod and play
Why the streamlets dance all day
To an undiscovered tune
Older than the sun or moon—
'Tis the voice that turns to scorn
All that is of woman born—
'Tis the chuckle sharp and shrewd
Nature in her impish mood!
'Tis the laughter, shriek and wild,
Nature mocking her own child!
Waving shadows, warning lights
Nature in her moods unites,
Giving partial scope to none
Of her wild dominion.

John Cowper lectured a good deal, in English, on the Continent, making a hugely relished appearance before Royalty in Dresden, and sooner or later involved in his perambulatory lectures Louis Wilkinson, who was a public success, and Llewelyn, who was not. His first invitation to the United States (whether or not one considers it ill-fated) took him to Philadelphia where in January, 1905 he gave his first lecture under the auspices of the American Society for the Extension of University Teaching. His own reminiscences show far more interest in the boat-journey out than in the work, but his rhetorical genius did not fail him, and he was soon burning-up large, enthusiastic, popular audiences from the Atlantic to the Pacific seaboards. Punchinello he might love to call himself, 'a prophetic Dan Leno and a comic Savonarola' but 'I was no mere Pierrot of culture but had in me "something dangerous"'. 'There was a formidable daimôn which ... can be reached somewhere in my nature, and which when it *is* reached has the Devil's own force.' His appeal to the shoulder-chipped and nonconforming cultural aspirants of a young civilisation was phenomenal—above all, Jews took him to their hearts. 'He lectured more to please himself than to please others' commented the invaluable Bragdon in *The Hidden Springs*. His message was regenerative and trespassed generously on the political. To audiences of those days his unconventionality was sometimes startling; as when he observed in Rochester, N.Y. in 1907, 'You know, ladies, we all like to have our sexual life go on pleasantly.'

He projected himself with overwhelming energy into his

lectures, even leaping down among the audience, shaking them by the hand, thumping them on the back and bidding them come to Dostoievsky as a salvationist might exhort them to come to Jesus. He rather exulted in this *abandon* than sought to contain it. 'I howled and whimpered and chanted and burbled like a dervish ... a Dionysus of East 14th Street ... for these people I tore my heart to pieces. For these people I gouged out my most sensitive nerves with my own finger-nails, and wrote with them in blood on the trembling air.'

It was not under any official or scholastic auspices that John Cowper's torrential expositions really flourished in Theodore Roosevelt's America. He became a 'Circus' privately organised by an impresario, and tapped a new reservoir of aspiration among those to whom a faint feeling of outlawry attached and who were to a great extent attracted by his embryonic socialism. Arnold Shaw, a droll and sceptical businessman from Yorkshire was his first circus-master, and he was as much devoted to John Cowper as to the box-office. John Cowper was equally fortunate later in Shaw's second-in-command, Glass, a quieter but exceptionally conscientious and reliable personality. Public lectures are now, of course, a big industry in the States, but in these days of all-pervading universities and lower-middle-class society it is difficult—and fascinating—to try to envisage those early audiences. For this was, in truth, popularisation of literature, with only commercial, lay backing; and the public was not the public of today, higher education was not a widespread cult, and contemporary literature had no prospect of being accepted as common currency. Punchinello was a portent and a cultural circus a novelty.

John Cowper made something like a thousand pounds a year, a useful sum which he either sent home to his family at Burpham or dissipated with incautious open-handedness. He was never able to refuse a wheedling acquaintance or a tramp. He spent much of his summers in Europe but gradually became engulfed in America, if the word can be applied to one to whom *coelum non animum* so plainly applies. With his good nature and desire for experience he accepted the United States cheerfully, almost enthusiastically; though, as so many Britons still do, he liked the people far better than their ways of life. His analysis of the paradoxical character of the American male remains one of the most shrewd and probing ever penned. He startled middle-class opinion, but little more than he was liable to do in England. Despite the 'oceans braid' his intense study of all things Welsh, his desire to go back to his romantic-ally-envisaged forefathers and be Celtic, was intensified. From 1902 his mind was committed to the almost perverse yearning which after three-and-a-half decades was to carry him to his hilly fastnesses in Cambria. A moderate linguist, he was a passionate mythologist. In all this attraction, the elemental and occult factor was of course very strong.

He travelled a good deal in the Old World, especially in France, Spain, Italy and mid-Europe. Usually he had the stimulating companionship of Louis Wilkinson or Llewelyn, whose violent and tenacious attack of phthisis in 1909 was a great shock to the older brother, intermittent invalid as he was himself. 'Not Lulu, not Lulu ill!' he cried. It was more than two anxious years before the beloved younger with his Pagan-ism and laughing gaiety was restored to real activity. The most stimulating of John Cowper's continental adventures, later to provoke some of the best pages of the *Autobiography*, was the holiday in Venice in the early summer of 1912 with Llewelyn, Louis Wilkinson and Frances Gregg (the boy-girl to him) the beautiful art student from America who had married Louis in April. All three men were in love with her, including John Cowper for all his 'cold, planetary' heart, and the piquant situation inspired the pens of both Powyses. The marriage was commonly attributed to John Cowper's match-making activi-ties and it is a fact that his liking for marriage has persuaded him to advance several unions which his friends describe as, broadly, disastrous. The cynical may conclude from the records that the least enamoured of the Venetian trio was Louis Wilkinson, while the most ardent was Llewelyn; but that the husband was the only one free of jealousy. That this unusual *ménage à quatre* enjoyed the holiday of a lifetime is perhaps a tribute to the Powys genius for goodwill and sympathy.

However solicitous and helpful he may have been in Llewelyn's illness, John Cowper surpassed himself in self-neg-lect and wilful stoicism in his later thirties. It is a little sur-prising, sometimes, that he got round to his lectures at all, for he had to travel prodigiously. He underwent several opera-tions for his ulcers, culminating in 'gasterenterostomy' per-formed in London. He cast off the effect of this with his usual robustness and buoyant will-power, and joined more actively than ever in the life of American cities, for many of which, especially New York, he developed a certain affection grounded in close acquaintance. He sympathised with the common man and especially the negro. In these years he got to know, among many lesser literary characters, Edwin Arlington Robinson, Vachel Lindsay, Edgar Lee Masters and Theodore Dreiser. As shown clearly in the *Autobiography* these important writers were to have later a perceptible influence on his mind. Awareness of Dreiser is frequently to be sensed in his novels.

But, over all this willed participation of John Cowper's, there hangs a faint air of unreality. His mind was there, but not his true soul. He was no Henry James, enamoured of social reciprocities and urban solutions of man's loneliness. Despite his sentimental praise of togetherness, the unique quality of a man was more a reality to him than man's commonalty. Nature confined to human nature must always leave him desolatingly incomplete. He was as incapable of moulding himself to the American civilisation as he was of taking an aloof or unsympathetic attitude towards it. He remained 'Wessex' the whole thirty years he was steeped in the atmosphere (should one say various atmospheres?) and pressures of the United States. His novels have shown from beginning to end no background, no medium, no way of living outside the well-weathered English traditions. However great the eccentricity of these novels, it has always been eccentricity curiously *within* the Englishness.

CHAPTER IV

American Years: the 'Circus' and Early Novels

'My furtive and gingerly-stepped *pas seul* round the
maypole of life.'

IT is a little difficult to evaluate John Cowper's attitude or
wishes in the realm of achievement and reputation as a young
man. He inherited from his mother a leaning to abasement—
how Mrs. Powys hated success—and from his father a massive
indifference. He was obviously sincere in protesting his aversion from personal distinction or celebrity, and that is precisely
what he achieved in an almost sensational degree. On the other
hand he frankly hoped for some immortality for himself and
his colleagues in creative writing; and creative writing he can
barely be said to have essayed before the First War, when he
was forty-two. It seems probable that he was a good deal influenced by anxiety about the financial welfare of his family at
Burpham. With little real self-discipline, desperately active,
tortured bodily by ulcers and morally by his sadistic fancies,
distracted by his phantasmal Tantalus-lusts, he may well have
postponed his creative urges. He suggests his own love of unreality: ' "Sawney John" the King's jester, at his familiar
antics, paying himself with the tinkle of his own gold, and
feeding himself with the smell of his own goose.' It is difficult
to resist him in this vein—such candid self-knowledge is very
uncommon indeed—but to dwell on it too much is to risk mis-
understanding him. He was really in terror of discovering himself to be a humbug, and determined not for an instant to run

into the danger of becoming anything that he himself might come to see as a humbug. Hence such startling excesses as 'Quixotic puppet as I am, prophetic scarecrow as I am, draggle-tailed hermit-whore as I am.' That his Circus was no mere Circus to others is shown by such testimonies as that of a very clear-eyed fellow-Cantab, the actor Maurice Browne:

> Powys was then reaching the height of his amazing career as a lecturer in the U.S.A. He earned large sums which he sent to his family, travelling himself in endless discomfort, sleeping in pokey hotel bedrooms, suffering almost continuous pain from duodenal ulcers, never complaining. Incomparably the finest public speaker I have heard, not excepting John Burns at the turn of the century or Winston Churchill in recent war years. I listened to him scores, perhaps hundreds of times, and never heard him speak badly, not even when he was so crippled with pain that he could hardly stand upright; more often than I can remember he was like a trumpet calling to battle. He identified himself with his subject, almost invariably a literary subject, even if the author were one whose work he did not rate highly. When he lectured on Huysmans at Lincoln Centre, a social settlement on Chicago south side, sparks seemed to fly from his fingers, which were handling like an obscene object a Bible lying on the lectern before him; the audience hated his guts—as he intended. When he spoke on a subject near his heart, he inspired his hearers. Once I heard him talk on Hardy for over two hours to an audience of over two thousand in a huge auditorium in the heart of Chicago's slums; throughout those one hundred and thirty odd minutes there was no sound from his listeners save an occasional roar of applause or laughter; and when he had finished speaking we rose like one person to our feet demanding more. The man was a great actor.[1]

Most of us find it difficult even to envisage a crowd of two thousand at a lecture on literature. As these public harangues were nothing if not impromptu there is, of course, no close record of them; but traces of the popular lecturer are very evident all through the miscellaneous articles John Cowper was beginning to collect for *Visions and Revisions*. A certain diffuseness and over-emphasis very characteristic of the platform were to be a perpetual weakness of John Cowper's critical presentations, and indeed of all his writing. *Visions and Re-*

[1] *Too Late to Lament* (Gollancz).

visions displays more evident traces of visions than of revision: but there is obviously *some* revision. There is little suggestion of the compelling personal urgency of the lectures. It is a pity that we have not a tape recording of just one of these.

Until long after the First War he was migrant, Burpham being domestically his only headquarters, while his spiritual home remained Wessex. There was much in the United States, of course, that he regarded with horror, just as there were qualities in the American character that lent themselves to his occasional sentimentalisings. Louis Wilkinson has quoted as an anticipation of the most Cowperian passages in the novels an undated letter of about this period:

> I *couldn't* write before. I've been absolutely in hell. Madly hunting for somewhere to live in Virginia. It was hot as the devil. I landed myself finally in an Inn on a marsh by a sea-estuary among reeds and black decaying tree-trunks and indescribable mud—and on the other side of the water black cypresses and the *House of Usher.*
>
> The place heaved and palpitated with the life of putrescence like a horrible great heart. The shore was strewn with dead turtles as big as pigs and the salt water when you bathed tasted of Death.
>
> My head has only just stopped aching. It *was* a place! A sailor was always drunk in the next room and kept me awake, *moaning* 'God damn you all, and the whole lot of you' all night long. It was the cradle of all the physical night-mares that prey on morbid nerves. It heaved with horrible death-in-life. I shall never forget it. I went in the middle of the last night in my pyjamas to my landlord and told him I was going to clear off at six o'clock in the morning. Then I 'phoned long distance to New York to stop May coming. She was out. They said 'had gone'....
>
> In fact *now* I don't care for anything. I have—really and truly—looked at unmitigated horror with naked eye-balls. The place *heaved* with unspeakable life—with forbidden life. It was like black blood breeding *snakes.* And the House of Usher was in the midst of it. A dead tree as tall as a mast had a heron's nest against the sunset and great shrieking cries of some sort of fish-hawks died over the water.

The masochistic strain in him which so irritates Louis Wilkinson was never so alive as during his thirties. It is the vein which was to recur constantly in the anti-heroes of the novels, in Wolf and No-man and John Hush. But despite this much more real weakness, he continued haunted by his 'sadic' guilt, and began to feel for the first time some puritanical compunction about his sylpholeptic indulgences. As Rook Ashover in *Ducdame* he was to write of himself 'This blending of an irresistible attraction to the feminine body and mind, with an absolute lack of emotional passion, was nothing less than a monstrous deformity'. He frequented forlornly the most repellent peep-shows and vaudevilles. The 'burlesque' shows in the States, to one of which he actually dragged the sceptical and disillusioned Wilkinson, overwhelmed him with a sense of his lack of sexual normality and gave him an increased distaste for the common man's predilections, without lessening his incongruous enthusiasm for the common man. A typical frustration in his strange erotic quest occurred when, on a visit to Paris, he was drawn to a 'gala night place'.

> To see a person, and a fairly good-looking person, belonging, or apparently belonging, to the same sex as the most ravishing of my sylphides, tossing up a flurry of petticoats and displaying a flurry of under-garments and then drumming on her rump with her fist while she screamed 'Bon face [*sic*]! Bon face! Bon face!' in the very tone that Punch on the donkey-stand at Weymouth used to cry 'Toby! Toby! Toby!' was a spectacle, so far as I was concerned, calculated to freeze into Arctic ice every lecherous impulse in the human frame. In the end I set out alone for Rouen in order that I might enjoy—while I struggled to get that obscene cry 'Bon face! Bon face! Bon face!' out of my head—Ruskin's favourite facade of St. Ouen. It's a wonder, however, that I didn't behold, poised above those flamboyant buttresses and battlements and pinnacles, some colossal Gargamellion rump, pedestalled on that heaven-aspiring pile!

His inward recoil from ordinary urban society contributed to his rather sentimental idealising of the negro, whose apparent humility would in any case strike a sympathetic chord in him. '*Inching along*, like the poor inch-worm, waiting for Jesus to come,' they appealed to all his love of primitive simplicities and of those simple acceptances which his own supersubtle mind found so tantalisingly evasive. 'The only imaginative Christians left,' as he sweepingly put it, probably meaning the literal type of imagination to which his sophisticated longings strove so persistently in his great creative period. Actually his relish for the negroes, as for Wessex peasants in his

books, springs largely from his desire for lost, elemental innocence. These folk are of the unchanging and incorruptible
earth.

John Cowper already had an emotional leaning to what he
called Socialism. He was indeed—and has with some quali-
fication remained—one to whom funny peasants are funny
peasants, negroes are negroes and tramps are tramps. He had
little more notion of levelling than most men of the day. But
he desired 'to smite this cursed economic system some shattering blow', and in 1914 those who had vision as well as goodwill
were with him here. That all John Cowper's politics are sentimental is hardly to be questioned. His quaint addiction to
nuns, whores, hoboes and anarchists is a fairly clear pointer
here, and we have seen the appeal he had to minorities among
the educated of the West. The Cooper's Union hall was the
arena of several of his lecturing triumphs. On one occasion the
authorities, having let the hall to an anarchist speaker, can-
celled the letting. In protest John Cowper declined to give the
lecture which had been billed. He affirmed years afterwards
that 'the Anarchist Ideal, which is of course the perfect one,
has never been tried'.[1] But he cannot be said to have enriched
the literature of anarchism. Whatever the elemental and the
anarchic may seem at first blush to have in common, it emerges
fairly soon that elemental feeling inclines us to an extreme
conservatism in mere human affairs.

The year 1914 proved a doubly catastrophic one for the
mellow Montacute background that had watched the emer-
gence of so strange a brood. In July Mrs. Powys was taken
violently ill, and on the 31st July she died. 'I don't think I've
ever seen anything so tragic and full of sorrow as that face,'
Llewelyn wrote. John Cowper arrived at the vicarage on the
next day, and his mother's funeral took place on the fatal 4th
August. Her senior by six years, her sturdier husband had still
another nine years to live.

Though the War does not seem to have inspired John
Cowper creatively, it stimulated his almost too ready flow of
words, and persuaded him into writing as apart from talking.
His first novel *Wood and Stone* was not published until 1915—
though I cannot help believing that its tone and matter are
earlier—while his first small prose volume *The War and Cul-*

[1] Letter to Louis Wilkinson, October 13, 1939.

ture was issued by Arnold Shaw of the Circus, recently turned
publisher, at the end of 1914. (It appeared shortly afterwards
in England as *The Menace of German Culture*, a title obviously adopted over here with jingoistic or recruiting purpose.) The essay is in fact a reply to an American professor of
Bismarckian leanings. Although John Cowper's magnet
always responded more quickly to the North than to the
South, he had in fact for some years been hostile, as an individualist, to the authoritarian and monopolistic views now
current in the Germany of his beloved Goethe and Nietzsche.
In 1916 he published with Llewelyn the *Confessions of Two
Brothers* (Manas Press, Rochester, New York) which has never
been issued in England. The two contributions are separate,
and the elder brother's is by far the more substantial, the
younger's being only superficial reminiscences. John Cowper's
confessions are inward confessions, egoistic and important. In
these pages, and in those of *The War and Culture*, most of his
recurrent philosophical ideas are to be found in embryo, and
they can best be discussed together with his later essay-books.
His sensationism is here, his then emphatic repudiation of free-
will, his tentative Pyrrhonism, his aestheticism, his polytheism,
his dislike of himself. 'A little too inhuman, a little too
analytic . . .' was Llewelyn's verdict 'they were also too
modest'.

Wood and Stone is an extremely English work in spirit and
setting; no doubt affording John Cowper some tacit relief from
'Residential sections' and other brashnesses of the 1914 American scene. For all its zest in national description and its careful
studies of character and motive, it must be considered a pren-
tice novel. More concerned with expression than art, with ideas
than surface plausibilities, John Cowper still combined unquestioning acceptance of the English social scene with a lively
economic 'socialism'. Without being in any way autobiographical the story—if story is the word—is largely bounded by John
Cowper's earlier life. Leo's Hill is obviously drawn from Ham
Hill near Montacute, and the Leonian sandstone which figures
so prominently is inspired by Nevilton stone. The Catholic
dialectician Mr. Taxater is drawn closely after Williams. Luke
Anderson would hardly be Luke Anderson but for the strong
traces of Llewelyn in his make-up and the self-deprecating
Maurice Quincunx is one of John Cowper's less extreme

travesties of himself. Much of the behaviour and psychology fails less by being impossible than by being unconvincing— after all, John Cowper was to become a great master of the convincingly impossible. A large number of ideas and indeed some vivid conflicts are projected. The issue most persistently presented is the relation of Catholicism to Christianity in general, and of both to the senses. It is the Achilles heel of this early novel that so far as issues are realised it is in conversation, and weakness in conversation is the weakness no Powys has ever been able to surmount in writing fiction. The family are tone-deaf to ordinary talk. *Wood and Stone* is not only dedicated to Thomas Hardy, but forcibly recalls him by its setting and by its elaborate descriptive overture. But it is scarcely akin to his work and curiously deficient in the dramatic interest that never failed to lend vitality to the great Dorset writer.

Not that *Wood and Stone* is without interest today or that it is difficult reading. It is too full of ideas not to throw some light on the pre-1914 scene, and in style it is the least involved of John Cowper's novels, except perhaps *Ducdame* which was simplified at the earnest solicitation of Llewelyn.[1] *Wood and Stone* is, however, much less mature in tone than its immediate successor *Rodmoor*, which unfortunately has never come out in England. Not only is the earlier book wanting in freedom of imaginative expression, but it lacks the frankness in sexual and religious matters that is so refreshing in John Cowper's mature work. The publication was barely noticed in London, but *The Times* reviewed it in 1917, calling it an 'immense novel'—little did they know of what John Cowper was to be capable! The writer found the novel pretentious and on the whole rather repellent, though he recognised its intellectuality and commented on its power of depicting the many-sidedness of love. With *Rodmoor* we are far more conscious of a poet's world. *Rodmoor* may still lack something of ease and assurance, it may still be careless of artistic restraint, it may have few superficial graces to lend it sheen; but there is no doubt of its imaginative power. It is the work of one possessed—of devils possibly, but certainly possessed.

---

[1] Louis Wilkinson recalls that once Llewelyn told John Cowper 'the less the better', to which the elder replied, 'No, no, the more the better'. It proved a costly heresy.

In 1916, with America perilously poised on the verge of a world war, the public was in no mood for experimental or even good novels. Although there was a fairly persistent vogue for British authors, Wells's highly topical *Mr. Britling Sees it Through* met with little success, and Bennett's *The Lion's Share* and Hugh Walpole's *The Dark Forest* were no more fortunate. Works of the calibre of *Seventeen, Just David* and *When a Man's a Man* were topping the best-seller lists. It is scarcely surprising that *Rodmoor* found a discouraging response, though John Cowper's reputation as a speaker was then at its zenith. There is no apparent link between the propagandist for the war effort which he had now—in complete earnestness—become and so remote a poetic extravaganza as *Rodmoor*. It might indicate the quality as well as the limitations of the book to call it a *Wuthering Heights* manqué.

Rodmoor has its setting not in the mysterious and legend-haunted west, but in the breezier openness of East Anglia, a country John Cowper was to revisit only once, and briefly, in the overture to *A Glastonbury Romance*. This migration was almost certainly an attempt to avoid dominance by too potent native associations, and it is not without its significance. For John Cowper was never a mere elementalist in fiction: psychology already had him in fee. Man's relation to woman, and man's relation to the sea, are alternating *motifs* in this strange romance, and it is only under the waves that human love is allowed in the end to triumph.

Rodmoor is indeed more a challenge than at first it appears to be. There is already stirring in John Cowper a half-conscious dissatisfaction with past treatment of human character in imaginative art. John Cowper's characters are realised a little differently, they are franker, odder, more magnetised by fetichism and animism. They have something of the irrationality of Dostoievsky's people, but are drawn by a simpler, if not indeed a simplified, attraction to the earth.

From early in *Rodmoor* it becomes evident that John Cowper's novels will be irrelevant to criticism of twentieth century society. Each of his real characters, his major introverts, is a society to himself and living in a timeless world of his own. The other-worldliness of *Rodmoor* is manifest after one brief uneasy London chapter: there is no pretence of the circumstantial as in *Wood and Stone*. *Rodmoor* itself is 'a place where one loses one's identity and forgets the rules', though never quite so destructive of identity or oblivious of rules as John Cowper's later Wessex and Wales. The Italian Adriano Sorio (a very Powysian Italian!) is adrift, in what was to become the classic John Cowper fashion, between two women, the sympathetic and the more demonic intuitive. He is engaged, as later the parson Hastings in *Ducdame*, on the manuscript of a nihilistic work, and we are invited, rather confusedly at times, to witness nature's revenge and how much more demonic is nature than the demonism of mere human intellect. It is more than probable that the destructiveness and the Nemesis were born of John Cowper's sadic self-accusation. 'I want to show—' says Adriano,

'what is simply the truth—that the pleasure of destruction, destruction entered upon out of sheer joy and for its own sake, lies behind every living impulse that pushes life forward. Out of destruction alone—out of the rending and tearing of something—of something in the way—does new life spring to birth. It isn't destruction for cruelty's sake' he went on, his fingers closing and unclosing at his side over a handful of sand. 'Cruelty is mere inverted sentiment. Cruelty implies attraction, passion, even—in some cases—love. Pure destruction—destruction for its own sake—such as I see it—is no thick, heavy, muddy, perverted impulse such as the cruel are obsessed by. It's a burning and devouring flame. It's a mad, splendid revel of glaring whiteness like this which hurts our eyes now. I'm going to show in my book how the ultimate essence of life, as we find it, purest and most purged in the ecstasies of the saints, is nothing but an insanity of destruction! That's really what lies at the bottom of all the asceticism and all the renunciation in the world.'

Philippa, the intuitive young squireena, is filled with much the same destructiveness, and it is she who draws Adriano on to his death by drowning in a scene forshadowing the cosmic catastrophe of *A Glastonbury Romance*. The triumph of nature over man is no mere triumph of matter over mind, but the triumph of a higher over a limited animism. There are several, sometimes conflicting, strands of speculation running through *Rodmoor*: the melancholy of the modern world, the hopelessness of meliorism, the impossibility of undivided love;

but the dominant theme is the destructiveness of destruction with the certainty that the destroyer will himself be destroyed.

Adriano has to be not only the embodiment of pessimistic and destructive moods, but from time to time unmistakably John Cowper himself.

I *know* I've got it in me to give to the world something it's never dreamed of—something with a real madness of truth in it—something with a bite that gets to the very bone of things.

The very bone of things. Do the jaws close on it in *Rodmoor*? One must be candid about this. The book is a completely disinterested, one might almost say in the circumstances heroic attempt to ignore accepted values and penetrate to the truths of poetic psychology. It succeeds as expression, but hardly as art. Imaginative argument never quite becomes transfused into a convincing re-creation of life. This is due not only to a certain indecision in the writer's mind as to the real issue on which the central action hinges; but to faults of construction and inequalities of style, some incidental, some never to be wholly surmounted. The handling of language, especially in passages of description, can be very remarkable and convey an extraordinary freshness of perception, as in showing the deadness of a dead sea off Norfolk:

The blazing sunshine, pouring down from a sky that contained no trace of a cloud, seemed to have secured the power that day of reducing even the ocean itself to a kind of magnetised stupor. The waters rolled in, over the sparkling sands, with a long, somnolent, oily ripple that spent itself and drew back without so much as a flicker or flake of foam. The sea-gulls floated languidly on the unruffled tide, or quarrelled with little, short, petulant screams over the banks of bleached pungent-smelling seaweed where swarms of scavenging flies shared with them their noonday fretfulness. On the wide expanse of the sea itself there lay a kind of glittering haze, thin and metallic, as if hammered out of some marine substance, less resistant but not less dazzling than copper or gold. This was in the mid distance, so to speak, of the great plain of water. In the remote distance the almost savage glitter diminished and a dull livid glare took its place, streaked in certain parts of the horizon by heavy bars of silvery mist where the sea touched the sky. The broad reaches of hard sand smouldered and flickered under the sun's blaze and little vibrating waves danced like shapeless demons over the summit of the higher dunes.

But when concentration of purpose relaxes, the style can veer between the Book of Revelations and a superior novelette. The effect is, of course, distracting. Nor had John Cowper's writing acquired yet that peculiar tang which gives a persuasive unity of character even to the conversations of his maturest work. A still more serious strain on the reader's suspension of disbelief, and one that goes far to mar a much greater work in *Jobber Skald*, is the multi-centred construction. In a novel of ideas and one that is emphatically psychological and not panoramic, it is essential to concentrate on the protagonists, here surely Soriano and the two girls Nance and Philippa, and see other characters in relation to them. But these other figures, the sinister epicure Balthazar Stork, Nance's half-sister Linda, the parson Traherne, the world-weary Mrs. Renshaw, Fingal the arresting doctor, take the centre of the stage time and again and have enough vitality to keep the reader in a state of perpetually divided interest.

A war-time American Press was not highly responsive. We must recall that though the modern novel has long reached a phase that has little dependence on narrative or dramatic probability, in 1917 a serious novel was expected to be realistic. Though not a pioneer technically or in the sense of Dorothy Richardson or Proust or Joyce, John Cowper was a pioneer by reason of his novel standpoint. The *Bookman* was pained, having shown some appreciation of *Wood and Stone*, which it considered 'a better story'—a judgement surely relating only to the better construction and greater clarity of the earlier book. The reviewer, H. W. Boynton, who was not blind to John Cowper's intelligence, found the new novel 'a sort of gruesome jest on the part of a brilliant but eccentric performer' and, more enlighteningly, 'such a romance as might have been compounded by a Brontë and a Russian, and supplemented or decorated with the jovial speculative humour of a Peacock'. The ordinary newspapers, awake to John Cowper's publicity value, gave the book some superficial recognition. A more important, though much tempered, appreciation was that of Lawrence Gilman in the *North American Review*. Gilman was a fashionable critic of some influence, in whom a mildly tonic astringency was marred by persistent cheap

E

sarcasm. He knew John Cowper, who portrays him with his usual kindness and vivacity in the *Autobiography*. Gilman had drawn attention, rather deflatedly, to Louis Wilkinson's recent novel *The Buffoon* with its vigorous caricature of John Cowper and to a small selection of *The 100 Best Books* written by John Cowper himself. *Rodmoor* inspired him with a little more respect: [1]

> For unity's sake the scene is carefully harmonised with the inner motive of the story. It is worth remarking that the kind of unity that is most highly prized by a certain type of writer is the unity of effect conferred by landscape and environment, and this leads sometimes to a kind of childishness, a kind of old-womanish superstitiousness, a Castle-of-Otranto-like romanticism. Mr. Powys does not altogether escape this tendency. In his story nature sometimes ceases to be an Arctic void, and is suspected, like any old witch, of 'exercising a malign influence', the sea (which is really the chorus in the drama) is accused of hypnotising otherwise sane persons with its ceaseless terrifying voice; at critical junctures fiery clouds point threatening fingers at poor bedevilled mortals. An owl pecks at a dead woman's eyes, merely to remind us that nature may be as gruesome as a folk-story. But it would be a mistake to suppose that *Rodmoor* is merely a study in the effect of environment upon sensitive spirits. The meaning of the story goes deeper than any 'call of the wild' or than any of those psychological hypotheses that in the hands of certain writers lend themselves so agreeably to dramatic development. It delves down into the irrational, into the sub-human, and it finds awful realities just under the skin of consciousness. . . .
>
> The qualities to note are the extraordinary and disturbing reality of the thing; its awful plausibility; its terrible sympathy in raising sympathy and quelling it; its insane humour and its humorous insanity. . . . Oh yes, there is a world of common-sense, and satisfying feeling, and 'human' joys and sorrows—and ginger shall be hot in the mouth. But is *our* world *the* world, or anything like it? Genius may work towards the super-rational or toward the sub-rational. Neither theme is understood. Perhaps, sometime, the broken will be joined, and then we shall see how the unknown above joins the unknown below. Perhaps this story of Mr. Powys is just a pathological study; but perhaps it is something more: it possesses at least the thrill of the unknown which is also the thrill of beauty, and this gives it a claim.

[1] *North American Review*, December 19, 1916.

A comment that is highly understanding and more than a little prophetic. Unfortunately for his creative reputation, John Cowper did not follow-up with any more fiction until *Ducdame* nine years later, excepting a few short stories of which the very titles are difficult to authenticate[1] and which their author disliked in common with all short stories. Indeed he had little fellow-feeling for anything short.

In the later war years and for some time after John Cowper had a temporary Bohemian home in New York City, but he travelled continuously and was for long stretches in England. With a complete faith in those who went to the war, and little in those who directed it, he tried hard to enlist despite his appallingly unhealthy condition, which was never worse than in 1917. He underwent a further gasterenterostomy operation in New York. Llewelyn in those days was openly apprehensive lest the telegraph's 'pink messenger' should arrive with news of the death of his beloved Daddy Jack, and Louis Wilkinson, a more sceptical observer, was seriously alarmed by both the ulcers and the bread-and-milk asceticisms. John Cowper exploited himself further by stumping Great Britain on behalf of Lloyd George's War Aims propaganda; but he was inwardly relieved when his application to visit the Front as an entertainer was turned down. He would indeed have cut a memorable figure behind the lines in Northern France! An incident too typical of his satisfaction in self-humiliation is recorded at this period of war hysteria. Asked in public why he was not fighting, he replied that it was for fear of German bayonets; but he was forty-five, he was wretchedly ill, and he had tried obstinately to enlist.

Many of John Cowper's letters dealing with public events and local experiences in the later War years border on the brilliant, but they never reach quite the mellow level of those of the 1939-45 period when, like most of us, John Cowper was a good deal better informed about what was really going on. For all his over-mastering humanity he has never been in the least persuaded by the pacifist creed, and for all his fondness for Germans he has never sentimentalised German nationalism. The practical insight of this impractical man must never be overlooked. It is one of the qualities that have kept him

[1] e.g. *Romer Mowl* and *The Spot on the Wall* (both early, probably very early).

immune from all passing intellectual and sentimental fashions. The attraction which Roman Catholicism and anarchic communism have for him has never weakened, but this is due to something in his temperament: he has never accepted either of them.

CHAPTER V

Wessex and *Ducdame*

JOHN COWPER himself put down his comparative diligence in writing after 1914 chiefly to Arnold Shaw's becoming a publisher, and so personal and so unaccountable are his moods that the explanation can by no means be put aside. Whatever started him off, he now wrote a good deal. It is difficult to date the composition of most of the poems collected in *Wolf's Bane* (1916) or *Mandragora* (1917), but the copious literary essays included in the two volumes *Visions and Revisions* (1915) and *Suspended Judgments* (1916) were largely written with book publication in mind, some being obviously worked-up from lecture material. Reviews and full length miscellaneous essays began to appear in American journals, though not until a long time after can the name of John Cowper Powys be found at the foot of articles published in England.

The great difficulty in appraising at all tidily the books John Cowper wrote between 1914 and 1925 comes from there being at least three different streams with no apparent confluence, odd as this may sound in the case of a man of exceptional honesty and single mindedness. *German Culture* and the *Confessions* belong with the extensive series of earlier essay books; *Visions and Revisions* and *Suspended Judgments* call for suspension and revision of judgement beside later and more considered criticism. The novels containing so much more of the real, the future Powys, are totally independent, while the poems (including the still dormant *Lucifer*) are virtually a fourth stream, if that can be called a stream which flows so faintly from its sources. Yet John Cowper still looked on verse

as his true medium, which it had never been and was never to
be. The explanation of the difference in depth between these
streams lies partly in his not taking his early publications,
despite their earnestness, wholly seriously. The view of himself
as a prattling Pantaloon, goring his own thoughts out of professional necessity, died hard. He must, in the idiom of the
hour, keep the home fires burning. He failed in this to distinguish between talking for money and—what no Powys can
achieve—really professional authorship, meeting the reader.

His essays, his empirical socio-moral books have achieved a
certain currency from time to time, but they have from the
beginning puzzled his serious admirers because they are not
the John Cowper of the *Autobiography* and the letters and
still less the John Cowper of the novels. The *Confessions* were
followed by a series of small 'philosophic' booklets in blue covers
and bound with wire, issued in the States by Haldeman-
Julius, which in one course led up to *The Meaning of Culture,
In Defence of Sensuality, The Pleasures of Solitude* and
other elaborated essays. All these books are in essence the same
and it is impossible to remember them apart. There is little or
no development—John Cowper's general intellectual views
show very slow and slight *progress*—and they are dominated
by sensationism and the spirit of compromise. The gulf in
quality between these essays and the autobiographical writings
has much to do with his aiming in one case to give help to
readers and in the other to give help to himself. His literary
essays, though superficially less individual, are more satisfying
than the essay-books. He emerges in the long run as less a
philosopher than a critic; and less a critic than an empirical
psychologist.

He has always written better when his eye has been on himself than when it has been on the outer world, though he does
not admit this. Actually he resents his personality's being rated
higher than his speculations, and discounts mere biography.
His literary essays show his speculative capacity and his
imagination better than do his 'philosophic' essays because so
much less compromising and pragmatic and because although
he does talk down and over-tolerates, he talks down and over-
tolerates less. *Visions and Revisions* and the far superior *Suspended Judgments* had a temperate reception from the more
critical, who were not disposed to buttress this adventurer's

peculiar standing on the cultural fringe. They were critical largely of his generalised indulgence and his easy tendency to 'cancel out'. The early literary criticism is in truth facile as well as subjective, though it flows entrancingly where his fiction stumbles. No man, he made it obvious, was so well equipped to be a critic, could he but concentrate his mind on something definite. His amazing power of allusion and his international range have never been shown more dazzlingly than in *Suspended Judgments*, which is indeed mainly devoted to French writers.

His life, though not his mind, definitely centred now in the New World, where he experienced great kindness and (in his own way) happiness and for which he developed an affection strengthened by familiarity. The old domestic roots were almost finally torn up by the death of his father on the 5 August 1923. The old man's substantial fortune had been very considerably impaired by the devaluations of the War. Unfortunately his uncalculating first-born, whose popular success had made him independent of any financial sheet anchor in youth, was to be seriously in need of one in later years.

Oddly enough John Cowper's prolonged love-affair with America did not evoke the characteristic virtues of either. He was deeply grateful that the U.S.A. was different from the England of that intensified Englishness (of the public school, for example) that, for all his kindly tolerance, he disliked. Yet the particular ethical warmth, the communal goodwill, in which the U.S.A. is ahead of the world was not congenial or even very apparent to his peculiar temperament. The liaison was remarkably uncreative; but it must be remembered that after his boyhood John Cowper was little influenced except by books. His earth-spirit was destined to repulse, and his aestheticism was not greatly affected by, the environment he accepted. This was all food for the autobiographer, no doubt, but hardly for the speculative novelist. Cosmopolitan in culture, the writer never becomes a cosmopolitan. We might almost say of him, however long-lived, for all his Celtic dreams and his American philanderings

'in spite of all temptations
To belong to other nations
He remains an Englishman.'

If England has never taken to him very generally, America, apart from his minority-minded lecture audiences, has shown still less avidity for his achievements. Neither to America's vital academic establishment (so much more extensive and pervading than any in Europe) nor to her general readers— three times our number here in Britain—did John Cowper become a definite force. Both America and he had their particular conservatism, and American conservatism is perhaps as intolerant of the aristocratic rebel as Powys conservatism is intolerant of *newness* and of what we may roughly call the planning inclination in modern life. John Cowper has never lost, in his own words 'a certain reverence for man as man'. However superior to earlier centuries otherwise, the twentieth is inferior in what touches the essential dignity of the human soul.

In this consideration the mind that was incubating *Ducdame* was separated by an impassable gulf from its lively social contacts. The United States is least of all lands the happy home of the individualist, the man indifferent to the values of normality. John Cowper was not only indifferent to these values but distrustful of them. In almost every response to life he remained and remains 'pre-War' and non-conforming, seeking 'the courage to live like a tramp'.

While the *Autobiography* leaves no doubt of its writer's fondness for the United States, it may throw some light on his temperament to record that he had difficulties with Canada, which apparently reminded him of England without being English enough, and of America without being American enough.

> My roguish manager Arnold would always be announcing to me 'John, I've got a mean jump for you *now*!' and one of the very worst of these jaunty trips was when he acquired the habit of sending me into Canada ... Canada and the Canadians puzzled me. I do not yet understand them. They are certainly very different from Americans.

It was typical of John Cowper to find an extraordinary way of comforting his discomfiture:

> I certainly have derived immense satisfaction from prowling round the walls of the convents in Montreal. What queer feelings of attraction, pity, dismay I used to experience towards these harmless dedicated persons! The fact is I have a mania for nuns. It is true that I instinctively rev-

ere all priests—for I have always felt a romantic and superstitious tremor of credulity in the presence of what, after
all, *may* be a superstitious magnetism, evoked by the anonymous intention of generations of human faith. But towards
any nun I feel an emotion that combines superstitious
reverence with something else ... I believe it is connected
very intimately with what the ancients felt for Demeter
and Persephone.[1]

So, *Rodmoor* half-forgotten, the aesthetic exile-from-the-earth
continued to exhort a capitalistic society from many platforms,
bidding them read the classics, urging them to come to Dostoievsky. There were changes in the Circus, for a good while
the Western States supplanted the Eastern as his centre of
operations, for a long time he deserted the tutelage of Arnold
Shaw and some years after the War Glass, of the Lee Keedrick
Bureau (who had once handled J. M. Stanley) succeeded the
Yorkshireman as his impresario. But although true creative
work was almost at a standstill, he was becoming ever more
deeply influenced by Dostoievsky who like himself 'dipped his
pen in his own nerves', Dostoievsky, always the greatest influence on his novels and the one who most deepened his
psychological approach. As he is almost the only major novelist
of English whose contribution has been primarily Dostoievskian, who has actually advanced the insights of the great Slav
rather than follow other gods (yet tempering Dostoievsky's hell
with a wholesome whiff of the earth) it is well to stress this
allegiance. It is John Cowper's deepening concern with the
problem of evil and the hope of a new revolution through pity
that makes progress in the nine years between *Rodmoor* and
Ducdame, for all the later novel's limitations. He did indeed
take from the Russian 'a prophetic sensation that some vast
spiritual change is coming over human life'. To John Cowper
Dostoievsky explicitly stood above all other novelists: 'a
greater psychologist, a greater prophet'; and his *Memoirs of the
Underground* did more than anything else to deepen—if not
precisely to direct—the moral intensity that fused nature-
worshipper and psychological questor in the Englishman's
earthier phantasmagorias.

John Cowper in fact entered the sharply changing and much
evolved English novel of the middle 1920's with 'Something to

[1] *Autobiography*, p. 520.

declare'. He was perhaps more aware at that time of the climate of fiction in the States than that prevailing over here, and he first sought publication for *Ducdame* in New York, with the firm of Doubleday. The atmosphere of literature, in advanced circles at any rate, was changing very rapidly into post-war disillusion and symbolist influences. *Ulysses,* most sensational of experiments in technique, appeared under great difficulties in 1922. In the autumn of the same year Marcel Proust died prematurely, and the blaze of glory that flooded his achievement illuminated the whole world of the novel. Dorothy Richardson, whose new focus and integrity fascinated John Cowper, was making her comparatively modest contribution and Katherine Mansfield in her brief pathetic efflorescence had brought liveliness and informality as well as sensitiveness into play. *Mrs. Dalloway* appeared in 1925 and Aldous Huxley's pert acerbity (scarcely recognised then as Puritan) shocked more conventional social commentators. T. S. Eliot's *The Waste Land,* though the work of a great conservative, had shaken traditionalists severely. In America a new, indigenous urgency was appearing. The great D. H. Lawrence, made acrid by his disease, was now past his best: but his influence was only beginning really to penetrate. In short the wind of change, as we say, was blowing; but not altogether in a direction favourable either to the Hardy or the Dostoievsky element in John Cowper. His counter-religious mood (so far as it was counter-religious) was very different from any prevalent in the 1920's. His culture was not really that of a *nouvelle vague,* nor was his laboured earnestness nor his grave reverence for nature at all in the fashion. The Powys family were unrecognised in Great Britain. It was not till after 1923 that John Cowper—a little piqued as he admits—ever had to face the surprising recognition that 'Powys' did not mean himself. For external even more than for internal reasons it was scarcely surprising that *Ducdame* should create no furore in London.

Ducdame is the nearest approach in John Cowper's fiction to the common forms of the novel, and in the style of its presentation is the easiest to read, his tendency to rambling being deliberately curbed. It is not multi-centred, Rook Ashover and the Ashover estate in Wessex being firmly lodged in the reader's attention. But that does not mean that the book is easy. Again we feel it is the work of a man possessed, but again

we have to ask: possessed by what? The stress is almost inevitably on this question, for we are dealing with an author
who is not really concerned with the technique of presentation,
but only with what is presented. It is inner experience and
problems that are balanced against each other. What is evil? Is
it something eternally ranged against goodness or—as more
clearly in the mind of the later Wolf Solent—something inherent in goodness? It is the more difficult to realise all the
questions raised because Destiny is planning the directing
force and not human will—John Cowper's characters have
little more will than Hardy's—and because the writer, so
largely involved in Rook, confuses the problems of human fate
with the tensions in his own character. Metaphysical dilemmas
abound and overlap.

Scarcely any critic seems to have drawn, in 1925, any coherent inspiration from *Ducdame*. Most readers in the ranks of
the minority that was positively impressed were confused by
the apparent multiplicity of the writer's aims. John Cowper's
content with relatively simple narrator perspective (almost
'dear Reader') concealed from many his passion to push
psychological enquiry to new and strange depths. The anti-
hero was still an unfamiliar and even a slightly shocking
phenomenon. The subjective conception of Rook and indeed
of other principal characters was apparent in itself; but it was
less immediately clear that an elaborate self-projection and self-
clarification was the motive. The writer's possession with
nature was seen as an embellishment—still fashionable—
rather than as an inescapable identity. Still seeking some
external probability in a novel the *Times Literary Supplement*
reviewer was disconcerted to find the unsympathetic Lady
Anne the only normal character, and detected a 'dual mode' in
the whole book: 'the impression of a vast plot forced into a
narrow mould of ideas'. An article carefully commending the
novel, by Milton Waldman in the *London Mercury*, can well
be quoted today to remind us how difficult the approach to
John Cowper could be.

> The three Ashovers, Netta, the mistress, Hastings, the
> mad priest, and his wife, the bastard relative, the repul-
> sive gypsies and the country folk make up a *Dramatis
> personae* worthy of Trollope's [!] attention. They talk
> and think intelligently and often amusingly, feel strongly,

act sensationally but extravagantly, and do all manner of
things, but none of them ever becomes quite independent
of his author's supporting arm. Here is the chief reason
for the sense of excessive length of the novel—Mr. Powys
is continually forced to explain *ex post facto* the factors
in a character's, usually his hero's, psychology which
impelled him to do such and such a bizarre thing. Mr.
Powys also, following Mr. Lawrence, devotes long passages
to finding sexual meanings in landscape or other associations: certain days are women days, in others men
more easily triumph.... Yet he has an undeniable feeling
for landscape, even though his interpretations of its moods
may be rather fantastic and unconvincing. He has, further-
more, a very real power of conception on a large scale, a
feeling of seeing logically down long corridors in relation
to their ultimate significance. *Ducdame* is a far better book
than the only other novel of its author's that I have read,
Wood and Stone, and if the next one shows the same
growth it will be, beyond doubt, a masterpiece.

Reference to Lawrence does indeed go some way to suggest
John Cowper's direction, though (a less aggressive character)
he has always been free of Lawrence's didacticism. And more
remarkable than in Lawrence was the domination of the ideal
in the Powys moral motive, a great contrast to the preposses-
sions of the new novel at that hour. A satirical acceptance of
the sceptical, material shrug-at-life was indeed more alien to
John Cowper than to D. H. Lawrence. *Ducdame* and its successors were as uncommitted to moods of the twenties as they
were tolerant of human vagary.

We have already implied that *Ducdame* is more a promise
than an achievement. How much actual achievement is there?
There is undeniable ground-work in self-study. Nature, in
many intimately realised aspects, is brought on easier terms
with intuitive human beings than in *Rodmoor*. The nature of
evil—so obsessive with John Cowper—is posed as a problem, if
little more than posed. The Freudian loading of character, still
novel, is carried into tolerably confident practice. An urban
generation is reminded that man is influenced by animistic as
well as human powers. Indeed in *Ducdame* the hero or anti-
hero Rook is bravely launched on that career of animistic
sensationism that recurs in all the vital novels, and he is ex-
hibited without that defiant resort to fetish which grew on
John Cowper later. It is indeed not in the rather overstressed

and perfunctory problem of the Ashover inheritance, territorial and psychic, nor in the riddles of family promiscuity, nor
in his relations with his sick brother Lexie (that slightly satyrish version of Llewelyn) that Rook is really most himself to
us:

> He passed out at last into the orchard; and from the
> orchard into the open uplands. The slope of Battlefield
> as he made his way between gorse and bracken was sweet
> with the irresistible scent of thyme. It was difficult not
> to tread upon tufts of euphrosia and milkwort; and when
> he reached the top of the hill the hot, merciless suction
> of the noon's leonine month had filled the air so full
> with the odour of pine, bark and turpentine and fir
> needles that he felt as if the trouble of human thoughts
> were a kind of foreign intrusion, an ill-mannered and
> irrelevant guest, amid the largesse of all this earth-life.

But the gulf still yawns between self-comprehension and
imaginative comprehension. It is not only a question of
amateurishness, of frequent maladroitness, though in *Ducdame*
with all its humours and fascinating awareness of life the awkwardness in narrative (and especially talk) which John Cowper
has never quite overcome was not yet transfigured by all-con-
suming purpose. There is something unsatisfying about several
of the characters in *Ducdame*. Parson Hastings and his manuscript and his mania are not quite convincing, and the clumsy
anti-climax of the plot, where he kills Rook with a rake and dies
is nearly fatal to the book's whole integrity. Mrs. Ashover, compared with her later development into Wolf Solent's Laodicean
mother, is almost the Roman matron of melodrama. The likeable, rather pathetic and bedraggled mistress Netta is a success,
as is in harder lines Lady Anne. But here again the more intuitive young woman Nell Hastings is tentative. Her story never
achieves the solidity of those chapters in *A Glastonbury
Romance* in which the love of another mismated Nell is so
gloriously portrayed.

In *Ducdame* John Cowper, whether in quest of the occult or
whether by nostalgic impulsion, has leaned more heavily than
elsewhere to the regional. It is important to note this, for the
rural convention was alternately his Achilles heel and his
strength. It could inspire him and it could date and limit him.
The failure of verisimilitude in his novels was often related to

this rustic drive; and on the other hand his closeness to nature often lent him a needed sanity. Hardy's influence, never afterwards quite so strong, is palpable in many passages of *Ducdame*. Who can fail to recall *The Return of the Native* in this passage about the moths?

> 'Why didn't you catch it,' he cried indignantly: and the sudden consciousness of what had really happened— of these two feathered amorists moving together over the dark currant bushes in a mysterious ecstasy; of their being drawn towards a flame that desired them not and indeed knew not of their existence; of their being separated with an absolute and final separation; of the one he had thrown out fumbling vaguely with antennae in that immense darkness, from under the shadow of a peony leaf or a dock-leaf, fumbling and uttering—who knows?—lamentations and moanings that would sound like the voice of Eros himself if there were ears that could hear it—struck like a spear into Rook's brain.

Only a disciple of Hardy could write on a match:

> he watched with interest the tiny Promethean flame lift up its eternal living protest between cold moonlight and cold mortality.

The rustic humour is even more inescapably linked to the same pattern:

> 'Me old woman be snappish in winter, prickish in ploughing-time, and all heads and tails in harvest. But come summer, same as us has now, and she be sweet as oil of Lebanon.'

But in the 1920's this England of Hardy's, in the remoter parts, still existed. It was soon to pass away altogether, and concurrently John Cowper was to part company with the 20th century entirely, defiantly confronting the present with the immemorial in *Maiden Castle* and preserving his faith often by strained symbols and impossible fidelities.

But *Ducdame* remains an unforgettable landmark, and one whose direction is unmistakable. Though the feeling out for the fantastic in the gypsy scenes does not carry conviction and Cimmery land, the 'Elysian Fourth Dimension—out of Space and out of Time', remains too shadowy, the total impression is one of fresh and positive promise. There is no concession to either the conventional or the modish.

It was inevitable that John Cowper's challenge, however cultured and sensitively aware, should fall athwart the main stream of the English novel, set definitely in an intensified social awareness. Technically speeding-up and tightening, far from intensified rumination, was now the accepted mode. John Cowper found his champions—that outstanding critic of fiction, H. C. Harwood of the *Outlook* especially welcomed *Ducdame*—but it was really as a minority man, an eccentric, the individualist of a strange religious twilight, that he was recognised. Artistically more vital, more easy to classify and range, his brother Theodore's crowning work *Mr. Weston's Good Wine* appeared in 1927 and found a more positive acceptance. It is indeed an allegorical masterpiece, placing the name of Powys for ever beyond neglect, and revivifying (though this is not its theme) in a narrow and intense way the rural element in life. In religion it is the complete negation of John Cowper's polytheistic questing tolerance.

The death early in 1928 of Thomas Hardy, removing from our literature its one unchallenged and unshakeable standard, was bound to lower the esteem of the novel grounded in nature. The view that the writer who sees man against the elements is nearest to the bone of things died very hard, and indeed it has never been convincingly discredited. The countryside (a limited aspect of nature) had become perhaps a cult, through never an ignoble one. Over-specialisation had certainly recoiled on its authors, and in the long years since Hardy had abandoned fiction reputations had wavered and waned rapidly, curiously diverse fates awaiting John Halsham, George Bourne, Eden Phillpotts, W. H. Hudson, R. D. Blackmore, Halliwell Sutcliffe, Morley Roberts and countless easily forgotten American followers. English life had ceased to be primitive enough to inspire such elemental masterpieces as *The Seasons* of the Polish Ladislas St. Reymont. Yet even in the 1920's Henry Williamson, Mary Webb, Phyllis Bentley, Adrian Bell and others could bring something fresh into life lived close to primitive unchanging things. But it was left to John Cowper and Theodore Powys to restore a real significance, to give a vital undercurrent to the evolving novel's social and urban awareness. To them God was not wholly anthropocentric.

In the early 1920's John Cowper seems to have come to

rather easier terms with life. Reading between the lines of the *Autobiography* and noting in particular his correspondence with Llewelyn (who became very sick again about this time) one can conclude that his physical health was better and his psychological balance definitely steadier. His sadic guilt gradually subsided after the end of the War. The stubborn Puritan legacy from his father was imperceptibly yielding to the long slow pressure of his humane culture; and it is notable that he almost ceased to feel that common human instincts call for apology. He moved easily in the atmosphere of genial enquiring tolerance that marks his mature novels.

CHAPTER VI

Full Creation (i): *Wolf Solent*

DURING the middle and late 1920's John Cowper (still centred in New York city and not yet an 'up-state' rustic) was unprecedentedly active in writing, though he was not yet planning seriously to abandon the platform. Besides journalism and minor pamphlets he wrote *The Meaning of Culture*, *In Defence of Sensuality*, the study of Dorothy Richardson and the first of his three outstanding mature novels, *Wolf Solent*. Even more definitely than its mighty successor *A Glastonbury Romance* (written in the peace of rural New York State, which he came to love so well) *Wolf Solent* is the book of an exile. *Wolf Solent*, he wrote many years after, 'is a book of Nostalgia, written in a foreign country with the pen of a traveller and the ink blood of his home'. It is clear on every page that he was an exile not only from his fatherland but from the earth and the past. However keen his interest in, and even his love for (so to speak) the guy in the subway, on the deepest imaginative plane he could only belong to Wessex.

Though not the most passionate or poetical of John Cowper's novels *Wolf Solent* has a strong claim to be the best. Not only because it is the most coherent structurally, the least multi-centred, of the riper works but because it comes the nearest to its author's aim. Although *A Glastonbury Romance* is vaster (in more senses than one) and *Jobber Skald* far outvies it in atmosphere, in beauty and wealth of description, in sheer imaginative exaltation, in Aristotle's 'something exceptional', both the later novels are burdened with more unabsorbed and difficult stuff, more that has to be allowed for, or taken on

F

trust. *Wolf Solent*, firmly centred in one who is the most psychologically convincing of all John Cowper's anti-heroes, provokes no disbelief but carries the reader on steadily to an end apparently inevitable even as it is enigmatic. The rhythm of the earth itself, so deeply sensed, is matched by the rhythm of Wolf's inner evolution. It is safer to say evolution than development, for the word has less possible overtone, and in this pilgrim's progress there is no better or worse, but only maturing self-enquiry. *Wolf Solent* is supreme in its toleration and non-engagement: of all novels it is the least didactic and has the least design upon any possible reader.

Wolf Solent (lone wolf?) is of course in the main a projection of his author, though wholly different in origin and heredity—this adjustment is very subtly handled. The great genius of autobiography has never used his own external life for purposes of fiction—a very rare and gratifying case. Wolf is indeed the book. It is misleading to call him, as some did in 1929, a modern Hamlet. Hamlet is Everyman: he includes other men while Wolf does not even know what other men are like. Wolf is more nearly a development of Jude the Obscure, beginning much where Jude left off. But parallels must not be pushed too far. Jude, like Hardy himself, was an intellectual with much of the common man in him, while Wolf is an intellectual doomed by his very nature to see in other men mainly variations on his own inwardness. He lives in the Powys cave.

But while it is easy to see that Powys-Wolf, with his fidelity to inner experience and his social incongruity, *is* in one very real sense the book, it is not so easy to say just what the book is about, for like most vital modern art it is bursting with problems. Indeed it is in the French phrase a *roman à thèse*. It poses presuppositions and plays upon them. But what is the thesis, if the word is not too inelastic for John Cowper? First the many-sidedness of truth and second the positive value of all forms and modes of experience: these concepts are the very essence of the novel's life. Both concepts characteristically are passed through the subjective mind of Wolf. We are here in full revolt against the naturalistic tradition: John Cowper always subordinates existence to essence. We find no sceptical side-glances at everyday life: neither a La Rochefoucauld nor an *Erewhon* Butler—nor indeed an Ibsen—exists for John

Cowper, who repudiates the satirical view of conduct as one of his principles. Everybody and everything is received with sympathy: there is no rejection. One is forcibly struck, it is true, by a strong view of disillusionment in the story. Wolf, hoping in his thirties for happiness, even some ecstasy, ends by comforting himself with typical John Cowperish sensationism. 'Well, I shall have a cup of tea,' he says in the book's last words. He is even disillusioned as to the reality of good and evil. His ideal affinity with Christie Malakite can be felt as less *definite* than the smell of pig's urine 'mingled with the scent of the flowering hedge', while the sadic evil personified in the sinister Punch-like Squire Urquhart becomes unreal, possibly a joke, indistinguishable from Wolf's own moral ambivalences.

But John Cowper has his capricious strain; and disillusion, no more than the omnipresence of evil, must be lightly accepted as the novel's motive. Belief, a faith in the sanity of death, a goodness in the very variety of nature's moods, point other and conflicting facets of Truth—Wolf's own power to accept the self he despises is a good. The simpler an experience the more valid it is, provided it be consciously intensified. The very quirks of human nature are the guinea-stamp of its authenticity, as well as being its most positive feature. Eccentricity is supremely valuable: valuable not only as a defence, or a means of fighting life and hardening one's individuality, but as a force making for tolerance. And moral force, for John Cowper, has a life of its own, living on in the air and inspiring even those not yet born. It is like the face of the man on the Waterloo steps that had haunted Wolf with its haggard suffering ever since he left for the West Country, inspiring compassion in characters a hundred miles away who have never seen it. While John Cowper's 'sylpholepsy', (of which he had long felt ashamed) transferred *in toto* to Wolf Solent, acquires a moral ambiguity.

This duality, the coldness in lust detached from the warmth of sexual love felt to be equally essential, poses for Wolf a yet further guilty doubt. Which side of him is the more destructive, which the more valid? Fragmented (though not quite in a clean-cut way) between Wolf's feelings for Gerda and for Christie, the author's sexual awareness becomes an amoral moral problem. He is desperately concerned to make both pleas dispassionately. It is difficult to think of anybody else who could do this in quite this way. So pretty, animal Gerda with her many negative qualities becomes for a long stretch a positive force while the subtle and almost ethereal Christie, with her many positive qualities, can become a negative force. It is emotional experience of both perhaps which matters to Wolf, which builds up in him a sort of moral stature. It is a casuistical act of choice, a righteous act, which is capable of shattering Wolf and so the novel. To make a decision, to qualify for approval: that is what could destroy tolerance and pure enquiry.

As *Wolf Solent* is so important it may be well to give some outline of it, ill though John Cowper accords with outlines. Wolf is a teacher of history in London who has been asked to resign because of a semi-hysterical outburst in class. (There is an echo here of the author's last Sherborne adventure.) He returns to Sherborne, where his childhood was passed and his slightly scandalous schoolmaster father lies buried, in order to assist the necrophilous Squire Urquhart in writing a scurrilous local history. He lodges with a Mrs. Otter, whose elder son Darnley is an agreeable schoolmaster and whose younger son Jason is a very fantastic poet, *calqué* on Llewelyn Powys. ('The facts he tries to smooth down are the porcupine quills of God.') Wolf becomes involved with the elderly Salena Gault, an old intimate of Solent senior and own cousin to Miss Havisham. He is later joined—or descended on—by his mother, a tough poised character at odds with Miss Gault and determined to play a dominating part in her son's life. Even more disturbing, Wolf meets two girls, one primitive and the other elfin and intuitive—the familiar John Cowper pattern. The beautiful, vital, physically conceived peasant Gerda, perhaps the most *distinct* of the author's characters, makes an immediate appeal to Wolf's 'cold planetary lust'. As primitive as Wolf is involuted, Gerda fixes herself for ever in his (and the reader's) imagination by her imitation of the blackbird's song, deceiving and captivating even the country-bred Wolf. The description of Gerda's bird-song, untouched with irony, is actually one of the loveliest passages in a book which has little of the conventional picturesque.

Gerda gives (perhaps improbably) her tepid affections to Wolf and they marry, with a fine disregard of what the future must bring. But in the meantime Wolf has discovered a far more pregnant affinity with Christie Malakite, reputedly daughter of an incestuous old bookseller, a girl physically and mentally Gerda's complete antithesis. Christie who, whatever her reputed parentage, can only have been begotten by John Cowper Powys upon Sue Bridehead, is a very Aeolian harp of ethereal emotions and philosophical imaginings. To her the strangeness and variability of truth is less a concept than a condition of being. Not so egoistic as Wolf she is equally intelligent and equally free of the conventional and the preconceived. Their relationship is at the same time deeply sophisticated, homely and curiously innocent.

The obstacle to it, the complication, is that while both strongly feel their relationship to be significant (even unique) both despair of relating it to their individual truth. Truth, like deity, is impossibly multiform to John Cowper.

Despite his girl-bride's jealousy, Wolf perseveres in exploring experience and sensation, trying apparently to reconcile the world with his 'mythology' (as he calls his questing life-illusion). Such dogged, such scrupulously undeterred introspection of necessity makes personal relations desperately insecure. But his idealism holds. The Squire, whom Wolf suspects of sadism, becomes a more intrusive problem. Oddly enough Wolf's scruple is far less about writing his employer's lubricious chronicle than about taking payment for it, urgently though he needs this.

The ideal defeat, the loss of his self, is finally bound up with his yielding to Gerda's importunity for the cheque and with his failure to respond to a pathetically awakened Christie. The chapter 'Mr. Malakite at Weymouth', in which Wolf and Christie pass an evening in her bedroom in agonies of love and frustration, is masterly in its subtlety and above all in its exploitation of the trivial to release the infinite.

It is not only Christie Wolf fails, it is 'old Truepenny' and his mythology and the hope of imposing a constructive ideal upon life. Scepticism thrives upon disillusion, and Christie's affection and even Urquhart's evil become suspect. Gerda's blackbird whistles again and she finds consolation—it is not clear how much consolation—first in the odious larrikin Bob Weevil and secondly in the breezy worldly Lord Carfax. Wolf's mother and Selena Gault fight for his possession and his salvation in vain, and the bizarre, almost frightening poet Jason

Otter, always satisfied that 'Truth flies downwards, not up-
wards', furnishes a cackling commentary. Christian values
emerge vaguely in the tipsy vicar Tilly-Valley (a character
surely borrowed from brother Theodore), but, through all, a
divided rather than shattered Wolf can see, in the last resort,
only that ravaged face on the Waterloo steps. The eternal
tragedy of the Waterloo face and the inevitable return to
sensation: these are the residue of experience. But there is
nothing dogmatic, indeed nothing narrowly definite at all in
the total impression of a narrative that has inner compulsion
but little outward sequence or logic. Questions (in the true
way of poetry) are not answered but largely, imaginatively
posed. The story as it draws to a close moves more and more in
a dream. 'How could there be so much salt water in one tiny
skull?' muses Wolf over Christie's tears. In all our skulls? one
is left wondering. The trees dissolve in mist: the wood remains.

Wolf is the most fluid of all men—excepting of course John
Cowper himself. He is the most revealing of John Cowper's
anti-heroes, the best medium, because he impedes nothing.
The life that flows around him is peculiarly rich and richly-
sensed—which does not mean, of course, that *Wolf Solent* is a
good representation of actual manners. The writing is quite
unworldly in the sense that John Cowper's scene has no protective colouring: the characters know no inner restraints and
few outer ones. It often appears as if the author cares only for,
and deliberately extracts, the *timeless* elements in existence. In
character the abnormal is always shown as beside the abnormal; it is never contrasted with or pointed by the normal.
Introversion and undirected speech are ubiquitous: John
Cowper's men and women can scarcely speak directly to each
other about happenings in the outer world.

Although in *Wolf Solent* it is already clear that the essential
matters more than any external probability, we are not yet so
far in the realm of dream and incantation as in the later
novels. In *Wolf Solent* there is obviously some deliberate
adherence to the earth and to everyday life, and the degree of
dramatic success cannot be wholly regarded as irrelevant. The
book is in a sense the novelist's last gesture of homage to
actuality.

The more direct impact of *Wolf Solent* owes much to the
fact that the author's views are mainly concentrated in Wolf

and not splintered-off among a number of interacting characters, as in *Jobber Skald* for instance. Wolf indeed, 'gnarled and
knotted and earth-rooted' is not quite John Cowper: he is
pantheistic and consistently anti-religious and altogether more
prone to disillusion. But the approximation is close and
cleverly manipulated.

It is Wolf himself who shrewdly remarks (he has many
shrewd remarks[1]) 'Reality's always different from the way
people put it.' Even in John Cowper's most inevitable and
purposive novel we have to face a lack of external verisimilitude in 'the way he puts it'. There is always a sense of watching
what is happening in the author's mind rather than being persuaded that here is actual life unfolding.

If we accept that *Wolf Solent*, whether or not John Cowper's
most substantial creation, is his best novel *as* a novel, this is a
suitable occasion to enlarge a little on the subject of his
equipment. Why are readers resistant to him? And what are
the positive qualities that emerge from his fiction, and not
from the other writings of this man who is fundamentally not
a recorder of manners but a poet of the earth?

Firstly there is the question of his dialogue, which is at its
mixed best in *Wolf Solent*. Broadly, the men and women of
the novels talk well when they are being self-revealing but
badly when, so to speak, the voice is the voice of Jacob. There is
generally in the dialogue of all Powyses a mixture of the naïve
and the intellectually conscious; and its tone clashes with the
reader's experience of people talking. Yet John Cowper's dialogue (which is really soliloquy) can at best achieve exceptional naturalness. He tends to identify consciousness with
speech, which marks his great difference from Joyce and his
distance from the stream-of-consciousness manner he so much
admired in Dorothy Richardson. How exactly Jason, the disconcerting *poète maudit* who feels that 'in this world Truth
flies downward, not upward', reveals himself:

'Darnley sentimentalises about his death, which was unfor-
tunate, of course, but perfectly natural—he died of pneu-
monia, as any of us might!—but what drove me to distrac-
tion was this playing upon a person's pity. He always did it

[1] As when he says to himself 'There's something horrible about a male
servant, especially a big male servant . . . when he drops his professional
discretion.'

—from the very first day. Darnley yielded to it at once, though he never liked the boy. I resisted it. I am of iron in these things. I know too much. But by degrees, can't you understand, though I didn't yield to it, it began to bother my mind. Pity's the most cruel trap ever invented. You can see that, I suppose? Take it that there was only one unhappy person left, why, it might spoil all the delight in the world! That is why I'd like to kill pity—why I'd like to make people see what madness it is.'

We get the very voice of a completely natural country girl in Gerda as she watches a vole:

'There's one! There's one! There's one! Oh, throw something to make it go faster. Throw something! Quick! Quick! Quick! No—I didn't mean to *hit* it. To make it swim faster! There! I *can't* throw straight. Oh, do look at its head breathing and puffing! Oh, what ripples it makes! Swim! Swim! Swim! ... It's gone! And you *did* make it swim! I liked to see it. Let's go rat-swimming often. It's wonderful!'

But a genius for creative psychology is not necessarily the same thing as a genius for drama. Through all the vast expanse of *A Glastonbury Romance* one searches in vain for dramatic verisimilitude, for anything that can be long accepted without discomfort, in the conversation of Dave Spear or Red Robinson or Paul Trent or John Beere or even the mighty Bloody Johnny Geard himself, the most massive character in all John Cowper's *dramatis personae*.

John Cowper's rustic dialogue however, over-stylised rather than under-stylised, comes in a separate category. Here also the level is higher in *Wolf Solent* than in more relaxed later books, where peasant talk often smacks of late Phillpotts rather than of early Hardy. In Mr. Torp, Gerda's gravestone-cutter parent, there is a good deal of shrewd, terse, vivid commentary:

'Life be a wink o' the eyelid, these times: and only them as jumps the ditches goes dry to bed.'

Occasionally he reflects a brooding semi-macabre vein of humour distantly recalling Shakespeare and Hardy:

'Some relatives do like to use a common sheet. But I do say it's the corpse's feelings what us have to reason with. These here shrouds'—and he tapped Wolf's knee with the carpet-bag—'be calculated to lie as soft and light on they, as lambs-wool on babes. T'was one of these here shrouds that thik bull-frog Manley cheated his wone mother of, by his dunghill ways; and her a woman too what always had a finicky skin. But don't 'ee say more than just that one word, mister. Missy up there, 'tis only likely enough, will give no more attention to these here shrouds than if she were tucking her dad in 's bed. But "leave it to Torp" is what that corpse would say, were speech allowed 'un. They be wonderful touchy, they corpses be, if all were told; and it be worse when folks' tongues run sharp upon 'un, as we know they do on he above stairs. 'Twere me thoughts of that, mister, that made I reckon Miss Malakite would be glad to see I, sooner than they death-nurses, who be all such tittle-tattlers.'

But generally John Cowper's rustic dialogue, though amusing, has the general weakness of his peasants in being too quaint, too patronisingly presented, and out of line with the twentieth century and the realistic mood of the novel's psychology. Comic relief, in fact, rather than comic contrast. John Cowper, in spite of his somewhat sentimental championship of the working-classes—the rural working-classes especially—does un-intentionally betray them. They talk stagey Wessex, and are rather decoration than an integral part of the human scene: they are hardly to be taken seriously as thinking, rational men and women. All this is related, of course, to John Cowper's unwillingness to face the realities of a changed social life in the English countryside.

The cultivated timelessness has a certain attraction for those many who find contemporaneity distressing, and it may even help to underline the abiding quality of John Cowper's psychological explorations. But it can lessen verisimilitude. A puzzlement about period can intrude. John Cowper is capable of filling the heavens with aeroplanes and leaving the roads virgin of motor-cars. The 1914-18 war is never mentioned nor are any changes attributed to it. There is something almost perverse about the way his characters dispense with modern contrivances: the kettles are all iron kettles, the loaves cottage loaves, the lights oil lamps. For *Wolf Solent* we have to accept datelessness.[1] The atmosphere is late Victorian or Edwardian,

---

[1] *Jobber Skald's* period is given as 190– but motor-cars abound in the provinces, while *Maiden Castle* with action approximately dated has still more incongruities.

the tone often studiously old-fashioned. John Cowper presents without comment that after Wolf's marriage neither he nor his in-laws even consider entering into any closer relationship to each other. In spite of his extremely homely ways, Wolf remains the gentleman, apart, and they peasants, in a way outside twentieth century England altogether. In his hostility to everything mechanical Wolf gives a clear indication of his creator's sentiments—we can only feel here that Wolf and John Cowper are one. There is a very Litany in Wolf's plea for deliverance 'from the brutality of mechanism, from the hard glitter of steel, from the gaudy insolence of electricity'. Aviation repels him violently.

> The Powers of the Air! No, he could *never* yield to them. While a single grass blade grew out of the deep earth, he would never yield to them!

In *A Glastonbury Romance* aeroplanes were a regular background to the ruthless Philip Crow, supreme enemy of King Arthur's Glastonbury and the living mythology of the Grail.

So in John Cowper's ripest novels we are faced with a certain unreality due to his writing in the psychological idiom of an age and at the same time shrinking from acknowledging its characteristics. In the period romances of his old age, almost prophetic in their psychological speculation, he sought another solution, the careless anachronism: but all this does invite the paradox that his historical novels are modern psychological essays while his modern novels are mythological reconstructions!

By *Wolf Solent* John Cowper's narrative style, a good deal more complex than in the early novels, is fairly set. It is easy to see that many readers must feel a certain resistance here. 'The gift of what is commonly called *style* has been denied me,'[1] says the writer himself. Louis Wilkinson on his friend's prose is amusing. 'Sometimes a sentence of his will resemble some queer mythical invertebrate animal, or even monster, breeding from itself as it goes, as it uncoils itself along.' A certain gracefulness, the product of natural fluency and intense literary culture, is in conflict with a persistent harshness. The harshness is due to a highly conscientious resolve to push natural sensation to the limit. The supreme limidity and elegance of

---

[1] Preface to *A Baker's Dozen* by Ll. Powys.

a Thackeray, so dangerous to integrity, have always been quite foreign to John Cowper, though one of the Powyses, Llewelyn, was far less allergic to them.

> The acrid, ammoniacal smell of that casual retreat brought back to his mind the public lavatory on the esplanade at Weymouth, into which, from the sun-warmed sands, he used to descend by a flight of spittle-stained steps. This memory, combined with an access of pervading physical comfort, drew his mind like a magnet towards his secretive mystical vice. Once more, as he gave himself up to this psychic abandonment, he felt as if he were engaged in some mysterious world-conflict, where the good and the evil ranged themselves on opposite sides.
> He rubbed his hands together in the old reckless way as he walked along; and it seemed to him as if all these new impressions of his took their place in this mysterious struggle. That ravaged face of the Waterloo steps mingled its hurt with what Jason, Valley, Christie were all suffering; while the sinister magnetism that emanated from Mr. Urquhart fused its influence with that of Jason's idol, and the cruelty of Miss Gault to Christie; and of his mother to Miss Gault!

The language cannot be faulted on 'literary' grounds: the choice of words is admirable; but it is impossible to deny the jaggedness and craggedness, the lack of easy readability. These are largely attributable to a certain want of natural drama in the novelist's make-up, theatrical though John Cowper himself may be.

And though John Cowper's larger-than-lifeness shows itself rather inwardly than outwardly in *Wolf Solent*, a certain quality of phantasmagoria, his only reminder of Dickens, does from time to time touch his descriptions, and not only his descriptions of nature. There are indications in *Wolf Solent* of a Dickensian esurience, later lost in a consuming psychological inwardness.

> he glanced away at the mahogany sideboard, where Mr. Smith's heavy pieces of polished silver met his gaze, with the peculiar detached phlegm of old, worn possessions that have seen so many family troubles that they have grown professionally callous, after the manner of undertakers and sextons. Wolf began to be conscious of the drift of the amazing discourse which the visitor was directing, like a cannonade of lumbering artillery, across the room into the ears of his sister. Selena's attire was in good taste

enough—indeed, it was superlatively ladylike; but it was the 'rich, not gaudy' attire of a person quite oblivious of contemporary fashion, and in some queer way it lent itself so well to the quality of that room that it seemed to bring the furniture itself to life in support of every thing she said.

The gathering darkness assisted at this strange play. It was as if all the ponderous objects in that room—including the silver, the chairs, the dark green curtains, the grotesque portrait of Mr. Smith's father, the leather backs of the *Sundays at Home* and the *Leisure Hours*, the leather back of a draught-board, with the words 'History of the World' printed on it, the bronze horses on either side of the mantelpiece, the enormous empty coal-scuttle combined together to give weight to the opinions of this aggressive woman, whose own childhood, like that of the silent person upstairs, they had ramparted with their massive solemnities!

This carries us back to Dickens. But also, in its power, it carries us forward to John Cowper's maturing conception of, not the lower creation only, but inanimate things, as partakers of a new animism. For in the new-found world of Bloody Johnny in *A Glastonbury Romance* everything that lives is holy, and everything that exists has some quality of life. Wolf, despairing of the First Cause, despairing of his former idealism, reaches out in this last reverie at sunset to a polytheism, half-mystical, half-sensationist. If only for a moment, even the ravaged face on the Waterloo steps seems accountable.

As he turned eastward, and the yellowness of the buttercups changed from Byzantine gold to Cimmerian gold, he visualised the whole earthly solidity of this fragment of the West Country, this segment of astronomical clay, stretching from Glastonbury to Melbury Bub and from Ramsgard to Blacksod, as if it were itself one of the living personalities of his life. 'It is a god!' he cried in his heart; and he felt as if titanic hands, from the horizon of the 'field of Saturn' were being lifted up to salute the mystery of life and the mystery of death!

What he longed to do was to plunge his own hands into this Saturnine gold, and to pour it out, over Mr. Urquhart, over Mattie, over Miss Gault, over Jason, over all the nameless little desolations—broken twigs, tortured branches, wounded reptiles, injured birds, slaughtered beasts—over a lovely stone on which no moss grows, on the heart of Lovelace Park, over a drowned worm, white and flaccid, dropped from the hook of Lobbie Torp into some

Lurt pool, over the death-pillow of old Mr. Weevil, depri-
ved now of his last conscious gluttony, over the lechery of
the 'water-rat' himself, so pitiful in its tantalised frustration! All . . . all . . . all would reveal some unspeakable
beauty, if only this Saturnine gold were sprinkled upon
them!

Wolf has perhaps no answer to the face on the Waterloo steps,
but to his creator there is at least some positive quality in all
existence.

Wolf Solent was fairly well received in England for a novel
so provocative and so unfashionable, yet so conventional in its
method. The *Times Literary Supplement,* the *Spectator,* and
the *Daily Telegraph* were among the papers that attached
weight to it. Unfortunately for John Cowper's lasting reputation he was now as hopelessly an item of a trinity as one of the
Three Musketeers or the Three Men in a Boat. It had been
the fate of Emily Brontë. One of the best reviews of *Wolf
Solent* was by Conrad Aikin in the *New York Post,* although
the book was actually not to be published in the U.S.A. until
1936 after the success of *A Glastonbury Romance* and *Jobber
Skald.* 'Leisurely, copious, humorous,' Mr. Aikin was anxious
to communicate the scope and grasp and grandeur of the inspiration and at the same time appreciated its 'genial philosophical expansiveness' and its wealth of 'renunciation and
comment'. The *Times Literary Supplement* reviewer, contrasting *Wolf* favourably with most novels of the day and specifically Joyce's, remarked especially on the unfaltering idealism of
the author and his abstinence from all admonition, so contrasting with Joyce's tone. The reviewing was on the whole
reasonable and generous, but unfortunately the literary world
was already divided into Powys and anti-Powys, despite the
great differences in the brothers; and those who did not then
accept John Cowper have ever since most effectively ignored
him.

CHAPTER VII

Full Creation (ii): *A Glastonbury Romance*

'The Cause of the Unseen against the Seen'
—Introduction

IN *A Glastonbury Romance* (1933), John Cowper's imagination passed clean beyond the world of his journalism and essays and revealed his displaced religious sense as seeking to evoke a life-sustaining magic from the earth. The failure of the heavenly was to be magnificently compensated in the realms of the occult. This vast romance of nearly half-a-million words, probably the longest undivided novel in English, is less a novel without a hero than a novel with two heroes and an anti-hero. Around the anti-hero John Crow—a quite undisguised projection of John Cowper—the complex narrative is very loosely strung; and while Bloody Johnny Geard is the most robust of all his author's personalities, even he is less the hero of the book than is the Grail. That is to say, the absent presence of the Grail, its potential experience. And the power of this sense is to be measured by the immensity of the unwieldy epic it sustains and holds together. Although John Geard its prophet has been aptly summarised as a vulgarian Christ, the symbol of his Glastonbury is inevitably a Celtic rather than a Christian Grail. Geard, whatever else he is, is inescapably Merlin *redivivus*.

Naturally, the scene—satisfying the mythology of Arthur and John Cowper's hunger for the earth and his early life—is the Glastonbury *terrain*. For the Grail, for the soul of this countryside, for the spirit of Merlin, John Cowper has staged a vast and impressive, if involved, conflict. Bloody Johnny ('dipped in Christ's Blood' is his style) has inherited a fortune from the clergyman grandfather of John Crow and Mary his cousin, and masterfully acquiring the mayoralty of Arthur's capital, stages an ambitious Pageant. This is to be run on communal principles and as things develop Geard and his associates envisage a sort of Commune in the island-city. Set against them is the industrialist Philip, another Crow, the very incarnation of capitalist enterprise and modern mechanics. (It is due to John Cowper to say that Philip is never overdrawn or allowed to become inhuman.) The period of this formidable conflict is described somewhat mendaciously as 'The Present' and forty-eight 'principal characters' are set out in the *Dramatis Personae*. It is not altogether surprising that the London publishers of *Wolf Solent* should have taken fright at this Leviathan; but another firm, the Bodley Head, so often the champions of adventurous causes, soon found courage to issue it. Materially their enterprise was not ill-rewarded, for rather surprisingly John Cowper was able to describe the romance as 'the best hit of all my books in England'.

This is a great novel if you seek out and accept what it gives; it is but a qualified masterpiece if you look for the rest of what makes novels. Never has the author been so deeply aware of the earth, but rarely has he represented so arbitrarily the behaviour of the beings who people it. Despite the essential resemblance between all John Cowper's writings, *A Glastonbury Romance* is to *Wolf Solent* rather as a phantasmagoria to a psychological diary. In the *Romance* a reader has to surmount, but will in the end surmount, a frequent sense of irrelevance and a sometimes embarrassing suspicion of absurdity. Even these who scoff at the colossus as unreadable remain to find it urgently re-readable: the deeper you go the richer are the realities that come to light. It is not surprising that the *Romance* should be the Koran of the most devout John Cowperists: 'Perhaps the greatest work of our generation', says Professor Wilson Knight exuberantly, adding justly enough that the author 'pushes understanding of sensuous amatory and mystical variations of experience, both in their contrasts and interpretation, to all but superhuman limit'. Indeed even in this book with all its deeply felt magnificence of setting and its poetic pantheism the author remains interested above all in psychology and psychological motivation. Though the interest of the characters in their own psychological abnormalities is less laboured here than in *Rodmoor* or *Wolf Solent,* it still operates to the peril of surface realism. The introspective loses the outer world. John Cowper is far more convincing about woman in love than he is about sadism which he studies subjectively.

The author was right when he called the *Romance* 'this tumultuous tale': there is no form, no 'art', and there is abundance of vitality. There is much power in the conception of Bloody Johnny, though this earthly prophet is not so much the theme of the book as the release of the action, the demonic force that triggers off the conflict. Geard is to some extent John Cowper's desire for a simpler, a mere physically effective reincarnation, not sicklied o'er with the pale cast of thought. If Geard's language is often unreal, there is no doubt about his personality. More sensitive votaries of the Glastonbury legend are dangerously lulled, as John Cowper himself is, by 'tender false mandragoras', but there is nothing tender false about the champion of the legend, with his 'exceptional animal magnetism', his 'big, white face', his 'unholy eyes' those 'diabolical black eyes, now gleaming like two fuliginous mine-shafts out of some Tartarean tin-mine'. His nature is 'about ten times as thick as most men's'.

> He had never been an artistic man. He had never been a fastidious man. He had got pleasure from smelling at dung-hills, from making water in his wife's garden, from snuffing-up the sweet sweat of those he loved. He had no cruelty, no culture, no ambition, no breeding, no refinement, no curiosity, no conceit. He believed that there was a border-land of the miraculous round everything that existed and that 'everything that lived was holy'.

It is this solid fantastic field preacher John Cowper (himself so much of a field preacher) has made ostensibly the minister of Merlin and the Grail but even more the prophet of his creator's own earth-worship. It is in keeping with John Cowper's honesty and realism in fundamental things that Bloody Johnny is not successful in the quest of the Grail. A vision of it is reserved for Sam Dekker, the parson's son and adulterer

turned saint, who may fairly be regarded as the embodiment
of John Cowper's suppressed evangelicism. As to whether the
author himself hopes for or despairs of the Grail, he is as the
Sphinx. Geard is drowned, virtually a suicide, in the great
flood that overwhelms the island-city—'the excuse found by
God when his world got beyond his control: "The Flood." '

But, Geard, though he may fall spiritually between the
stools of Christianity and Arthurianism, is a great artistic
achievement. His ruminations and his public speeches (that,
for instance, delivered from the Rotunda) are often out of
character, too educated and in fact soliloquies of his author's,
but dramatically he is as forceful and undeniable as the other
characters are uncertain. He solidifies more and more, a person rather than an idea, and he can transcend his author. He
acts the other characters off the stage. He is unforgettable, all
through the richly-drawn-out scenes where he visits Lord P. at
Mark's Court and sleeps in the haunted room amid the ghosts
of Merlin and Vivien or when he delivers the cancer-patient
Tittie Petherton from her agony.

> 'Let this cup—' howled Mr. Geard in a tone that made
> even Mr. Wollop shiver, for it seemed more like the bark
> of a great Sedgmoor fox than the voice of a man; and
> even as he cried he flung the thing with all his force upon
> the ground, flung it just at Crummie's feet, who was run-
> ning, laughing and weeping, in wild hysterics towards him.
> When he reached Tittie, whose voice had now sunk again
> into moans, he snatched her up in his arms, as a fireman
> in a whirl of flame might seize a burning woman, sank
> down in the chair with her on his lap, and began, in his
> own natural voice, that familiar refrain that had won him
> his nickname, 'Blood of Christ deliver us! Blood of Christ
> save us! Blood of Christ have mercy on us!'
> His voice got lower and lower as he went on. Then
> it fell into complete silence. Still he continued hugging
> the figure in his arms and slowly rocking himself and her,
> backward and forward, backward and forward. There was
> such a dead silence in the room all this while, that the
> voices in the other rooms became like the intrusion of
> revellers at an execution or at a childbirth.
> Then there came a grotesque and even rather an un-
> pleasant sound. It was the stertorous breathing of the
> sleeping woman.

In such passages as this we forget that there is occasional over-
writing and even melodrama in the book.

G

For Geard is, like John Cowper himself, more than normally alive. Yet if the other intuitive characters, with their subtler inwardness, sometimes pale a little beside him, he does not eclipse them. There is enough individuality and novel perception in them to make many lesser stories. The great limitation of the *Romance*, apart from its lapses from verisimilitude, is in its Hydra-headed quality. So many individualists have their own significant experiences. The many strands are loosely interwoven if interwoven at all. Everything, certainly happens around Glastonbury and Glastonbury is an ideal unity: she is autonomous, an island-city in more senses than one, sundered from the outer world administratively, socially, economically. In John Cowper's terms the city could indeed become the timeless commune of Geard's dreams. But the many richly realised personal relationships have so little to do with the Grail or with each other. The loves of John and Mary Crow, of the saintly Sam Dekker and Nell Zoyland, of the delightful (and extraneous) Lady Rachel and her farmer poet, of the conventional Persephone and the hard-faced Philip, of Cordelia Geard and the sad sadist Evans are all studied, if flickeringly, with the insight of genius. But their interactions are casual and distracting; and they are simply too multiform for any novel to carry. Similarly the political conflicts of capitalists, Christian socialists, ideal communists, anarchists and philosophic Radicals—far less intuitively handled—are confusing and really incompatible with the progress of any sort of novel whatever. Such politically seen figures as Dave Sheer, or the odious Red Robinson, or Paul Trent, simply do not come to life at all because John Cowper is not at home with them, he cannot create in terms of a *political society*. He can only form living characters from the inside, psychologically, developing them from fragments of himself. He is incapable of a distant, panoramic view of society. It detracts further from any developing unity in the novel that Evans, undoubtedly a tragic Dostoievskian figure, has to live out a spiritual crisis without being in any way absorbed into the great theme of Glastonbury; he remains a separate subject yet urgently calling for attention. It is for all of these reasons that *A Glastonbury Romance,* despite its amazing amplitude and richness, does not really surpass or eclipse *Wolf Solent* as a novel, a compelling human document. One must, too, mention that among the intuitives[1] there is some uncertainty in the realisation of character. Owen Evans, antiquarian and sadist, a projection of one uneasy preoccupation of his author, never seems to me quite convincing; and the scene of his quasi-Christlike agony and fainting on the Cross at the Pageant is one of the action's dubious culminations. Sam Dekker's conversion to evangelical asceticism, following directly on his blissful *amour*, is too arbitrarily achieved. And while the mingling of John and Mary, both 'rooted in fen mud and vicious heathenism' is a marvellously subtle projection of John Cowper in love, John Crow, Geard's earth-worshipping lieutenant, does drift out of the action after his vision of Excalibur at Pomparles Bridge. There is an insistence throughout the book that John belongs to the Devil, but we wait in vain for the Devil to make the slightest attempt to claim him!

On the contrary involved, not too convincingly, in the local Geard-Philip struggles, he is gradually drawn back into the author from whom he has so little emerged. His individuality fades beside that of Sam Dekker the newly awakened evangelical saint, who has a vision not merely of a sword but of the Grail itself. In Sam, it may be noted, the formidable shade of the Vicar of Montacute once more overshadows the scene. John Crow, however, is not a character to be overlooked by the student of his author. He is a John Cowper who has found his complement in love, his affinity although he may have failed to identify himself with the spirit of Avalon. His subtleties are manifold. Like—one may venture—John Cowper he 'simply cannot understand what people mean when they talk of life having a purpose' for 'life is simply the experience of living things'. In describing him John Cowper perhaps hints at a still deeper understanding of his own strange elusiveness:

> It might indeed be said that the whole of John Crow's life was a series of 'other sides'—'other sides' of roads, 'other sides' of thoughts, 'other sides' of ideas, religions, labours, activities....

John Crow prays to his dead mother as John Cowper to his dead father. He hates a noisy, dusty early motor-car: rather than have to do with it he feels he should die upon the road. He sums himself up in the Powysian words

[1] I think the valuable classification 'intuitives' was originally due to Mr. Roland Mathias.

'I'm a hard, round, glass ball, that is the mirror of everything, but that has a secret landscape of its own in the
centre of it.'

Mary is brilliantly realised as his feminine other self: the element of kinship between them is perfectly suggested. As a
study of a woman in love she has no superior even in John
Cowper's gallery. The concreteness and the passivity of feminine passion are consummately touched on.

> One quaint feeling often came to her, in the oddest
> moments of his 'sweet usage', namely, that he was one
> of her old, faded, wooden *dolls*; yes, the most dilapidated
> and injured of all four which used to belong to her, come
> to life again, but this time full of queer, hardly human
> exactions that she would willingly prostitute herself for
> hours and hours to satisfy, so long as she could hear those
> wooden joints creak and groan in their joy.

A Glastonbury Romance has many of these unexampled
passages where the author's almost clumsy-mannered laying
bare of the roots of feminine emotion and action leaves the
reader half-fascinated, half-stunned with incredulity. The
deceptively homely scene where Nell Zoyland prepares to receive her lover Sam is lit up again and again with those brilliant insights.

Somewhat apart from the central struggle for the soul of
Glastonbury in this teeming narrative stand the saint and the
sadist. There are differing opinions about their success, their
reality. It must be admitted that beside the limited positiveness of a Will Zoyland both are a little abstract. We must bear
in mind the reservation of Mr. Roland Mathias, probably the
best of all critics of the *Romance*. Its characters, he says,[1] 'are
not products of society, but foci of intellectual, genealogical,
geological, and vegetable processes'. Sam Dekker is less a fragment of John Cowper than a gesture of reconciliation and
compromise made to the spirit of the Rev. Charles Francis
(Mat Dekker, Sam's father, the Vicar of Glastonbury, is indeed
a slightly less robust and less innocent version of the Vicar of
Montacute). Sam is vouchsafed his vision of the Grail after
resigning Nell Zoyland and their unborn child to embrace a

[1] *Dock Leaves*, 1956.

complete faith in Jesus. Though growing into an asceticism so repugnant in theory to John Cowper, he is touched with his author's polytheism: 'I am considering Him as a God who is against cruelty of the great Creator God,' he protests. Many and strange powers are active against the First Cause. Having renounced his own world to labour with and for the humble, Sam is in fact on the eve of administering an enema to a sick and rather repellent old man when his vision comes to him. None the less it is Sam the lover and not Sam the saint who lives on in the memory: his love is more convincing, not to say more holy, than his asceticism. This is almost certainly unintentional; but it does indicate that religion unless fortified by fetish has a dead quality for John Cowper, while all that pertains to the sexual seems to be in some measure sanctified for him. But true religion or no, spirituality or no, Mat and Sam Dekker have a *positive* impulse. The emphasis here is little on the problem of evil; but much on the problem of creative goodness.

If the goodness fails to transport us, it is surely because the vastness of the book has tired even John Cowper a little. If the problem of evil, the Dostoievsky legacy, is less of a general motive in the *Romance* than in *Wolf Solent,* it is because evil is too narrowly canalised into sadism, embodied in Owen Evans, who moreover remains a dim and imperfectly vitalised exemplar of the vice.

It is conspicuously some of the women, Nancy Stickles and Crummie Geard as well as Nell, to whom a simple, refreshing faith in life lends the sap and vitality which can mitigate the *longueurs* of the book. The lovely and likeable Crummie, who studies and adores human beings as well as her own flawless legs, is not only vital in herself but something of a prosaic Chorus to the torrential play of man and the elements. Nancy Stickles, married to a sticky stingy pharmacist, has a *joie de vivre* as memorable as it is simple. Never surely has sensationism come to terms with untutored living better than in her.

> She shared with her great aunt a certain Rabelaisian habit of mind, or at least a habit of mind that liked life none the worse because of its animal basis.... When not in acute physical pain, or in the presence of acute physical pain, Nancy Stickles enjoyed every moment of life. She liked

to touch life, hear life, smell life, taste life, see life; but she went far beyond Mr. Wallop and Bert, as she did indeed beyond everybody in Glastonbury, except its present Mayor, in the enjoyment of religion. To Nancy Stickles, God was a dignified, well-meaning, but rather helpless Person, like Parson Dekker, Christ was a lovable, rather disturbing Person, like Sam Dekker; the Holy Spirit was quite simply and quite reverently, a very large and very voluble Wood Pigeon; but all these entities moved to and fro in an inner-behind stage Glastonbury; a Glastonbury with greener fields, a redder Chalice well, yellower apples and even bluer mists, than the one Nancy knew best, but one—all the same—that she felt frequently conscious of, and towards which her deepest feminine soul expanded in delirious waves of admiration, hope and love.

Most difficult to assimilate of all these loosely associated personalities is Owen Evans, the other-worldly sadist, through whom John Cowper evidently yearned to cleanse the stuffed bosom of much perilous stuff that of old had weighed upon his heart so long. It is easy of course to sympathise; and it is easy to appreciate the passion that has been spent in entering into the heart of this guilty, marked-out victim of obsession. But the trouble is that Evans is faceless, something short of human; and never for a moment is one convinced that this deficiency is really the *consequence* of his sadism or sadic guilt. Neither wickedness nor suffering acquires any vivid reality in him. So his redemption at the last from hideous indulgence by the love of Geard's glamourless elder daughter Cordelia is something of a false climax—touchingly though it is depicted. Evans in his inconclusive introspections and in his collapse as the crucified Jesus in Geard's Passion pageant, is too heavily charged with John Cowperism. When we read for instance that 'Dante was his favourite poet' or that he was 'beyond any Latin or Teutonic mind' we are forcefully shifted from his reality in the drama to awareness of an idiosyncratic John Cowper, directing it all.[1] Evans on the whole is not so much sadic horror, living and challenging, as a projection of the idea of shamed, struggling sadism.

A Glastonbury Romance is then on the face of it, a vast, powerful shapeless phantasmagoria, dramatically often halting and full of improbabilities of action. One must of course look

---

[1] Persuasiveness is by no means added by habitually calling this strange figure 'Mr. Evans.'

much deeper to grasp all its significances and extricate all its
conflicting themes: its studies, to name a few, of sadism, saint-
hood and the eternal harlot in woman. The bold confronta-
tion of magic and reality is itself a novel challenge. Never,
surely, has any writer so made us feel that the forces of
mysterious nature are inextricably bound-up with more than
natural forces.

Undoubtedly, like his John Geard, John Cowper 'believes in
psychic radiation', but he believes in a great deal more. Very
great and patient intimacy, very convincing observation, a
strange intensity of contemplation, goes to the generation of
such ideas as that 'at certain epochs in the life of any history-
charged spot there whirls up an abnormal stir and fume and
frenzy among the invisible elements or forces that emanate
from the soil.' The prophet of an earth-mysticism must have
been very close for very long to the earth before he can hold us
with his experience:

> And the voice replied to him [Evans] again and it was like
> a wind stirring the horns of snails and touching the hairs in
> the throats of night-jars, and moving the antennae of
> butterflies, and blowing the gold-dust from the droppings
> of weasels, and rippling the brown rainfall in the cups of
> fungi, and fretting the light scurf on the brittle skulls of
> the new-born, and the rheum-drops on the eyelids of ex-
> treme old-age, and the sweat-drops on the forehead of death.
> And the voice whispered—'For those that are forgiven there
> shall be a new heaven and a new earth!' And Mr. Evans
> groaned forth his retort to this: 'But what of those that
> *cannot* be forgiven?'

Description, however inspired, could never—least of all with a
John Cowper—be an end in itself. But who can fail to feel
deeper implications underlying such an experiencing as Cordelia's of the rain?

> The wind rose about her as she stood there, in wilder and
> wilder gusts. And then Cordelia, gazing directly into the
> wide-flung branches of the biggest of the two giant trees,
> was aware of something else upon the wind. Those enor-
> mous branches seemed to have begun an orchestral mono-
> tone, composed of the notes of many instruments gathered
> up into one. It was a cumulative and rustling sigh that
> came to the woman's ears, as if a group of sorrowful
> Titans had lifted up their united voices in one lamentable

dirge over the downfall of their race. It kept beginning afresh, this solemn moan upon the air—a moan which always mounted to a certain pitch and then sank down. Sometimes, such were the vagaries of the wind, before this portentous requiem started afresh, there was a singular humming and droning in those huge branches, as if the tree wished to utter a private secret of its own to Cordelia's ears, before it recommenced its official chant. Yes! the peculiarity of this humming sound was that it shivered and shook with a special intention for the woman standing upon the bank! And Cordelia knew well what that message was. The great tree was telling the hillside that there was rain upon the wind; but it was telling Cordelia something else! Then all was absolutely still; and in that stillness, a stillness like the terrible stillness of uttermost strain in travail, there came the first day of birth, the fall of a single drop of rain. That first drop was followed by another and that again by another. Cordelia did not hear them in the same place. One drop would fall upon the roadway beneath her; one upon a dead burdock leaf; one upon a faded hart's tongue fern of last year's growth. Then the sound of the falling drops would be drowned in a reawakening of that orchestral dirge. Then the wind would die down over all the upland, and once more an absolute stillness would descend; and in the stillness again—only now in an increased number—the big raindrops would splash to earth, one falling upon a dead leaf, one upon a naked stone, one upon a knot of close-grown twigs, one upon Cordelia's bare forehead. Her feeling at that moment was that some deep psychic chain had been broken in her inmost being. Hola— Hola! She could not restrain herself from giving vent to a wild cry of exultant delight as the first bursting deluge followed those premonitory drops.

The truly creative initiate is one in whose inmost being the occult can forge some psychic chain. Such an initiate is John Cowper Powys.

It is not easy, as we have seen, to concentrate on one overriding theme in the *Romance* and certainly we are not asked to review any of its problems as a problem *solved*. John Cowper's insatiably philosophic rejection of philosophy refuses the master-key. Is it Merlin *versus* Mammon? Or nature against science? Is it the conflict between evil and the healing acceptance of the earth? Or is the master motive the desire to escape into magic? To set magic against evangelicism: the Cymrian gleam indecisively contending with Montacute Vicarage? Or are we to feel, underlying all the rest, that the rhythm of the earth, responded to with unprecedented intensity, can and must be reconciled with human love? The clue may elude us, but the groves of the labyrinth blossom and bear fruit eternally.

A Glastonbury Romance was a landmark in John Cowper's reputation. The minority who accepted him could now only accept him as a major figure. With most contemporary novelists there was no common measure. He o'ertopped their puny world like a colossus. The *Romance* was only sharing the common Powys fate in being overpraised (as art, recklessly) by its admirers and being disproportionately undervalued by everybody else. To keep this in proportion, it must be remembered that John Cowper really needs exceptionally intensive reading, which not all give him, to yield up his quality. It is good to recall that more popular novelists, J. D. Beresford, J. B. Priestley, Hugh Walpole and L. A. G. Strong, were in the early 1930's liberally acknowledging his stature. In America, where the *Romance* was published the year before its London appearance, the counter-émigré was joyously acclaimed, all the more because most famous migrations had been the opposite way across the Atlantic. The first important article on the *Romance* to appear in London was, actually, prompted in 1932 by the American edition, and was by J. R. Theobald in the *Bookman*. Mr. Theobald revealed a sustained sensitiveness to

> the three-dimensional subsidy of the hills, houses and rooms; the sculptured clarity of every scene; the astonishing *presence* of colour and scent, down to the most ˙imponderable fragrance'; the subtlest fall of light that alters with the time of day and change of season; and none of these merely as they are objects in themselves, but as they move across the consciousness of the characters, either singly or in groups, like momentous inscriptions on the course of their lives. All this has been done with the assistance only of a large-scale map, at a distance from Glastonbury of three thousand miles of space and twenty years of time. But the independent reality of the characters and of the scene never distracts the idealising tendency of the book.

Mr. Peter Quennell in the *New Statesman* was more sceptical, if not impercipient, as when he noted that 'for Mr. Powys, as for the followers of Cornelius Agrippa, there trembles between man and the surrounding universe a fine cobweb-mesh of esoteric bonds.' On the whole, though, Mr. Quennell was amused:

> his narrative emerges, yard by yard, wallows up blowing and snorting from the depths of his mind, all a whole fantastic continent is revealed to view. All barnacled, encrusted and over-grown ... Appropriately, the book ends in a tremendous flood, with a swash, gurgle, a great noise of chasing and rumbling, leviathan takes its leave of the exhausted reviewer and seeks its playground in the mystic erotic deep.

About this time the journalistic assumption began to be established in England that John Cowper, though no longer to be dismissed as the least of several Powyses, might well be dismissed as the oddest. Lively critics adopted the notion of a whale of a book and a whale of a writer, overlooking, perhaps, the distinguished role played by the whale in great neglected novels. Meanwhile in the far peaceful hinterland of New York John Cowper was occupying himself with the *Autobiography*, the palpable masterpiece which critics really have no excuse for not understanding. In his almost adopted land he championed modern marriage against Bertrand Russell in a debate before an enormous audience, and on a vote he all but won the day. This side his experiences were less happy: the owner of the caves at Wookey thought himself slandered in the person of Philip Crow and John Cowper was constrained to settle the claim out of court. This fostered in him his incurable fear of the law. He was writing side by side with the *Autobiography* the novel *Weymouth Sands* and this he kept back from English publication until he had disguised (or tried to disguise) all the place-names and altered the title to *Jobber Skald*, with its unlucky suggestion of Norse saga. So this sea-drenched offering to the gods of Hardy's Budmouth did not appear on his native shores until 1935. Lyrically his most exciting work, *Weymouth Sands* had come out in the States soon after *A Glastonbury Romance,* preceding *Wolf Solent* by two years in the New World, where it called forth an enthusiasm often discriminating and by no means confined to the exiled and the nostalgic. All the same, John Cowper's conservatism in language and perspective left him, in the age of Joyce, far less fashionable than were several lesser novelists. He had of course little more than Joyce or Virginia Woolf of the common touch which could bring middle-class readers to Hardy or Bennett; but it was a shade disconcerting to find even brother Theodore riding ahead of him so easily into the gilded arena of the paper-backs.

CHAPTER VIII

Full Creation (iii): *Autobiography*

'There is a gap in all the shelves of all the immortal libraries, only waiting to be filled by the one person destined for such a task—the life of a man by a man' —to Llewelyn Powys, 14 September, 1932.

OF all forms of writing autobiography has obviously best suited denizens of the Powys cave, and considering John Cowper's make-up we cannot be surprised that this intimate and often formless art should come the most naturally to him. His subjective nature, his self-consciousness, even his rambling are here rather a strength than the weakness they appear to be in his other books. Our literature is not particularly rich in autobiography, owing to the national reticence and primness; and until recently this was even truer than today. Our popular successes, our Colley Cibbers and Creeveys and Charles Grevilles and Margot Asquiths are really diarists and society correspondents: they have little inwardness. For outstanding self-depiction, if we do not go overseas straightway we look to Pepys' *Diary* or De Quincey's *Confessions of an English Opium Eater* or Newman's *Apologia pro Vitâ Suâ*, works widely different in aim and by no means set autobiographies. Since the first World War self-portraiture has been much more frankly and successfully practised, but such esteemed declarations of the self as *Memoirs of a Fox-hunting Man* or *Goodbye to All That* are superficial beside John Cowper's *Autobiography* or even Llewelyn's *Skin for Skin*. In frankness and seriousness and self-understanding John Cowper is comparable with a Rousseau or a Bashkirtseff, and in idiosyncrasy and 'ego hood' there are few to set beside him. When has an Englishman of comparable scope and sensibility drawn himself so fully and ruthlessly? One could claim for the *Autobiography* without extravagance that it is the best in the English language.

John Cowper is interested in everything in life. His contempt for boredom is significant in one to whom contempt is almost an unknown foible. 'I believe the most unphilosophical, irreligious and immoral word in the English language is the word "commonplace".'[1] As all that lives is holy to him, so all that happens is full of interest. All phenomena are to be studied, even exhaustingly.

It is difficult, even if it is desirable, to isolate and describe the quintessence, the unique quality of John Cowper as a writer on himself. It could be said of course that he writes always on himself, whatever his form of composition. But when he writes explicitly of himself the endearing and child-like element in his frankness holds the attention much more compellingly than when he attempts to be extraversive or objective, when in fact he tries to subordinate his relish in being John Cowper to exhorting his readers or to setting an imaginary world before their eyes. You feel that in the *Autobiography* or his intimate letters, revelling in introspection, he is truer to himself than when preaching or telling a story. And deeply as he loves direct self-revelation, there is quite as much self-abasement here as glorification. This, added to his depth of capacity for experience, challenges compassion with the great name of Montaigne. In their ultimate nature the two men could not be more unlike. Montaigne's being was a harmony: he was above all men at peace; and all his work was a deeper growing into that peace. Perpetual division, perpetual inner warfare renders exciting all John Cowper's efforts to pin himself down. The reader is almost as excited as John Cowper himself by this butterfly chase, and complete success eludes both the writer and the reader—the writer perhaps enjoying a little both the reader's mystification and his own! But no Wedding-Guest was ever more completely mesmerised by any Ancient Mariner, and if he does not emerge a sadder man he will certainly emerge a wiser one.

[1] *Autobiography.*

John Cowper does not fortify his book by any special skill in construction or arrangement: apparently the form is as casual as in the rest of his writings. Nor does he pause to point or elaborate his effects: the carelessness of wording almost excludes the idea of revision or indeed of much premeditation. But if the book appears artless in shape it is supersubtle in inner development. The outward story is fairly regular, though far from consecutive, from infancy to the climax of the first War. From that point until 1930 or so we have a general survey of retrospective and recent experience from the comparative seclusion of 'these Shropshire-looking hills' in the New York hinterland. Here he wrote in outward peace, undistracted by those aspects of American urban life which he could never wholly assimilate, 'filling-stations, sign-boards, cement highways, ginger-pop stalls and residential sections'. His brain has generally striven conscientiously to cope with urban values while his heart has remained immovable in more primitive places.

Autobiography does, none the less, provide a commentary on half-a-century of a whole changing civilisation. Here indeed is far more than introspection. Earth-man, naturalist, sensationalist, John Cowper evades many of the pitfalls of the more conventional intellectual and wears his aestheticism—a very pronounced aestheticism—with a difference. *Autobiography* can outline, to persons of very different temperament, an attitude to life. Psychologically always awake to the ideas of his age, John Cowper is also exceptionally alert to more timeless ways of living, living physically, emotionally, spiritually. He has kept his roots.

Though on the surface it is apt to appear that John Cowper's geese are swans, and his critical lance is blunted with a patrician courtesy, there are many lively and penetrating portraits in the autobiography. The most memorable of all, and that most significant for the study of John Cowper, is that of his father. In his simplicity, his solidity, his sleepy shrewdness, his implicit force of character, his period self-assurance, the Vicar of Montacute emerges all of a piece and utterly convincing. He is indeed the key to the whole Powys individuality, though for all his 'wonder at the mystery of life' he totally fails to suggest the subtlety or imagination of his artistic offspring. Indeed he emerges with the solidity not of some memorial of a static era but of an unchallengeable work of art. He is so much more vivid, in these pages, than most reality that we are only prevented by the testimony of others from believing that John Cowper, in a supreme and unusually objective mood, made him up.

The Vicar is defined as, like John Cowper himself but unlike Theodore, Homeric rather than Biblical, with a childlike sense of the 'incredible romance of his own existence upon earth'. If John Cowper had a cat-head his father, it seems, was more like a lion, with a 'peculiarly strong resemblance to one of the larger carnivores: a resemblance that was due not only to the squareness of his face but to his low forehead and his long quivering upper-lip'. (The long upper-lip is indeed the mark of the Powys.) He was proud and supremely indifferent —as he could enviably afford to be—to social life and public opinion: an attitude that re-emerged with a difference in his first-born. 'I like to be *independent*, John my boy,' the father would say. The vicar's religion seems to have been instinctive, uninquiring, lacking in spirituality and stubbornly puritanical. Louis Wilkinson, who has pooh-poohed the notion that John Cowper is sadistic, finds a repressed sadism in the father which has descended only to Theodore, the great man (to him) of the family. But John Cowper, in stressing and artistically delighting in his own perversities, has not emphasised any perversion in his father, envisaging him as the very type of monumental sanity. There is much art in this memorable conception, as well as much reluctant piety and affection. Every anecdote, every passage in the *Autobiography* about the father, seems to be not only building up an imperishable character but illustrating the source of what is most Powysish in Powysism:

> For all his contempt for science, and his preference for traditional pastoral lore, he was wont to utter such proud phrases as 'I am glad you have noticed that formation, my boy. It is blue lias,' or 'Here is something, Johnny, that is worth seeing, a piece of Kimmeridge clay.' He would say this just as he would say 'The Cormorant is the greediest of all birds,' or 'My brother once stared into a tiger's eyes till he put the brute out of countenance.'
>
> Every phenomenon he referred to, whether animate or inanimate, became a sacrosanct thing, a privileged object like those objects in fairy-tales that travellers carried to work magic with. I think it materially increased his appreci-

ation of any landscape he was traversing when he could
gravely refer to 'Purbeck Marble', or say, 'Do 'ee see, my
boy, how uneven the "Rock Formation" is, in those cliffs
over there? Such a peculiar strata'—he would use the word
as if it were a feminine singular word, but use it with so
much authority and weight that as with a great many ex-
pressions he used, like the syllable 'goss' for instance in
place of 'gorse', his repeated misnomer finally became an
organic entity with far more substance in it than most
dictionary words can claim.

But in those days I even had the presumption—limb of
Satan that I was!—to want to tease my father! It was a
little later that I did this, but I always *wanted* to do it,
just as I always wanted to tease my younger brothers and
sisters. But it was a little later in our life in the drawing-
room at Montacute—knowing perfectly well how it would
annoy him—I expatiated at exhaustive length upon the
Seven Principles of Man, as interpreted by Annie Besant.
I went on till he lifted up his head from his netting—he
used to make our lawn tennis nets then—and burst out,
trembling with fury:
'She is a Demon...John...a Demon! *The woman is a
Demon!*'

The muscular Christian's innocent, sightless callousness is
vividly illustrated by his habit of dragging Theodore, delicate
when a child, here and there 'like a unicorn in a lion's den',
on walks longer than his strength could endure.

But oh dear! how well I can see little Theodore, white
in the face and with great forlorn eyes like an overdriven
animal, as he was dragged along some dusty road where
the very flies joined forces to persecute him!

Had John Cowper brought his mother likewise to life we
should have held a priceless clue to the Powys idiosyncrasies,
not to mention an enrapturing biographical fragment. But his
ban on 'Society ladies' forbade. How Mrs. Powys would have
recoiled from being characterised as a Society lady!

An extraordinary distinction of the *Autobiography* is that it
is never, in intention or effect, a record of achievement, a
success story (John Cowper deprecates success almost as much
as did his mother) but far more a self-avowal of inadequacy.
'This is my great rôle: to be polite and to bow and scrape.'
Whatever the writer thinks of his accomplishments, he never
loses his relish in implying that they are really fatuous and
valueless. His self-deprecation is extreme, almost pathological.

There is of course the Uriah Heep impulse, 'I love to be honoured for my humility,'[1] but that is secondary. Indeed it is probably without motive and masochistic in origin. 'Sawney John' or 'a cowardly Celtic neurotic' is mild disparagement for himself. 'Even more accountably than the word zany or punchinello, the word maudlin exactly describes the wool-gathering, absent-minded foolishness in my face.' He is 'a born clown, a born zany', a 'scarecrow Don Quixote with the faint heart of a Sancho'. It is true he regards these deliberate deprecations as part of the art of being authentically himself. 'There is an unmistakable ninney-look or zany look in my face. This look answers to what I feel, and to what I let myself feel, and to what I maliciously encourage myself to feel.' There is a world of implication in that maliciously, though the malice is always directed primarily against himself. John Cowper's sense of mischief, persistently gleaming through his pages, has no element of rancour towards the denizens of the strange unPowysian outer world.

Though the *Autobiography* is by no means our only source of information on John Cowper's early life, it is the chief (and quite inimitable) record of his childhood and school sufferings. His brother Littleton, though the soul of honesty and honour, was not by nature candid. And, though he did not exactly deplore his more gifted brothers as not being gentlemen, and wrote without the ordinary malice of a brother, he did deplore that they were not gentlemen of a more Christian and conventional pattern. Therefore he averted his eyes from the John Cowper whom John Cowper writes solely to emphasise. Llewelyn's loving and ruthless comments[2] on John Cowper and the *Autobiography* did not of course begin till later, as he was not born until 1884.

From the *Autobiography* it is clear that the child was not only father to the man, he *was* the man. Early and late his days were linked each to each by unnatural piety. His account of the boy Johnnie—and this enhances its value—is not coloured by distance any more than his account of himself at sixty. There is no *quantum mutatus ab illo*! In that sense he is his own anti-hero, gloriously of a piece through the long

---

[1] Letter to Louis Wilkinson, 7 June, 1944.
[2] See letters to J. C. Powys and A. R. Powys, Autumn 1934 (*Letters of Llewelyn Powys* ed. Louis Wilkinson.)

H

years. The school chapters of his life gain savour from the fact
that he never disowns his past, his immaturities. I am, he
seems to say, as shamelessly what I was as I shamelessly am
what I am today. In fact John Cowper, limiting as always the
freedom of the will, accepts all his behaviour as virtually inevitable not to say preordained. Oddly enough, this definitely
makes the *Autobiography* more exciting and endearing as a
document. A Laocoon who laughs conspiratorially as he
writhes in the coils of his own fatality proves a figure not to be
resisted. He disarms, too, moral judgement.

School oppression did however definitely harden in him two
tendencies, the retreat into the rural and his wilfulness. The
retreat was, according with the depths of his nature, to enrich
his individuality as a novelist and the wilfulness was to stultify
greatly his art. 'Moony' grew into a youth set against urban,
modern man and he also became completely defiant of all
restraint in artistic expression. Moony might be the most
affable of mortals in society, he might 'bow and scrape', but
once escaped into the heaven of his study he was not going to
deny himself the indulgence of literary intoxication, just in
order to communicate with readers.

No vindictiveness colours those early reminiscences, whatever the suffering. Conventional schoolmasters and even
hearty athletes are drawn with generous impartiality. Institu-
tions as such are never attacked in the modern fashion, and
indeed this most subjective odd-man-out is on balance a refreshingly detached chronicler of Victorianism. His tone is
never superior and never grows irksome. But it is nearly
always the inward searching that produces the most memorable
passages.

> I am afraid I was often cruel to Littleton; not always
> with sadistic pleasure as when I once ran him down 'The
> Slopes' in front of me till we collided—or rather Littleton
> collided—with the iron rails at the bottom, rendering him
> breathless and speechless and white-cheeked; but with a
> kind of arbitrary capriciousness and fantasticalness. It was
> in this latter mood that I would threaten to 'beat him
> like a dog'—which must have been a phrase picked up in
> my readings of Harrison Ainsworth—if he allowed it, or
> God allowed it, *to rain*! Like my father I had an extreme
> hatred in those days of rain and mud, an unpoetic attitude
> which I am proud to say I subsequently outgrew; and it

was my custom at the beginning of these long walks, where
the meadows, the lanes, the copses, the rabbit-holes, the
glow-worms, the ploughed fields, the yellow bracken, the
stubble, the clamorous rooks, the peewits and yellow-
hammers and starlings, all lost their charm for me if I was
getting wet, to demand imperatively of Littleton like some
touchy Nebuchadnezzar of his chief astrologer—whether it
would rain or not; and then, if he said *not* and the heavens
in their wantonness refuted this prediction, I was accustomed to behave towards him as savages behave towards
their medicine-man. Thus, as in the streaming rain Powys
Mi. fled from the fury of Powys Ma. down the long hill this
side of High Stoy, the elder brother tripped over a grotesque umbrella it was his wont to carry, before he was
allowed to carry a stick, and fell heavily on the wet road.
If Littleton was treated like a dog when it rained, he was
menaced with a wrestling-bout in the ditch if he so much
as looked at his brother when that blunderer fell on his
face, as he was wont frequently to do when descending a
hill; so on this occasion he took to his heels and fairly
buggered off; a proceeding which by no means allayed the
smart of my indignity and pain.

(Nebuchadnezzar's astrologer and the medicine-man here are
two delightful examples within one sentence of John Cowper's
felicity in allusion.)

John Cowper has indeed so much of Rousseau and Boswell
in him that he always seemed preordained to take his place by
right among the great portrayers of the self. And, after all,
what a self it is! However little of a mixer he may be by
nature, every chapter of the *Autobiography* is eloquent of his
vitality, his wide acceptances, his curiosity, his interest and his
contempt for boredom, his relish of congenial spirits and sympathy in keeping them alive for the world's enjoyment. Louis
Wilkinson, who calls him a super-introvert, proclaims none
the less his 'extraordinary gift of drawing-out the mental and
emotional resources of everyone he met'.[1] It is astonishing that
this least mannered and most easily readable of his many
books has achieved so limited a currency in England. *Autobiography* is, certainly, an American product and fertilised by
long residence in the United States, to which it is a resounding
tribute; but in a deeper sense it is equally an affirmation of
English values and loyalties. *Coelum non animum mutat.* His
descriptive style achieves a rare poise and grace as, years after,

[1] *Swan's Milk.*

in rural New York, he recreates for example the atmosphere of Gloucester in the days of his youth:

> Gloucester too was a city I got especially familiar with and to this day I think of it as fulfilling some deep craving in my nature, a craving that I would be hard put to it to define. Something about those particular ancient streets, those ancient bridges, those ancient cloisters, those old inn-yards, those romantic, upraised stone footpaths under Gothic masonry, used to give me again and again as I returned from my afternoon walks a certain vague obscure delicious feeling, quite impossible to put into words, but of extraordinary value in my secret life. How can I so much as approach a definition of it? It was clearly not directly connected with any aesthetic loveliness; for when I call it up now, after all these years, what pleased me most in these walks it is not of the precincts of the cathedral that I think. I think of a somewhat dilapidated entrance to this old city, a lingering twilight-darkened highway, leading up from certain vague, misty wide-stretching water-meadows. This highway, I remember, as it approached the region where in old days the city walls must have been, crossed an ancient stone bridge. Beyond this bridge, in that obscure evening light in which I always see it, the road trailed upward, *itself lingering*, so I almost feel now, as if it were loth to leave the river-mists and to face the traffic, till it led me into the heart of the town. And there was an intermediate region, between the bridge and the town, where this entrance into Gloucester seemed really, in some obscure way, enchanted. Between straw-smelling stables the road went, where, amid darkened shapes of great wagons, lanterns seemed to be moving of their own volition. Under rain-washed sign-boards and weather-stained roof-eaves it led me on; and it seemed to be always passing cavernous warehouses and medieval looking shops in the dark interiors of which there seemed to be flickering candles.

He is here of course, as nearly always, in the timeless; but not entirely in the past.

The finesse with which John Cowper plays Sancho to his own Quixote, his rare gift of passing through his egoism to its very opposite, gives all his confessional writings a sort of serious vivacity. We can hardly fail to believe him, even if we are a little surprised, when this egoist declares 'I am a vapour hovering over and passing through all and dissolving in an ecstasy into all.'[1] It is true as its opposite, his subjectivism, is

---

[1] Letter to L. U. Wilkinson, 13 Feb. 1956.

true. Overwhelming sympathy with himself alternates in the *Autobiography* with overwhelming sympathy for tortured life, victim of the First Cause, as easily as the swings of a pendulum.

He is clear-eyed, almost mischievously clear-eyed, about his stabilisation of his own values through the way in which he archaises the present. 'The truth is,' he writes, 'I am a born *reactionary*; and so I think is the Devil. It is God who enjoys stirring things up and forcing the past to lose itself in the future. The Devil has a romantic passion for the past.' This conscious emphasis on the old is however carried to extreme only in his fiction, his *later* fiction. *Autobiography* and *The Meaning of Culture* are immeasurably more of their own time and world than *Maiden Castle*, the novel written soon after them.

John Cowper finds an automatic gratification in experience if not in action. But in his comparative—only comparative— serenity in rural New York at sixty he never lets us forget that his has been a tortured life. Not only tortured by ulcers and 'sadistic' obsession. A certain morbidity—the word is too disparaging, a certain hypochondria—nourished by boyish suffering has dogged him, and in being a part of him it has given a savour of intensity to his experience. His brilliant appreciation of the Free City of Hamburg, which he visited to lecture in 1901, closes with a sombre reminder of his segregation from any possible happy herd, a sort of *memento mori* of the spirit.

> The especial Demon, in the lunatic asylum which I keep locked up in my cat-head, whose pleasure to vex me with disgusting imaginations was so lively and obstinate, the same Demon, who had strewn the avenue to Court House with bullock's blood and black snails, now bestirred himself to attack my peace and to sap my energy.
>
> It was in Hamburg amid all those great sloping roofs and those massive warehouses and those dark canal wharves covered with snow that I had one of my miserablest occasions of wanting desperately to find a close-stool and not finding one. So deep an impression did this devilish experience make on me that even today, when I see snow on the ground, I am liable to feel a twitching in my nether gut as if I were holding back the excrement of weeks. But unforgettable though this experience was—and I have noticed that priests and ministers and clergymen, and doubtless their sons too, have more difficulty with their stools than

other men—my mind was more ruffled, although my whole personality was not so paralysed, by a certain coloured picture that appeared in a popular, possibly a *comic* German paper.

It was a picture that had a woman's breasts in it and in some way connected with these breasts a great deal of blood. But this blood, at least to my morbid imagination, was not ordinary blood. It was very pale, but it was also very vivid. Indeed it must have been due to a triumph of art in the colour-printing of that prosperous epoch that even from across the road this blood was visible. It seemed to have the power of leaping from the page and of splashing over my face; yes! even into my mouth and down my throat. Nor did this blood-stained Milky Way stop at my throat. It sank into me until it reached some deep-buried 'loathing-nerve' that licked it up with frenzy; licked it up as fast as those centuries blackened wharf piles licked up the plague-spotted waters of those canals! In regard to physical impressions *of a certain kind* I have, I am sure, nothing less than the Devil's own imagination. I *know* I am not being silly or conceited when I say that in certain directions I have as powerful an imagination as Swift. In certain directions, too—and with regard to certain unpleasant impressions—I am as one who goes to and fro *without a skin.* This morbid and indeed almost monstrous sensibility is something you have to pay a heavy price for.

One quality that lifts John Cowper's memories above those of most conceivable rivals—above Llewelyn's, for example—is that they are a *religious* document, and full of ultimate wonderment and doubt. At the bottom of his experience there is a wide-reaching, nearly an all-embracing, reverence. It is redolent of his father's gravity and his mother's humility. Whether he is absorbedly declaiming on Remy de Gourmont or savouring (if inhibitedly) the life of Paris or being disillusioned in the bedroom of a Birmingham street-girl, he has ultimately the Grail in sight. And it is part and parcel of his humanity that this does not restrict his abundant humour. An intimate associate of the more challenging figures of his day in American literature, he is probably the only man who has described them without lapsing into either solemnity or insular miscomprehension. Almost all his American vignettes show a sparkling awareness of the sitter's essential quality. It is perhaps a result of his rebellion against the British social conventions, but it seems that his understanding of Ficke, Dreiser and Edgar Lee Masters has been even more intimate than his

appraisals of his English friends. It is significant that he came
to the conclusion, in the 1920's, that 'to be a genius in America
is twice as difficult as elsewere'.

The vividness of the *Autobiography* never flags through its
652 tensely-charged pages. But Llewelyn (critical to a degree,
for all his love of 'Daddy Jack') drew a sharp distinction of
artistic sincerity between the greater part of the book and its
last, less reminiscent chapters.[1] He censured that temperamental obliquity and self-dramatisation which is none the less
part of the essential quality of John Cowper's fertile personality. The prayers to Demeter and many another, the tapping of
the stones with the forehead, the rather posturing preoccupation with vivisection, the too literary and allusive semi-
religion, the intimate exhibition of physical sufferings, distressed the direct clear-eyed Pagan. All these and other too
human flaws are flamboyantly evident in the later pages of the
book; but this is a moral rather than an artistic criticism.
They are part of John Cowper's inner complexity, the complexity which makes the *Autobiography* its outstanding self.
'How the old Cacodemon,' Llewelyn wrote, 'is constituted of a
thousand elements—his nose of ivory, his claws of brass, and
his Long Tom of the tail of an adder that has forgot its good
trade. God bless us.' Beneath John Cowper's obliquities there
is depth, beneath Llewelyn's wholesome straightforwardness
there is rather less depth. For the profound writer existence is
always difficult, mysterious, menacing. Laying his hand on a
willow-tree in order to gain strength and comfort from elemental things, John Cowper can hope to find a new life at
sixty only in the belief that 'the astronomical world is *not* all
there is. We are in touch with other dimensions, other levels of
life. And from among the powers that spring from those *other
levels* there rises up one Power, all the more terrible because it
refuses to practise cruelty, a Power that is neither Capitalist,
nor Communist, nor Fascist, nor Democratic, nor Nazi, a
Power *not of this world at all*, but capable of inspiring the
individual soul with the wisdom of the serpent and the harm-
lessness of the dove. And this comes to pass, while we are still
in life, that when our soul loses itself in the long continuity of
kindred lives, it does not lose itself in any power less gentle,
less magical, less universal than itself.'

[1] Letters of Llewelyn Powys, pp. 189-192.

The last years in the United States, the wholesome, natural, congenial surroundings of up-state New York, not only eased the birth of John Cowper's most luxuriant novels but marked the slow end of his Puritanism. This is set forth in the chapter stirringly entitled 'There's a Mohawk in the Sky!' He had never been intolerant or didactic or censorious; and now he ceased to be—in that respect only—self-accusing. Llewelyn and Louis Wilkinson had driven out the murkier *manes* at last!

But with the closing pages of the *Autobiography*, as with the increasing unworldliness of *Jobber Skald*, one is forced to feel that John Cowper has parted with a good deal more than his hereditary Puritanism. His sympathy with the urban twentieth century, except only in its psychological questings, is now worn almost to nothingness. The freedom of nature henceforth implies for him freedom to see the past and present as one, to concentrate, except when he is engaged on pure journalism, on the timeless elements of existence. Continuity is all. In his New York years he finally lost not his passion for experience, but all acceptance of what is specifically modern in modernity.

> The country here has the very look of the old romances that I love best. Those who love tapestry say its hills offer some enchanted vistas as did the mediaeval backgrounds to the castles of the Gothic North. It is more like England, this district of upper New York, than any landscape I have yet seen in the whole of America. It is like Shropshire. It even makes me think of my native Derbyshire. Thus has the wheel come full circle and I am at Shirley again! In every direction, narrow lonely 'dirt roads' wind through faraway valleys and over remote hilltops, leaving behind them, as their perspectives diminish, that peculiar thrill that seems to come down to us from the generations, but which is so peculiarly hard to define. It is an impression that has to do with horsemen journeying, inn-lights beckoning, journeys' ends coming to lovers, to tramps, to camp-followers, to adventurers, to the life-weary Dead. It is an impression that has to do with all those mystic omens of the way that they are driven off like hunted wild geese by such things as 'filling stations', sign-boards, cement highways, ginger-pop stalls, and 'residential sections'.
>
> And, moreover, this vague sense of old-world romance, which I am trying to describe, is a completely different thing from the startling natural grandeur of virgin forests,

great prairies, vast deserts and towering mountains. It can only appear under particular conditions in the history of any landscape and it requires a particular kind of landscape for it to reveal itself at all. These conditions are precisely fulfilled in the hilly regions of 'up-state' New York of which I am speaking. The hills are not too high, the woods are not too continuous. Grassy slopes, park-like reaches, winding rivers, pastoral valleys, old walls, old water-mills, old farmsteads, old bridges, old burying-grounds give to the contemplative imagination that poetic sense of *human continuity*, of the generations following each other in slow religious succession, which is what the mind pines for, if it is to feel the full sense of its mortal inheritance. Where, moreover, by an incredible piece of luck I was allowed to settle, the actual earth-strata [*sic*] is peculiarly harmonious to my exacting taste. Grey slaty boulders lie in every direction, covered with the loveliest mosses and lichens, and intersected where the pines and hemlocks and birches grow by rich black earth-mould where the most delicate of wild flowers and ferns appear in their seasons.

CHAPTER IX

Full Creation (iv): *Jobber Skald*

JOBBER SKALD (or *Weymouth Sands*) marks an important turning-point in John Cowper's fiction: the point where his desire to escape the present in magnificent fantasy began to counterpoise his passion for deeper psychological reality. The third in importance as in date of his major Wessex novels, it is the last to show unrelaxed psychological drive. It is too, the vaguest in direction and loosest in construction, and above all distracting by its changing centres of interest. Though it is the most attractive of his works to many readers, its triumphs are not really a novelist's in characterisation or handling of ideas. It is extremely difficult to extract any sustained rendering of life from it, though attempts have been made to impose one. Its only true hero, as we have already observed, is a place; and its strength is more in poetry than in the world of human relationships. The background dominates and outlines the action.

The Powysian projection who holds the psychological stage most often in the book is not the longshoreman Skald but Magnus Muir, a middle-aged tutor in Latin. Nothing particular happens to Magnus except to be humiliated and jilted by a common lovely (vividly portrayed) of the familiar Gerda type. These connections, unequal socially and in age, are a recurring preoccupation of John Cowper's. Apart from beauty Curly's recommendation, a negative one, is freedom from possessiveness. She is a shade more unfeeling than Gerda or Wizzie; but the type is the same and certainly stands for something solidly human amid incarnations of super-awareness.

Magnus himself is rich in rumination: his passions are centred more unreservedly in Weymouth than in Curly, and he lives under the dominating, masterful shadow of his dead father. The Cowperian projection is unmistakable, extending even to the great walking-stick.

> The stick had been his father's. It was of some hard, heavy foreign wood, of a dusky colour, and possessed a smooth curved handle upon which Magnus loved to lean his full weight till he felt he was leaning upon the undying strength of the formidable old man.

Nowhere has John Cowper communicated more tensely the agonies of his own self-awareness:

> Magnus had the peculiarity of being thoroughly 'anti-narcissistic'; that is to say it gave him a real twinge of unendurable discomfort to think of his physical appearance. It is the more remarkable, therefore, that at this moment as he imagined himself holding his body by a leash he did get an intensely vivid feeling of himself sitting there on a sleeper and looking at those lights! There wasn't a muscular excrescence, or a long contour, or a fibrous hollow in his whole flesh-covered skeleton that he didn't feel, as he crouched there, hugging his knees and swaying a little from side to side. He felt the bone-points of his buttocks against the pressure of the sleeper. He felt the brittleness of the skull against the pressure of his cloth-cap, and he got the sensation that he was travelling through immeasurable gulfs of empty, black air, he and those four lights, Curly's, Peat Bog's, the White Horn's and the vessel's off Vorcliff, towards nothing and from nothing. Yes! and *with* nothing except an ultimate defiant-self-awareness, one skeleton's and four lights': destructible and yet indestructible, travelling; travelling through eternity.[1]

There is really a touch of moral sublimity in this striving to make consciousness more conscious through the quite unreserved study of introversion. If nothing happens to Magnus, something should ultimately happen to the absorbed reader through Magnus and the Magnuses scattered about John Cowper's intractable novels.

The Jobber himself is not wholly a success. An imaginative, classless, Dorset-speaking giant, he seems to have strayed in

---

[1] 'I always shrink away, as in a swift funk, as if I'd been caught stealing, when I catch the faintest glimpse of myself in a mirror.' Letter to L. U. Wilkinson, 19 November, 1955.

from Ibsen's *Lady from the Sea.* Though he runs a car (improbably in 190–!) he has little to do with either dry land or
the realities of workaday life. A purely poetical character, he
lacks plausibility and has no credible social *rapports.* He is a
legend and carries in his pocket a large stone with which he
has vowed—and planned in some detail—to kill the wealthy
brewer Dog Cattistock (another Philip Crow). The Jobber is,
more happily, the medium of the greatest elemental invoca-
tions in the book: through him Weymouth and the stars and
the oölite and the 'island' are magnificently realised. He does
not, foreseeably, kill the Dog in the end but sins more
pleasantly with Perdita Wane, a sensitive and really lovable
lady's companion swept off her feet, like another Ellida
Wangel, by the sea-god in him. But his behaviour in more
mundane moments, in a gossip of locals or at a whisky session,
for example, contributes little to the verisimilitude of the
novel.

Another projection of the author, slightly crossed with
Bloody Johnny Geard is 'Sylvanus Cobbold, a mystic' whose
public loquacity perturbs the police and who seduces young
girls. He really demands a whole book with himself as centre,
which could well include his brother Jerry Cobbold the
famous clown whose wife employs the Jobber's sweetheart.
Jerry, although he drifts in and out of the story with little
relation to its development, is a brilliant creation, a theatrical
character without a trace of theatricality. 'Sylvanus said once of
him that Jerry wasn't the child of human parents at all; but
that his father was the Ghost of Swift and his mother a
Lemur.' Entirely devoid of Powysian inwardness, he holds the
limelight with his virile personality, though all the while
under his surface he loathes life. Almost alone in the novels he
demonstrates memorably what John Cowper could have done
with externally studied characters. Jerry is not the traditional
clown who aspires to be a famous Hamlet but a Hamlet who is
in fact a famous clown.

Another aspect of John Cowper is embodied in a young
friend of Magnus's: Richard Gaul, who has a private income
and spends his life in composing an elaborate system of world-
philosophy. The system, very Powysish, has a certain interest;
but Richard, though he is smitten of Curly Wix, has no
recognisable role in the novel, except to act as an intelligent

interlocutor for Magnus and to crystallise a few precious moments in the life of Weymouth. The trouble is, once again, that he is not presented in the experience of Skald or Magnus or Perdita or Sylvanus but distracts by being a separate pivot. The same can be said of Richard Loder the young solicitor in whose maiden sister Ruth (as in Peg Grimstone) the author attempts to transfer his 'cold, planetary lust' to the female sex. Around the major foci of attention, revolve, much more vitally, a host of minor primitives and children and eccentrics: Gypsy May, Marret the Punch-and-Judy girl, Daisy Lily with her doll Quinquetta, 'Dr. Girodel an abortionist', 'Larry Zed a mad boy', the vivisector Dr. Daniel Brush, the Wuthering Heights family at the isolated pub *Sea Serpent's Head*, Tissty and Tossty the Hardy peasants turned dancers at the Royal, and a fishmonger who like Jerry is sick of the human round. The *embarras de gaucheries* is at the same time an *embarras de richesses*. You cannot summarise or impose coherency on such inspired prodigality: you can only submit yourself to it.

For somewhere behind the external grotesqueries there is always the glint of inner truth. The sense of life is intense. And the very lack of any relation to twentieth century society is a sort of fundamental criticism of that society, agree with it or no. In *Jobber Skald* at any rate John Cowper elaborates no comment on the environment he rejects: he transcends it.

But how, the reader may well ask, is *Jobber Skald* as a *novel* of the same order as *Wolf Solent* and *A Glastonbury Romance* when the story has so little significance, so little development, when the behaviour is so flagrantly inconsequent and any essential theme underlying it is so elusive? It ranks so high in spite of all this because its great vitality and its re-creation of beauty are reinforced by the same intense psychological penetration. And John Cowper does not intellectualise his characters, as does Henry James for instance, in scrutinising their inmost motives and instincts. He believes that human nature is really simple, rarely far from the child and the animal; and he is never afraid to assert this simplicity. The *petits moeurs* of his men and women and children are as convincing as their major actions are often irrelevant or improbable.

Never for a moment is a John Cowper character on the stage. But never for a moment, again, does such a character escape either himself or us. Here is Perdita in the swift realisation of the love that is to raise her and her Jobber for a brief spell to the company of literature's great lovers.

'Our love is no ordinary love' she thought, 'we could quarrel fiercely, we could separate in blind anger, but nothing could ever really divide us, now we've once met.'

Her thoughts sank deeper and deeper down into the nature of this eternalised moment, into the heart of the experience through which she was passing. The hardness of the wall, as with her body thus immobile she pressed the stones with her fingers, gave her the feeling that her soul was sinking into this vast promontory of oolite as into the shaft of a bottomless quarry.

'I'm glad I came straight to his home,' she thought. 'It's funny how I don't really admire or respect him or even altogether *like* him!'

She gripped the stone with her fingers so hard that her knuckles went white. That bony structure of her face showed itself now in her death-stillness, as if it were her very skull seen through the transparency of her soft, weak, drooping, fluctuating lineaments. Her intellect seemed clearer than it had ever been in her life before, and she derived a savage pleasure from tearing away every shred of sentiment, every tag of reverence from what she felt for this man.

'It's as if something of him were inside me and something of me were inside him. It's as if there were no need for him to take me, more than he has taken me already! It's as if when I hurt him I hurt myself and when he hurts me he hurts himself!'

Her fixed gaze, with its new 'skull look' transforming her sorrowful features, seemed to penetrate the very roots of that stone-crop at her feet and plunge into the substratum of this stupendous sea-rock, into the foundation of it, into what lay fathoms deep below the sea-surface.

'I'm sure I don't know whether people would call what we feel for each other "being in love" or whether it's even passion. I think if he *does* take me tonight he'll do it clumsily, awkwardly, brutally, *and I shall be the same*. He doesn't seem to want to kiss me very much, and I don't want to kiss him very much. It's as if we were digging into each other's soul to find a self that was put there before we were born.

The poetry of Jobber Skald is inspired by the terror and

glory of land and sea and the elemental; and these are experienced implicitly in relation to man. The moral, the human element is always involved; and indeed there is no truly creative art without it. As Middleton Murry once remarked, all values are anthropocentric. The 'Nature' specialists such as Borrow and Jefferies, as John Cowper has himself observed, are precious by comparison with Homer and Scott; and he himself is with Homer and Scott—you might add Hardy—in keeping nature in the *background* of the human comedy and tragedy. Yet, again, this is a dangerous distinction; for the life of nature is inextricably one with our passional existence, existence on any level above the artificial or suburban, and there is an inter-dependence that defies any differentiation between them. So to qualify a novel, except in a disapproving sense, as rural or urban is really false and uncritical: a man is no more being a complete man when he shuts himself away from the elemental than when he 'goes native' and indulges himself in a life bereft of intellectual culture. The genius Bennett and the talented Galsworthy are as deficient in wholeness as the regional ecstasiasts whom they so much excel in artistry, and even Jane Austen lacks something, because not only her men and women but she herself appears too often as a merely social being. Of such limitation, John Cowper is by nature incapable: never in the long length of *Jobber Skald* do we forget either that a town is something more than a town, or that a landscape is most a landscape when it is most closely identified with the whole mystery of human experience.

One of literature's grand grotesques, completely unclassifiable, *Jobber Skald* is far greater as a book than as a novel. Observing admirably the unities of time and place, but held together by no other unity, it is barely a novel at all. John Cowper's persistent weaknesses appear more obtrusively than in the earlier fiction—for example, his perverse love of childishness for its own sake in adults and children, his lapses into false West Country talk,[1] his sheer proliferation of characters existing through their inner eccentricities rather than in spite of them. (The lawyer's family, the Loders, are an intrusion of this order.) A more serious strain upon the reader is the inclination, already noticeable in *A Glastonbury*

[1] See Tissty and Tossty's mother on page 481, or Gypsy May and Larry page 133, or Larry page 199.

Romance, to attribute to characters trains of reflection quite foreign to their capacities as when, to take an extreme instance, Larry Zed contemplates the sunrise. It gives a certain cumulative feeling of unbalance, too, to find in all these intimately studied characters not one with any awareness of what is usually called religion.

Perhaps it would not be fantastic to say that the greatest achievement of *Jobber Skald* is in making inanimate life animate and animate life more animate. It holds the memory more compellingly than any other of John Cowper's writings; it has most of the direct, positive impact of great poetry. There are few occasions in Hardy himself more unforgettable than that Hardyesque scene where Gypsy May cuts off her own hair and burns Sylvanus the mystic's moustache-ends. It is John Cowper's particular *closeness of exploration* that triumphs in the two pages where he gives eternal vitality to Weymouth by a Punch-and-Judy and links all Punch shows for ever to the spirit of Weymouth.

> There, above, on the *dry* sand, there were for ever limning and dislimning themselves groups and conclaves of a rich, mellow, Rabelaisian mortality, eating, drinking, love-making, philosophising, full of racy quips, scandalous jibes, and every sort of earthy, care-forgetting ribaldry. But as those mothers and those fathers, those uncles and those aunts from hundreds of English cottages—for there is still a noteworthy air of real countryfied exclusiveness about the ancient town—formed and reformed their group of Gargantuan joviality and exchanged remarks upon the world that were 'thick and slab' with the rich mischiefs of a thousand years, while, I say, the *dry* sands of the place received the imprint of those mature glosses upon the life that went crying and weeping by, gathering I know not what of less human commentary upon its devious ways from the Queen's Statue, the Church Spire, the outlines of Shell Back, the wet sands that were imprinted by the 'printless' feet, light, immortal, bare of what might easily have been the purer spirits of an eternal classical childhood, happy and free, in some divine limbo of unassailable playtime legend beyond the smoke of our confusions.
>
> Between the donkey-stand, where the bathing machines hide the sea, where Magnus could remember in his childhood actually bathing from one machine that bore the Royal Arms, and the Council Clock, the sands die away. Here the pebbles begin and the water offshore almost immediately grows deep. It was here that Marret's father,

Mr. Jones, had set up this summer not only a permanent platform upon which to erect his Punch-and-Judy show, but also a private and personal tent of his own in the interior of which—although, properly speaking, he had no licence to provide public refreshments—he was wont sometimes to serve, or rather to make Zinzim and Marret and Tiny serve, tea and bread-and-butter.

At the moment, on this particular afternoon, when the hands of the Council Clock, across all its faces, pointed to the hour of four, Magnus, strolling along the beach, stopped at the out-skirts of a crowd of children gathered before the miniature stage.

'*Judy! Judy! Judy! Judy!*' screamed Marret's father from inside his coffin shaped stage.

'*Judy! Judy! Judy! Judy!*'

There was something unique—like no other sound in the world—about his brazen challenge. It was brutal, it was heartless, it was shocking, and yet there was about it, some indefinable quality—possibly simply the revival of his childhood—that flicked at Magnus' navel. Mr. Jones' voice was a very powerful one and possessed the penetration, and something of the harshness of those Babylonian sackbuts that proclaimed the worship of the Graven Image set up by Nebuchadnezzar. It was like a savage chorus of age-old mockery, as if all the Mimes and Mummers of Antiquity, without pity or sensitiveness or remorse, were jibing at our modern sympathies. . . . He seemed to hear this incorrigible beady-eyed little reprobate, this Panurge grown corpulent, with the huge red nose and the nut-cracker chin, who now was banging the stage so viciously, leaping up out of a rabbit-hole beside those despairing pilgrims and calling out in his ferocious Babylonian intonation:

'*Judy! Judy! Judy! Judy!*'

'Yes, there's something,' Magnus thought, 'profoundly unchristian, anti-christian, even, about Mr. Punch. And how this chap catches the character of the pot-bellied rogue—God! how he smells of sour brass and strident brutality, like the bawdy-house signs in those streets at Pompeii!'

But this disorderly giant of a book does leave us with one conclusion, whether John Cowper intended it or not. The deeper, the artistic self in him has repudiated society. His true instinct is no longer to temporise. The individualist, the solitary is the artist who creates; and not the over-conscientious citizen. Man as gregarious, as a civic unit so to speak, continues to guide his scrupulous pen in the essay and the ethical

I

pronouncements; but in the fiction the deeper self is revealed. In *Jobber Skald* the intuitives, the deeply felt characters, are non-social animals: Magnus, Sylvanus the ranter, the Jobber, Gaul with his lonely studies. The delicate Perdita, abandoning herself to the classless, rootless Jobber, opts for the elemental. No longer is the central characters' relation or adjustment to their fellows a vital issue. There is not yet a deliberate gesture of social indifference and not until *Maiden Castle* do we find the motive undisguised and fully aware—almost defiant in fact. In his novels henceforward he seems to be building up an alternative to a social milieu, a background that can lend his protagonists vital dramatic significance while they remain essentially solitaries. This is of course difficult in the *novel*. In narrative poetry and poetic drama the hero is not really expected to be seen in social perspective.

Jobber Skald in fact is achieved without the framework of any real social structure. But how magnificently the author makes nature and human nature respond to each other and creates, as it were, a more animated earth and a richer sense of human withdrawal into primitive worship. Sea Serpent's Head on the night of storm, the whiteness of the dawn, the outermost projection of Portland Bill above the swirling green waters, these may well be the last and most enduring memories evoked by John Cowper's poem in prose:

> Then came a time when the whole wide stretch of waters threw open its tremulous dawn-porches to their intense gaze. Grey, and yet not grey, metal-livid rather, like the dumb glimmer of ten thousand sword-blades, the sea unrolled its leagues of shivering expanse. It grew whiter and even whiter, and its whiteness was not the whiteness of death, nor yet the whiteness of light or of life. It was the whiteness of the spirit. It was the whiteness of that mysterious act of creation that came even before the word. Nor did this whiteness last for long. It lasted long enough to add something of its own immortal nature to the mortal weakness of their human feeling. But then, soon, too soon, it began to fade, and its place to be taken by something else. And what now took its place was the natural, the secular diffusion of ordinary daylight, of the accustomed, the familiar, the common day, one more day, just one more, among all the other days that had spread themselves out over two human lives.
>
> They reached the very end of this sea-jutting platform of solid rock. Here they found themselves standing side by

side upon what resembled some dancing-floor of the sea-nymphs, so smooth it was, or the level tombstones of some ancient sea-god. It was a floor upon which a herd of seals might have lain down to sleep, shepherded by Proteus. It was dark brown in colour, spotted with some variety ot yellowish sea-lichen, and in particular places its surface was roughened by living shell-fish that clung tenaciously to it, and by minute fossils whose indwelling entities had perished millions of years ago. Under it the dark-green water swirled and foamed and gurgled, and beyond it, below the tossed-up surf—for the waters of Shell-Back Point were disturbed by other agencies than the day's weather—there were endless whirlpools and revolving maelstroms of green water. It was one of those spots where Nature arrives at an extremity of contrast that suggests a sublime intention, for while there was gathered up in that rocky floor, which itself was about twenty feet long and about half that distance wide, the very absolute of immobility, there was flung abroad in those breaking waters the corresponding absolute of never-ceasing movement. Standing upon this platform a person felt himself held by gravitation to the very bed-rock of our planet's substance, whereas in that rushing whirl of waters he was aware of gaping holes out of which jets of the aboriginal chaos kept bubbling up.

CHAPTER X

The Philosopher at Large

'It is hard to be impersonal in a cosmos that runs to personality'—*A Glastonbury Romance.*

'I've learnt to get my happiness out of sensation. I've learnt, sir, when to think and when not to think'
—Wolf in *Wolf Solent.*

THE breadth of John Cowper's interest and receptivity—*l'âme et l'esprit hospitaliers* in Joubert's phrase—found prodigal expression in writing as soon as his lecturing commitments were relaxed. He was not at all too exhausted by the writing of his three meatiest novels, to elaborate a very different class of composition, the quasi-philosophical essay book—this, of course, in addition to his literary criticism and reviewing. The 'philosophic' vein, the personal guide to life, goes back to the *Confessions of Two Brothers,* through the series of small booklets issued only in America in the 1920's, *The Complex Vision, The Art of Happiness,*[1] *The Religion of a Sceptic, The Secret of Self Development* and *The Art of Forgetting the Unpleasant.* All the series, down to the *In Spite Of* of old age, is concerned with coming to terms with life in a spirit of sensationism and compromise. What distinguishes these essays from all John Cowper's other output, and accounts probably for their considerable popularity is that, though highly personal, they are written less for the author's self-release, or pleasure, than to help other people to live more fully and happily. The reason of their exhibiting a certain

[1] Not the later book of that title (London, 1935).

self consciousness and suggesting very little the author's imaginative power and depth is probably a Powysian un-reality about the rest of the human race—John Cowper's odd, and wholly mistaken, assumption that other people *au fond* think and feel as he himself thinks and feels.

The whole long series—and they are markedly homogenous, not to say repetitive—are written with a good deal of grace and a pronounced amenity of tone. Their timeliness and attraction are undeniable. Yet they stand to his other achievements much as journalism stands to literature. It might be said that the novels deal with essence and they are literature; the essays deal with existence and they are journalism: communication, and not the enriching of awareness, is the chief motive. We have much of the individuality of John Cowper here; but it is a temporising, by no means an elemental, questing John Cowper. Elsewhere, even in literary lecturing, he is talking unrestrainedly to himself; in the essay books he is consciously a preceptor. He is writing *at* readers. Never, of course, harshly didactic; he is still performing something prompted by conscience, by social responsibility.

His *credo* is a highly charged one—and, we need hardly say, intensely genuine. He faces life and his own temperament as squarely as he knows. He never deviates from his natural puralism, his conception that the universe is a multiverse, his gnostic view of origins. Of these presuppositions he has written with intimate frankness in a letter to Iorwerth C. Peate:

> But my quarrel with the Catholic church and the Greek church and the Anglican church and all the nonconform-ists and both super- and sub-rational is exactly the same quarrel I have with the rationalists and with the vivisec-ting scientists. In plain words, in spite of an almost mor-bidly Christian conscience which I have to restrain as I have to restrain my vices, purely for common sense reasons of legitimate self preservation and sanity—my attitude to all these questions if essentially agnostic and heathen and indeed *pluralistic* as opposed to *monism* of every sort, the sort of pluralism W. James wrote of—tho' they tell me Whitehead is a pluralist; but I lack the brain to cope with HIM! My pluralism is a temperamental intuitive prefer-ence for the Many over the One—and for a certain Anarchy in things over One Cosmos and One God and One Christ. I like absolutely free speculation in these things and *I like to question* not only the *existence* of God—the *desirability*

of following Christ—the *value* of the Family, etc., etc., etc.
Like you, I rebel at the tyranny of the Church as well as at
the tyranny of the new totalitarian state. . . .[1]

The Meaning of Culture is the best of John Cowper's moral
essays on living, though possibly surpassed in literary grace by
The Philosophy of Solitude. The discussion of culture includes most of the basic assumptions of the further discussions: the sensationism, the bias towards plurality, the
alternating epicurean and stoical strains, the rather unwilling
scepticism, the acceptance of compromise as an inescapable
modus vivendi.

Of all the resources for good living which John Cowper
elaborates, he certainly makes 'culture' the most persuasive. In
fact, his conception of culture is more elevated than the life to
which it is to contribute. This may well be because in his ideal
of culture, the impulse to truth predominates, while in general
he responds more instinctively to the criterion of freedom than
to the criterion of truth. He is indeed persuasive in this essay
so far as he strives to balance feeling and thinking; so far as he
postulates a deliberate realisation of the self, and so far as he
appreciates the deeper and richer awareness which is the
residue (not the product) of human requirements.

> A mind that is totally uncultivated gets its own especial
> thrills, no doubt, from a more direct contact with un-
> mitigated experience, but the cultivated mind approaches
> everything through an imagination already charged with
> the passionate responses of the great artists; so that what it
> sees is a fragment of nature double-dyed, so to speak, a
> reaching, a stretching of time's whirling tide that comes
> when its chance-tossed eddies, the pattern of something at
> once transitory and eternal. What an intensely personal
> culture is always seeking from literature is an enhancement
> of its own peculiar vision.

But what, to press him further, is the meaning (in the sense of
meaningfulness) of culture? Both definition and description of
culture are called for, and in what he modestly calls 'this
tentative and hesitant work' he tries hard to provide both.
'Culture' is used broadly in the sense prevalent early in the
century to mean artistic and philosophical reading and habits.
It is what goes to enrich intellectual and emotional life: to

[1] *Review of English Literature*, January 1963, p. 39.

foster a richer awareness than that possessed by the guy in the New York subway. It is quite different from mere education, not being directed to acquiring definable *knowledge*. 'The whole purpose and end of culture is a thrilling happiness of a particular sort—of the sort, in fact, that is caused by a response to life made by a harmony of the intellect, the imagination and the senses.' Culture is universal contemporaneity. It implies something of a bi-sexual awareness. It is the way out of all dogma, being the true and only alternative to religion. It seeks the same end or satisfaction as religion by totally antithetic means. The twain are, assuming that religion implies dogma, mutually exclusive. On the positives of religion, all that belief has 'kept open', all that acceptance offers, John Cowper is extremely clear and appreciative. On the *penumbra* of religion, taking Christianity as the essence of religion for the argument's sake, he is brilliantly illuminating. Culture implies, of course, some scepticism. Such a condition of culture is, with John Cowper's underlying need of freedom, inevitable. The timeless, universal, bi-sexual awareness that is the absolute culture, comprehending the many-sidedness of truth, includes an unlimited capacity for scepticism.

So far, John Cowper may seem to march with his favourite and antithesis, Arnold. But in their capacity for detachment and in the quality of their scepticism they are wholly different. Arnold was fortified by a philosophic turn of mind. Less involved passionally than John Cowper in the revolt from faith, he was not drawn by recoil to sensationism and compromise: and his negations, if more curt, were less violent, less absolute. Further than John Cowper from the earth, moving in a world like John Cowper's poetical, but less elemental, his own culture was not so exclusive of the values of the *dévot*.

John Cowper's sphere, as we say, the orbit of his psychological make-up and his psychological assumptions, is a poetical sphere, the sphere of the aesthetic, one in which these things are the essentials which touch the imagination. Thus, his conception of the pleasure of sensation is never one of *purely* physical enjoyment. We have seen in *Wolf Solent* how his intuitives live either in withdrawn sensitiveness or for timeless, elemental things. The earth-man, not unaware of his otherness, projects it into all his significant characters.

Arnold was as enamoured of certitude as John Cowper of

doubts. *Semper aliquid certi proponendum est* he wrote over
and over again in his notebooks. So various—happily!—are
the fruits of a devotion to culture. But some of the conclusions
which John Cowper attributes—almost directly—to the
culture he so enlightenedly propounds might well disappoint
others than the shade of Arnold. 'The habit of enjoying the
sensation of life' may be desirable, but it is less edifying to
learn that 'the only superiority worth anything is the superiority of being happier'. Almost we are compelled to conclude
that John Cowper is a mere empiricist in philosophy.

> The whole purpose and end of culture is a thrilling hap-
> piness of a particular sort, in fact, that is caused by a
> response to life made by a harmony of the intellect, the
> imagination and the senses.
> From Nature we get eternal whispers that happiness is
> deeper than pain. Yes—what we call culture is only an
> elaborate, intellectual cunning, directed towards the
> snatching of happiness under the very jowl of the dragon.
> Compromise is so profoundly of the inmost essence of life,
> that it might be called life's basic and fundamental law.
> The opposite of selling one's soul is suicide. The alterna-
> tive to compromise is death. Selling one's soul, however, is
> something that ought to be done quite frankly, and quite
> honestly, when it is done. Nothing that one does honestly—
> that is, with a childlike attempt to brazen out what one is
> ashamed of—hurts one's culture in the way that white-
> washing or idealizing one's meanness hurts it.

That the self must be deliberately fortified is the chief presupposition of John Cowper's cultural quest. Now, practically
welcome as all this sensationism, stoical or epicurean in
essence, may be, the arguments involved are anything but
philosophical. Such reasoning, unspiritual in inspiration, has
too little regard for inner truth to lead the soul to wholeness.
If compromise is indeed life's basic law, it is in the realms of
mundane expediency, not of disinterested thought.

The truth is, of course, that John Cowper is speaking two
languages. He claims that for the cultured, all truths are
equal: he does not aim regularly at a unifying truth. But he
does seek some central awareness that will make living possible. There seems to be some implication that we cannot live
comfortably with ultimate truths. Feeling and metaphysics are
violently sundered. For instance, most of us who are worthy to
be John Cowperians will delight in the *obiter dictum* 'any

boy, any girl who has spent an hour in happy dreaming has already fulfilled the purpose of creation'. But 'the purpose of creation' is a challenging phrase, and especially in view of John Cowper's gnostic assaults on the First Cause, one cannot help being made uneasy by a vagueness, a shifting of levels, a wonder whether 'culture' can serve happiness and truth in the same terms at the same time. For John Cowper does envisage through his 'culture' a creative morality as well as a formula for living.

Culture, if we may attempt to sum up this book (and there-fore, to a great extent, its successors) implies a meaningfulness that extends far beyond learning to accept the contem-poraneity and equal validity of all experiences and refining our capacity for reacting to and judging what is educative. It involves scepticism about all dogmas and especially about a First Cause. It assumes (more arbitrarily) in ourselves a willed quest of happiness and, in the sphere of behaviour, considera-tion and tolerance and compassion for other people, combined with non-interference and a certain withdrawal—the theme of *The Philosophy of Solitude*. The implications of conscious sensationism and hedonism, of moral scepticism and of in-difference to opinion, which he was to elaborate in the later essay books, are suggested more briefly.

Stimulating and enlightening as a commentary on living, *The Meaning of Culture* may seem a little stultifying as a contribution to philosophy. In the John Cowper canon it is important as summarising so eloquently so much of its author's essence, but curiously limited as containing so little hint of his creative imagination. The poet, the initiate of nature, the occultist, the psychologist with his magic insight, do not emerge. The popularity of *The Meaning of Culture,* as of the lesser essay books (each devoted to some particular problem of living) suggests his practical goodwill touched an audience a deeper and more demanding literature would not easily reach—the audience that indeed he had in mind to help. How personal, not to say subjective, how highly charged with idiosyncrasy is the attitude that underlies both his adaptation and his 'scepticism'.

The uncultured but educated man finds himself irritated, bewildered, nonplussed by the sophisticated childishness which exists in the heart of true culture. For it would appear that no scepticism has gone far enough till it has reached the point where almost any magical interpretation of the universe seems truer than any scientific one. The permanent mental attitude which the sensitive intelligence utilizes and derives from philosophy is an attitude that combines extreme reverence with limitless scepticism; and the result of this is that the temper of true culture will be found to be much more akin to the immemorial superstitions of the human race than to the dogmatic arrogance of the last mechanistic theory.

No refining of one's taste in matters of art or literature, no sharpening of one's insight into science or psychology, can ever take the place of one's sensitiveness to the life of the earth. This is the beginning and the end of a person's true education. Art and literature have been shamefully abused, have been perverted from their true purpose, if they do not conduce to it.

It was the wayward opinion of Jean-Jacques Rousseau, that great man whose excellent super-sensual sensationalism is so unpopular today, and whose very name is rarely mentioned without a sneer by our smart publicists, that the meaning of culture is nothing less than to restore, by means of our imaginative reason, that secret harmony with Nature which beasts and birds and plants possess, but which our civilization has done so much to eradicate from human feeling.

But taken all in all the book is a success, a personal success, a success of personality.

The Meaning of Culture was followed the same year by another shortish, fluent essay-book, the ill-named *In Defence of Sensuality*, a work of more dubious persuasiveness which attracted attention—and some opposition. The dominant mood is again one of rather sceptical sensationism; which is, indeed, all the author means by sensuality. The case for an almost primitive dependence on physical satisfaction; the life of the 'ichthyosaurus ego', is put with impassioned goodwill; but John Cowper exhibits sensation as a satisfactory defence against a too difficult universe rather than as the key to reality. He is well aware of his motives; but he does blur the limitations of the purely empirical, whereby he has not unnaturally incurred the disfavour of philosophers as well as moral idealists. In making sensation the basis at once of a stoical-hedonist metaphysic traced to Pyrrho of Elis, and of an empirical code for living by compromise, John Cowper does indeed expose a rather obvious dualism. 'For Mr. Powys there is no real truth in life,' wrote Mr. Hugh Fausset trenchantly, 'because there is no unifying principle.'[1] If there is a unifying principle for John Cowper it is in the realms of imaginative experience unexplored in his essay-books.

John Cowper had, indeed, in his complex make-up a strain of scepticism—not always given free play—but he cannot be classed as a thorough-going sceptic. He describes himself in the *Autobiography* as a 'natural born disciple of the greatest of all philosophers. I refer, of course, to the philosopher Pyrrho.' (That 'of course' is inimitable!) Now Pyrrho, so far as oral tradition has preserved him, was sceptical of everything. He accepted no axioms at all. Later and modified 'sceptics' accepted sensationism as real, and they based on the truth of physical experience their semi-sceptical systems. John Cowper avows *ultimate* scepticism yet assumes the reality of physical experience, even of conscious sensation. Further, he founds a moral system on the reality of sensation. Yet so disarmingly incautious is he that, immediately after the homage just quoted, he cites Pyrrho's reply, when asked whether he was alive or dead, 'I do not know'. John Cowper in his novels *knows*, factually or intuitively or poetically, many things without question. Not only is the novelist quite convinced that human beings have life and a supra-cerebral mind and soul: he demonstrates without reservation that the 'inanimate' has some sort of half-conscious life too. John Cowper does not merely differ from the legendary Pyrrho: the two are totally irreconcilable.

The trouble superficially with *In Defence of Sensuality* is that a reader not knowing his John Cowper might well doubt, not if the author believes in the reality of experience through the senses, but if he believes in the reality of any other sort of experience. A sensation is now unequivocally 'a conscious feeling enjoyed or endured through the senses'. We are led far towards a half-belief that happiness *is* sensation and sensation happiness. It is stressed that 'the *quality* of happiness is capable of an infinite refinement and an infinite assent'. We not only can, but must, move towards an intellectually sophisticated epicureanism. But the quasi-stoical note is even more

[1] *A Modern Prelude.*

insistently sounded throughout the *Defence*. The 'enjoy-defy-forget attitude, which is to permeate later the essay-books, becomes a counsel of conduct. In the name of positive morality, positive living, the First Cause is repudiated and with it, the 'cruel, evil-minded Puritan'. (Surely John Cowper's nearest approach to a defiance of filial piety!) He now accepts the implications of his long-implanted conviction that the First Cause is flagrantly cruel, though obviously the architect of a supremely beautiful universe, and cannot be acquitted on the ground that Man is given free will, since he hasn't, in the final analysis, free will. There is much we cannot go on facing; we must learn how to forget.

An unpersuaded reader may well feel, that the philosophy of this book, for all its sincerity and allurements, boils down very much to not worrying, or looking ahead: the stoicism is no Roman stoicism. *Carpe diem*. This feeling has some warrant; but John Cowper's writing is irradiated by a seriousness, a Wordsworthian wonder at the mystery of existence, a pity and reverence towards human endurance that separate him utterly from all facile fatalists of hedonism.

The last essay-book issued by John Cowper from rural New York was *The Philosophy of Solitude*—appropriately, perhaps, since in those parts the country is more primitive and the city more urban than over here. He continued to expound, unchanged, his stoic-epicurean sensationism, but with greater emphasis on the need for withdrawal. As his personal life and his novels show, he was now bowing his way definitely out of modern society. *The Philosophy of Solitude* is indeed largely occupied in showing how, by a process that includes defying and forgetting, one may deliberately escape from 'the crowd mind' into isolation and the peace of rumination. The reader may doubt the peace, and whether the solitude is not more valued for itself than for its mental opportunities, for the essay is palpably concerned with making life liveable, rather than with the quest of spiritual ultimates. Philosophy, driven out by science, must indeed be 'brought back' but beside this there is John Cowper's honourable concern that 'the daily life of men and women has to go on'. And John Cowper can quite easily assume that what solitude may achieve for himself, the poet, the elemental, it may as plausibly promise Everyman.

Solitude as a solution, just as philosophy as a description, remains a little suspect in spite of the persuasiveness of this essay. What really distresses John Cowper is his feeling that science has ousted philosophy: and he seeks to retrieve the situation by a revival of the *logoi,* a necessity before any 'subtle imaginative life' may 'become possible'. In the *logoi* he sees a practical, moralising vein in which all that is implied in poetry, in the mystical experience, in memory, in mythology, has a dominating influence. Since 'modern fashions of think-ing' especially the scientific 'have done a deadly hurt to the happiness of our race by their insistence upon the helplessness of the mind and the will', independence of the mind and the will must be fostered. Apparently this is to be effected as much with a view to happiness as to truth, and invites a considerable repudiation of society and communal values. Understanding demands a remoteness. 'It needs a passionate *loneliness*— whether practised in company or alone—to give us a real clue to the mystery of one single human being.' Loneliness almost becomes a heroic virtue in itself.

The book develops, in effect, into a frank assertion of the self by an unselfish egoist. All the chapters have such titles as 'The Self and the Past', 'The Self at Bay', 'The Self and its Loves' and 'The Self and the Bitterness of Life'. We are in-volved in solitude as a standpoint for sensationism and com-promise, moods none the less unphilosophical for the benevo-lence and perceptiveness and sincerity behind them. Always seeking for some device to 'control my thoughts' (if it is not his emotions he would control), John Cowper often seems to be seeking a way of life in which his own deeper impulses have no part. Is this an attempt to make communal existence toler-able for others on the part of an elemental man, a native man, whose imagination is really outside communal existence alto-gether?

This does not mean, of course, that John Cowper fails to bring riches of his own to the stock of our common life. His very refusal to be satirical about anything or anybody, and his almost childlike relish of everyday existence, impart a fresh-ness and compulsiveness to his comments. One always shares his awareness of the ubiquitous strangeness and richness of life. He has an indefinable gift of insinuating his moods into the reader, so that his humane but idiosyncratic devices for living become very difficult to question. Even his more superficial generalisations have a persuasiveness; and it is only the philosophically accoutred and the frivolous (those two extremes) who can fail to deepen their practical wisdom and insight by studying either *The Meaning of Culture* or *The Philosophy of Solitude*. Quite brilliant, for instance, is the analysis of the 'life illusion', that mirage of the self more superficial than the true self and terribly flattered and shattered by women; or again the reminder of the influence of *memories* with their supra-personal validity of which the mere brain is unaware.

But when we ask ourselves whether 'the undefeated self' which John Cowper proclaims can remain (in an age of general doubt and disillusion) really undefeated, by the aid of such arts and counsels as these, the soul gets a dustier answer. Even if John Cowper himself may be envisaged as 'undefeated' it is with reinforcement from tremendous imaginative experiences, poetic intimacies with the primitive and the magical and the occult, which remain quite uncommunicated in these essays in living. There is in John Cowper more of the poet than of the philosopher, intellectual though he be. So it is not really surprising that in his quest for life fulfilment or inner satisfaction, he should lean to the physical rather than the metaphysical. In *The Philosophy of Solitude* he first uses the word 'elementalism'; and thenceforth in his essay-books he inclined more and more to practical psychology and addressed more directly the Guy in the New York subway. The background of culture he demanded of his readers had indeed been a little unrealistic, for such a culture was accessible only to the highly intelligent and the early trained. Similarly, the isolation he was to go on desiderating is really aristocratic, not to say eclectic, though obviously genuine and generous in motive. It smacks of a defeatism which Geard of Glastonbury would never have countenanced! A cult of isolation can hardly be a positive, normal activity, just as lifting oneself by one's own braces can hardly be a philosophic solution of the problem of existence.

That 'the soul within us is a microcosm, not a micropolis' was the continual burden of *The Art of Happiness*, issued in 1935 and apparently the first book written in England by John Cowper after his return. Many critics were disillusioned by the more egotistic tone, the marked want of idealism, the apparent repudiation of Dostoievskian love. In retrospect, now, it seems simply that John Cowper, in conscientiously re-mounting his popular pulpit, was leaving a larger and larger part of himself out of his projections. He had developed a sort of sublimated journalistic personality oddly at variance both with the elemental questing novelist and the aesthetic ex-ponent of pure literature.

One of the sympathetically disillusioned, Mr. V. M. L. Scott, reviewing *The Art of Happiness* in the *London Mercury,* was resigned to recognise the abandonment of the Christian ethic, while still acknowledging the social penetration. John Cow-per, he wrote, was 'one of those who see that self-immolation in the cause of humanity is becoming a vice.... Happiness then is a stoic duty; self-pity, regret and even hope, the pro-found immoralities. We are to defy sorrow'. Because it was the core of his personal philosophy, as Mr. Scott justly observed, John Cowper placed too much emphasis on the stoic solitude which is an essential element in the well-balanced life. There was in effect a repudiation of St. Paul's and Dostoievsky's Christian-love. This was intemperate. Defy-enjoy-forget (almost grotesquely elaborated in this book) was spiritually nugatory.

All this is true enough. John Cowper's over-active goodwill was often at odds with the real poetry of him. Imagination was subordinated to purpose, almost to ingenuity. Our sense of happiness can possibly, as John Cowper contends, be elevated and refined through the will and right habits; and his in-sistence that the physical senses are always to be realised is realistic. But we are not born to a happiness, (or pleasure, or enjoyment), it is the by-product of our moral awareness; it is not a suitable aim for methodical seeking, it is what Aristotle called an incidental blossoming, ἡ ἐπιγίγνομενη ὥρα.

Though John Cowper's essay-books show a pronounced like-ness to each other and a certain sequence and are clearly de-marcated from his other work, the later ones (in which his idiosyncrasies were magnified by age) are much less expository of the ethic, the 'philosophy' of the earlier ones, and are chiefly notable for psychological observation. This observation is extraordinarily acute, though far less creative, more prosaic, less life revealing than in the novels. He himself, indeed, often contended, that your novelist is your most persuasive psychologist, and was well aware that 'the fiction I have written is worth much more than my lay-sermons'.

What makes *The Art of Happiness* memorable lies in the two chapters 'Woman with Man' and 'Man with Woman'. The nearest John Cowper ever came to the Rochefoucauld of whom he scarcely seemed aware is in the maxim 'it is better to be a shameless fool in Paradise than a discreet and honourable gentleman in Hell'. Perhaps over-zealous and unlucky as a matchmaker himself, John Cowper had become convinced that happiness—much as he disliked the 'bouncing babyishness of the word' is the *sine qua non* if not the sole aim of marriage. In his examination of the happy—or rather unhappy—sex association the pragmatist in John Cowper achieved his most obvious triumph. He in fact instructs, with many flashes of penetration, men how to let women be themselves as women and women how to let men be themselves as men. For

> So many of our modern intellectual *ménages*... are rendered unhappy because the man thinks it is unintellectual to be masculine and the woman thinks it is unintellectual to be feminine. They struggle to be distorted victims of intellectual modernity and intellectual sincerity, when all that is needed to make them happy is a taste of Helen of Troy's Egyptian Nepenthe—in other words, a drop of that primeval Duplicity which Nature herself pours like a blessed oil upon her sexes.

The admiring and indulgent account of woman's instinctive amorous and conjugal nature is as remarkable for its perceptive realism as for its humanity:

> It is the fact of a woman's 'possessive love' though equally shameless, being so much more diffused than a man's 'possessive lust' that enables her to indulge it so much more constantly and publicly than he can indulge his—women are very lucky in this. Their tactile sense is so much more polymorphic than man's that they have the power of 'feeling all over' at the least touch. Psychically they are far less sensitive than men, as can be seen in the way they can get beside themselves with fury, hiss forth the most deadly things, and a few minutes later, be as cheerful and normal as if their outburst of temper, which has left their men wounded and upset for half-a-day, was the merest scud of sea-foam as the life-wave rolls on, but their whole skin, thicker as well as softer than a man's, is so charged with diffused erotic magnetism, that it is wonderful what deep

satisfaction their possessive love can get from the least contact of fingers or lips.

Let him go on thinking in his folly that you love him for his humour, for his intellect, for his character, for his strength, for his humour, for his imagination, for his good looks. What you really love him for it is wisest never to reveal to him. Nature and yourself know what it is, that stripped, pre-occupied, heart-breakingly simple doll-man, whom you catch off guard sometimes and nearly give yourself away to him by the poignance of what you feel. But you must not give yourself away; for what he wants, unless he happens to have more of the woman in his soul than most of the tribe, is not just to be loved, least of all to be loved for his pathetic, reduced, poignant, tragi-comic identity, but to be loved with wonder and awe and reverence and admiration, feelings that come easily to you in the initial state of being-in-love, but which you are now surprised to find have extremely little to do with what makes you go on loving him.

There are two long essays which should be touched on at this point, both because they were apparently written in the late 1920's, and because though classifiable outwardly with his fluid, aesthetic, undidactic literary essays, they have little in common with them and they do bear some relation to the socio-ethical publicist. *Dorothy M. Richardson*, largely an essay on the feminine principle of life, is his only prolonged piece of literary advocacy of a contemporary. John Cowper in his little book was concerned not only to establish Dorothy Richardson's reputation more broadly, but to assert the desirability of bi-sexual awareness and the existence of a specific woman's world. Of this woman's world he sees Dorothy Richardson as the urgent witness, the artistic testifier that this world is quite independent of male thinking, male impressions, male pre-possessions or standards. He himself has been consistently concerned to see women, in Dorothy Richardson's way, as neither men see them nor they wish men to see them.

All authentic human genius is, in some degree, bi-sexual, and it is only because she is the first *consciously to turn the two elements upon each other* in a reciprocal fury of psychological interpretation that her achievement is so startling, so important and so new. All the way through

K

this extraordinary book the abysmal difference between the soul of a man and the soul of a woman is emphasized and enlarged upon. Upon this 'tragic tension' as Keyserling well calls it, depends the whole method of Dorothy Richardson's art.

Dorothy Richardson is, moreover, very obviously a sensationist forging a peculiarly intimate art out of closely recorded sensation. The scrupulousness of her self-observation and the thoroughness of her recording were quite as significant to her day as was her stream-of-consciousness method. If the author puts her as a pioneer with Joyce, the former rather makes her a small-scale feminine—or more feminine!—Proust.

John Cowper was quite consistent, while in his sensationist vein, in acclaiming her, for she was indeed a subtle exemplar of the sensationism he outsoared in his own greater novels. Her craving for closer psychology he shared, without by any means resorting to 'interior monologue' to consummate it artistically. But in the failure of his generous and sympathetic exposition, to point the limitation of her fiction, he points the limitation of his own critical sensationism. (His book, later, on Dostoievsky was much *broader*.) In *Dorothy M. Richardson* he fails to emphasise—or indeed to see—the limited end to which Miriam's inwardness leads: the *life* that is lost, the failure of imaginative significance. It is, of course, this very same ulterior vision which John Cowper's own art was a struggle to authenticate. But this essay fails to recognise the weakness of any position which makes the individual consciousness at once the medium and the ultimate. In the Miriam novels the medium too often becomes an end in itself.

The twenty-thousand word essay on St. Paul, though included in *The Pleasures of Literature* could only be omitted from his 'philosophical' writings and put among his aesthetic adventurings by an act of violence. (His American publisher in fact refused to print it in *The Enjoyment of Literature*—the title for the U.S.A.—holding reasonably enough that whatever its merits, it had no place in a volume promising recreation.) The essay, which is obviously deeply felt, really transcends and in great measure contradicts the views he was currently expounding in such books as *In Defence of Sensuality*, bringing back living faith as it were. John Cowper reveals a deep and possibly surprising affinity with St. Paul, or at least the St. Paul of his own perspective. Surprising, because St. Paul is the oracle of many Puritans and John Cowper abhorred 'the cruel, evil-minded Puritan'. But to John Cowper, the great ascetic is not really a Puritan in any negative sense, but rather one who has done more than anybody else to resolve a false dichotomy of the carnal and the spiritual.

It casts a revealing light on John Cowper's order of religious sensibility that he should love St. Paul's interpretation of Christianity and abhor the author of the Fourth Gospel. The Powys are ever mistrustful of the exotic and the recherché, and there is all of his father behind John Cowper when he disclaims (and in what a magnificent phrase!) 'the Johannine Love-Circle floating on the black waters of the Abyss'. St. Luke is to him the Gospel. What is important is to recognise that John Cowper is a Pauline Christian which is perhaps why he is so incompletely a Christian. Yet, as is evident, he wears his Paulism with a difference. Writing privately in his old age and lauding St. Paul for his humility he admitted 'I have never cottoned to Jesus, he is too narcissistic for me'.[1] Satisfying at once John Cowper's gnosticism, his hatred of the First Cause, and his craving for something less personal than a cult of Jesus, St. Paul appears to him the architect of Christianity as a religion and the true evangelist of stoicism. 'St. Paul, and St. Paul alone, created the Christian religion. He was the greatest God-maker who ever lived.' He inspires 'an unconquerable will to *heighten life to the very end*'. Not only is St. Paul a supreme psychological genius; the culminating *catharsis* towards which he strives is aesthetic. Not only does he struggle to change the actual nature of God; he succeeds in supplanting the objective Christ of the Gospels by the subjective ideal in the human mind, the 'Christ in our souls'. St. Paul the Puritan has no existence for John Cowper. The asceticism merges into stoicism, the stoicism merges into human sensationism, St. Paul 'becomes, in fact, as many of us are driven to become, a devotee of Prometheus against a pitiless Heaven'.

And it is as in page after vivid page as John Cowper develops—however arbitrarily—the Prometheus conception of Paul that he surpasses all his other argumentative writings and at the same time, assimilates the transmuted son of heaven most completely to his own sensationist humanism. St. Paul

[1] Letter to L. U. Wilkinson, 15th September, 1945.

rapidly comes to assume 'the huge and heroic spirit of the Pantagruelian philosophy'. The subjective process, the self-projection inevitably triumphs in the end, but it is not till after thirty or so pages that one finally envisages the apostle as a tall figure with high cheek-bones leaning on a ponderous oak walking-stick as he paces the street in Damascus that is called Straight, a very aged spaniel at the heels of his enormous boots. But what is important to recognise is how far more compelling John Cowper's sensationism can be when developed through religious enquiry than when developed empirically in the essay-books; and—further—how completely Prometheus triumphs over the heavenly powers in all John Cowper's conclusions. The elemental and the occult find their apotheosis where the mystical and the spiritual are most completely rejected.

CHAPTER XI

Maiden Castle and the Histories

'I am, too, a Welsh "wave of the first water" seeking my aboriginal level'—*Obstinate Cymric.*

ON the 8 October 1934, his 62nd birthday, the returned *émigré* took up his temporary abode in the old house in Dorchester which was to furnish the lineaments of Dud No-man's lodging in *Maiden Castle*. He was still at the peak of his mental powers and was bearing his blushing honours thick upon him, though his work was far from universally accepted. He was obviously glad to be back in England, though curiously coy in admitting it. In his homing to Hardy's Caster-bridge there was a certain appropriateness. The master, for all his defiance of Victorian taboos, had been far from contemporary; and the disciple was by now well aware that his own age could never satisfy him. His horror of modern science (rather illogically only, it seems of *modern* science) was almost overpowering. Antiquity out-of-doors and old, homely things indoors were essential to his being. He wanted to advance the frontiers of experience in psychology and the occult while rejecting all material modernisation. By the path of his father's Dorset he was on the way to the long yearned for Cymria of his forefathers, and the leisurely earth-dominated novel *Maiden Castle* is clearly the forerunner of *Owen Glendower* and *Porius*.

As a novel it shows a falling off from its predecessors—very obviously so in its want of motion or of cumulative fullness. No-man embodies little of the compulsive psychological drive that animates Wolf, and the vivid lyrical quality of *Jobber*

Skald reappears only in much subdued hues. Idiosyncrasy is heightened: often the book is a parodist's dream! Dud Noman (he has not even a real name) is the most whimsical of all the projections of his author, living in a phantom world of his own oddities; though there is certainly an advantage over John Cowper's two previous novels in that this hero (or rather anti-hero) provides a centre for the action and there is less disposal of interest. *Hamlet* has its prince. The strength, the merit of *Maiden Castle* lies in the deep awareness of race-memory and life's continuity and in the intensification of feeling by the passionate love of familiar abiding things. The old, the homely, the quaintly appealing, make a forceful assault on the reader's sensibility. A number of anachronisms and some improbabilities of psychology and behaviour do not seriously impair this achievement. So *Maiden Castle*, if no masterpiece, can be a memorable experience. Though the common life of man does not emerge, something essential in man's inner experience is undeniably preserved.

As social comment, comment on the life of its period, *Maiden Castle* has—except as a repudiation—no validity. It is a prolonged dance of Jonsonian Humours: the men and women are (except the circus-girl Wizzie, successor to Gerda and Curly) wraiths of the mind, of obsessions: intellectual wraiths, fundamentally dominated by the ruins and by nostalgic yearnings. They are isolated from the commonplace world and totally lacking in social defences, the reserves, reticences, surfaces of society.

Critics of *Maiden Castle* were for the most part nonplussed by the strangeness and the remoteness from normal human reactions; but the *Times Literary Supplement* reviewer put it rather well:

> It is certainly a curious, a tortuous even if not tortured, imagination he would express; one which sees men as spirits walking, and indeed all the manifestations of matter primarily as symbols comparable to the 'bubble cast up to the surface of a stream when a glittering fish passes by,' yet which is on the other hand deeply and persistently aware of life as 'sensual' thought and feeling, and of 'the actual substance of our planet down to the centre of the earth, with all the elements that work on it out of space, as an ever-present mystery, powerful for good and evil'.... The book has its own life, creates its own validity.

It will be seen how the book has a particular savour for those who love the essence of John Cowper rather than value novels as a representation of life as commonly lived.

But what, to get to the essential issue, is the trend, the special new contribution, since the ingredients, so to speak, seem much as before? We find No-man, a penurious, unworldly historical novelist, who communes in the cemetery with his dead virgin wife and is capable of 'inhuman detachment' combined with an overwhelming sense of his own nothingness. He is much possessed by fetichism; here centred in the knob of a wooden bedpost. He is involved with Wizzie who most improbably becomes his bedfellow, and Thuella Wye, painter of the stormclouds, a not quite convincing descendant of Philippa in *Rodmoor* and clearly related to the greater Christie Malakite. No-man, like Wolf Solent, fails both girls, who go off together to America. But these, and the other characters intuitive or supplementary really revolve about the sexagenarian Uryen, spirit of Mai Dun and the occult and all that is primeval and Druidic. He is really Dud's father, as is revealed in the course of the story, and it is in seeking reconcilement to this rather sinister figure, with ideas so congenial yet so violently challenging, that Dud sustains the leisurely action of the novel. Uryen is largely a reincarnation of primordial forces and a seer gustily condemnatory of all modern ways. *Hiraeth* is his slogan.

> 'What you women can't see,' the voice of their deranged giant was now whispering, and his voice was so low and yet so intense that it was like the wind lifting the tapestry in a royal death-chamber, 'and what these fools can't see, and what my son *won't* see, is that the Power of the Underworld that our old Bards worshipped, *though it was always defeated,* is the Power of the Golden Age! Yes, it's the Power that our race adored when they built Avebury and Maiden Castle and Stonehenge and Caer Drwyn, when there were no wars, no vivisection, no money, no ten-thousand-times accursed *nations*! They twisted it all round later, the sly children of gold and of burning, turning the dew of darkness into evil, and Bran the Blessed into a demon; but the Power that rushes through me when I go out *there*'— and he gave a jerk of his shoulder towards Maiden Castle— 'the Power that I *am*, under my name Uryen, lies too deep for them to destroy. Whether I'm Uryen or not—for all my mind is clouded with a doubt—this *Hiraeth* of my race, this

babbled, this thwarted, this hopeless desire, that from the
beginning of things has defied morality, custom, convention, usage, comfort, and all the wise and prudent of the
world, can never be destroyed out of the human heart now
it has once appeared! It moves from the impossible to the
impossible. It abolishes cause and effect. It strides from
world to world creating new things out of nothing! It takes
Nature between its fingers and Evolution in the palm of its
hand. Its more than desire. Its all the defeated longing, all
the babbled longing, all the forbidden longing, all the
beating against the walls, that makes the wind howl and
the rain cry! And it will break through.'

'The black man of Glymes,' he has inded a great if rather
bewildering forcefulness, and is plainly a passionately realised
embodiment of John Cowper's dreams of a better world—and
a better father? In the end he dies, acting all the other characters off the stage in a prolonged slightly melodramatic finale.

Curiously lacking in shape or planned development,
Maiden Castle is wholly occupied with the *essence* of life; but
especially, again, with the *essence* of memory, earth-memory,
race-memory. Mai Dun, Uryen, the ideal of *Hiraeth* are race-
memories. The author's possession with the idea of race survival and of our ancestors' being still alive in ourselves, part
of ourselves, is evident everywhere. The impressiveness of
Maiden Castle has in fact little to do with happening or expectation. There is no authentic present or futurity: whatever
happens, one feels, is already deeply in the past. John Cowper's
novels were becoming more and more timeless and in
truth almost demanding some classification outside that of
novels altogether. This is not however to imply that there are
not vivid, visible things in *Maiden Castle* which taken by
themselves would add to the stature of any novelist. There is
Dorchester on a Sunday evening:

> The return down the Weymouth Road coincided with
> the hour at which the burgesses of the town were lingering
> over their Sunday dinner, so that there was nothing to
> distract our friends from one another as they drifted *en
> masse* past the railings of the Amphitheatre. The massively
> built old town, surrounded four square by her umbrageous
> avenues, seemed to welcome their approach with her prom-
> ise of shady coolness and bodily refreshment. The absence
> of the weekly traffic had the effect of attenuating to a
> minimum all the usual vibrations interposed between

humanity and the mellow identity of the place. Like the
balmy air of a placid valley drifting over the graying backs
of the multitudinous cattle: 'All feeding like one,' the
combined scent of foliage and flowers, of dust and chimney-
smoke, of sun-warmed masonry and mossy walls, came
forth to meet them. But it was as if this 'Sunday smell' of
Dorchester contained something quite beyond all these
familiar scents. It seemed to bring with it—as if the whole
ancient place had been one deep vase of thick-pressed *pot-
pourri*—a subtle perfume that was like the sweet dust of
long-buried generations, a consecrated secular dust from
which all that was foul in mortality had long since evapo-
rated, leaving only a thrice-purged residue, a holy deposit,
the dust of what was insoluble in ashes, indestructible in
embers, destined to perish only with our human senses.

There is Wizzie's farewell letter to the ruminant she had so
improbably accepted as a lover:

'Everything,' she wrote, 'was too mixed-up. I simply
couldn't stand it any more. I leave you quite free. It'll be
only what I deserve if you get another girl. Only, if you
do, I advise you'—here there was a sentence crossed out on
which Dud pondered in vain. 'And if you do,' the letter
continued, 'I think I'd let Lovie stay on with Jenny and
Claudius. I don't want to defend myself, D. I know I
haven't been as nice to you as I should, and you've always
been'—she had put nice first, but crossing it out had sub-
stituted good, instead—'and considerate to me. It was my
longing to get back to the Circus and my work that made
me do it—and other things too, but that was the chief
thing. If I'd been cleverer, about books and all, it would
have been different. Don't be sorry or sad, and don't let
Lovie feel bad, or think bad of me. You *were* good about
Lovie. No one but you would have been like that. Don't
think I don't know it. I wouldn't like any other girl to see
my things all about. Give them to Jenny, and if she doesn't
want them, let her give them away. They know a lot of poor
people. When I was in a bad mood the other night I hid
all your bootlaces—those you bought from that tramp—
under the mattress. And those bits of paper by the statue
which you *did* go and pick up, for I found them in the
drawer where your shirts are, I threw into the fire. I'm
sorry, D., I ever said I hated you. It isn't true'—this last
sentence was underlined several times—'and perhaps some
day we may meet again. But don't think about me'—here
there were more scratchings out; but No-man, after puzzling over these erasures, concluded that the sentence went on
'as you did about', but he could not decide whether the

final word was 'Mona' or 'Mary'—'and don't let Lovie forget me. I'm sorry I was angry that night when Claudius was talking; and I'm sorry about *all* the times I was angry. Thel has been seasick, but I haven't at all, *not once*. Kiss Lovie from her affectionate Mummy. And don't wish you'd never seen me. Wizz. P.S. Write me a line how your father is, to General Delivery, New York.'

It is interesting to conjecture what John Cowper would have made of a whole tale peopled for once by extraversive, earthbound characters in the style of Wizzie.

In his nonage, as we have seen, John Cowper had taken only a secondary interest in history. Historical truth had seemed to him of far less urgency than poetic or psychological truth. That he had the aptitudes to have made him an academic historian of note can never have been in doubt. His grasp, memory, power of absorption were colossal and his insight into motive was discriminating. Actually the first Extension lecture he gave at Oxford for J. A. R. Marriott, in 1901, was on the Arthurian legend. He had fortified himself by reading John Rhys's well-known *Studies*; and it was very soon after this that his abiding passion for Welsh things, for thinking himself back into a Celt, began to possess him. In the course of the next 35 years he became a formidable authority on Welsh folklore, legend and antiquity. Historical lecturing had much less attraction for him: early in his public career the Oxford authorities who had rashly entrusted him with a course of instructional talks on the Roman emperors, were constrained to remonstrate with him for giving the students nothing but 'gossip from Suetonius'! The first book he wrote after migrating to Corwen in 1936 was one of his least happy, *Morwyn*, a fantasia directed against vivisection; but his major occupation for the next four years was *Owen Glendower*, almost as long as *A Glastonbury Romance*[1] and, even for those more sensible of its artistic gaucheries than of its greatness, an unexhaustible mine of curious erudition.

Covering the first sixteen years of the transitional and turbulent fifteenth century and centred in its hero's revolt against the House of Lancaster, *Owen Glendower* is the greatest of

---

[1] John Cowper calculated the length of *Owen Glendower* as 336,856 words, but this seems a considerable under-estimate.

John Cowper's histories. It marks the end of exploratory psychology as the dominating motive in its author's creation: from here on he was as much concerned to illustrate, and increase understanding of, the past as to enlarge man's future consciousness. 'Freud among the bowmen' may well be one's first impression, and familiar John Cowper themes do constantly recur; the mannerisms are unabated and the young Oxford lawyer Rhisiart is recognisably a self-projection. But psychology is now ancillary to imaginative reconstruction, though the characters' idiosyncrasies often predominate over and obscure action and background alike.

Bringing a half-buried world to life, *Owen Glendower* is a massive and awe-inspiring reconstruction, yet violates the first principle of historical fiction. The background, the framework, the detail are consummate; but we are living all the while in the twentieth century as well as the fifteenth. The tone, the tempo, the idiom, fail to convince: there is incongruity. It is just impossible to believe that people in 1400 were or thought or spoke or acted as John Cowper's intensively projected men and women are or think or speak or act. This defect, obviously attributable in a great degree to the *furor psychologicus* of John Cowper and indeed of the 1930's, really is fundamental and permeating: it disqualifies the writer from ranking, as he was so richly equipped to do, among the supreme historical novelists.

We have long become accustomed in John Cowper's fiction to timelessness in place of time and human beings who often seem rather to be walking spirits, but in the novel of history, which demands more and less than the pure novel, an element of period realism must enter. That the history in *Owen Glendower* is presented seriously is obvious, even if it were not emphatically implied by the masterly 'Argument' which John Cowper appends to the novel. There is as a matter of fact in *Owen Glendower* no suggestion of any but the most serious motives, as there increasingly is in the later histories. Poetry, colour, gorgeous fancy, magic and witchcraft there may be; but we are to accept a world of real happenings and real values: almost a selective segment of history. Otherwise the Argument, and indeed the whole elaborateness of the story's framework, are pointless.

The big bow-wow is indeed valiantly repudiated—perhaps

John Cowper has put the big bow-wow finally out-of-date.
(Further, John Cowper seems to have felt with a sort of personal scruple that the least approach to romantic sentiment or
cloak-and-dagger would betray his truth.) But the big bow-
wow—and it is not wholly mute even in Feuchtwanger or
Robert Graves or Jack Lindsay at their brilliant best—does
not destroy *essential* credibility. It does not, in the better parts
of John Cowper's revered Scott, involve being inherently un-
historical. But John Cowper's intimately modern speech and
psychology—all the more for the very closeness of his approach
—do shatter perspective. The behaviour, the self-consciousness, the sexual prepossession, are too essentially Cowperian to
go with the Middle Ages at all. The absorbing men and
women of *Owen Glendower* are not products of their own
starker, simpler, more formal times. Their very idiom denies
the medieval consciousness altogether. Master Young, Owen
Glendower's Chancellor, can say

> Well, at any rate, Owen's palace is safe 'pro tem'; and if
> it gets known outside that the place is manned to such a
> tune, those Ruthin fellows will clear off, even if they *are* on
> the prowl. Yes, they've lost their chance, the fools; just as
> Owen has lost *his* by telling the world what he's going to
> do—oh, my dear young man, I sometimes feel as if the
> whole human race is so brainless that it *deserves* to suffer
> what it does! But here's your handsome cousin; and, by
> cock, he'd make a pretty Lord Chamberlain to the little
> Dauphiness of France! Where do you suppose he picked
> up that pattern for his tunic? It's the very mate to the
> one my Lord Beaufort wore at the King's coronation!

You really cannot endow a nobleman of the Age of Faith with
the mingled sophistication, humility and self-doubtings of
John Cowper at his most fluid and unconventional. Nor will
you avoid anachronism if medieval men and women are
shown as constantly inhibited by typically modern scruples
and hesitations, by the consciousness that makes cowards of us
all in the twentieth century.

Yet a vital work of the imagination—so long as it is an
enlargement of human experience—has not always to be committed to period authenticity nor even to be an organic unity.
One may still say with Squeers 'here's richness'. Viewed as
poetry, as a timeless creation, *Owen Glendower* is richly
dowered with John Cowper's prodigious and prodigal wealth.

It is as illimitable as it is uncontrolled. The slow, rambling, inconsequent narrative is again and again raised above itself by passages of a luxuriance that almost startles in a low-toned age. Unforgettable is such a scene as the death of the bard Iolo Goch in Llewelyn's hall. Of the warmth and colour of the book—and these were not characteristics of John Cowper's earlier novels—Professor Wilson Knight has aptly written:

> We scent the perfumes of the chamber, the tang of smoke, the odours of vegetation. Colours are everywhere: the greens, yellows, scarlets, black, silver and gold of costume and accoutrements and the varied colourings of flowers, vegetation and sky. Red and gold dominate, in emblazonry, in people's hair, in the flames of torches reddening or yellowing the passages of castle or fortress, and from the great sun. And there is blood, and the agony of wounds. Over the action loom the twin threats of burning at the stake and the blood-ritual of the scaffold. As dawn's crimson gives way to gold, gold, at high moments, dominates Owen himself who is often described as a golden figure: the dragon-emblems of his standard may be either gold or red.[1]

The very soil exudes primitive mystery and the highly-individualised, often bizarre men and women achieve again and again a larger-than-lifeness and a strange otherworldly intenseness of reality.

Although Glendower and his rebellion are ostensibly the central theme of the story, Rhisiart (his cousin who becomes his secretary) is the chief experiencing character. Rhisiart, with his 'itching insect nerve', is a young John Cowper projected into the Middle Ages while Glendower, far more picturesque, is more objectively envisaged. So arresting is he that he overshadows the Civil War and its participants, and in the end its significance and motives become only his significance and motives. He illuminates life from a height while at the same time Rhisiart experiences and analyses it on a more everyday level. It is in Rhisiart's inwardness and his evolution that familiar John Cowper themes recur: there is the uneasy love for two girls simultaneously, the tinge of homosexuality, the tormented self-questioning, the spasm of disloyalty, the recurring lapse into sadistic craving and (as with John Crow and Dud No-man) the absence of full sexual intercourse. Glen-

[1] *A Review of English Literature*. January 1963. pp. 41-42.

dower we do not see chiefly through Rhisiart's eyes but in his
narcissistic solitudes and his lordly self-dedication. This is no
Glendower known to T. F. Tout but a subtly elaborated
genius whose aura is almost overwhelming. Here is no failure
to call up spirits from the vasty deep: he calls up all too
many of them. A fabulous ensorcerising, larger-than-human
figure; though at the same time profanely seen as 'the old
conjurer, at his tricks again' and one who can lapse into his-
trionics and spasmodic savagery. He bestrides the high poetic
scenes of the book—how admirably he is contrasted with the
sophistical churchmen, with his cruder henchmen, with the
neurotically-conceived Lancastrian princes!—while Rhisiart
pursues his own way through the jungle of psychological
eccentricity.

So heroic an artistic failure as *Owen Glendower* can hardly
be thought of as an artistic failure at all. John Cowper's vitality is very great, but no vitality could wholly animate so
labyrinthine a plot and such a swarming galaxy of characters.
There is also a certain failure to come to a point: there is no
climax or inevitability. We travel, often in glory, often tedi-
ously, rather than arrive. Cymria indeed remains, triumphant
and unforgettable. But this is by the poet's genius, not the
novelist's.

Owen Glendower won for John Cowper a lasting place in
the affections of an enthusiastic Welsh people—since the War
he has been virtually one of them and has even been crowned
as Bard in the Powys Eistedfodd. The reviewers were, understandably, in two minds as well as two camps. The devotees of
the exploratory novels of modern life were half-dazzled by the
depth and brilliancy of the fresh gifts displayed, half-discon-
certed by the looseness and lack of artistic restraint and by
discovering that John Cowper in the fifteenth century could
be even more uncompromisingly John Cowper than in the
twentieth. It was felt that he was asking too much of readers:
a feeling that *Porius* was to enhance. The slowness of movement proved especially provocative. It was possible to feel that
there was laziness or perversity as well as energy and understanding in this sprawling self-extension; and some feared that
a great writer was lost in the hierophant of a cult. Critics may
well have been right in deploring that John Cowper made so
little concession to his readers; but they were wrong in not

seeing that his genius was incapable now—perhaps had always been incapable—of formal discipline. Any perverseness in him, as a novelist, was quite unconscious.

John Cowper's second long reconstruction of Welsh history, *Porius*, was written (and he actually revised it!) between 1942 and 1950. *Brut Dinestow* was the Welsh basis of this 'great buggerly book of 33 chapters' as he called it in a letter. He had now brushed aside coherent structure and mere daylight reality altogether. He had no delusions about his own subjectiveness, writing frankly—

> in Porius I masquerade sometimes as Porius; but much more naturally in pre-puberty boyness of nine to ten or eleven, to which in 'Porius' and henceforth in all my future tales, till I die, I shall naturally revert—as 'Myrddin Wyllt' or Merlin the Wild; the Shape-Shifter, as he was also called.[1]

The book was conscientiously reduced several times; but ultimately expanded again by addition of a final chapter, so that it occupied in the end 682 biggish pages. From the fifteenth century he now went further back, to the legendary fifth, and from largely historical characters to figures of Arthurian myth, conceived in exaggeratedly unconventional and modern, not to say Freudian terms. The necromancer, the brooding presence, the magnet of the dark forces is not now Glendower but Myrddin Wyllt, or as we will say Merlin.

There are some, and they are perhaps the most devout Cowperians, who find wandering in the nightmare glades of *Porius* the most joyful experience its author has to give them. But the 'Romance' as he calls it is likely to remain a bone of contention between the Cowperian enthusiasts and his critics however sympathetic. It can be seen as both a triumph of the human imagination and a bad, almost wilfully bad, book. Slow and meandering, it contains much inept dialogue as well as some of the most penetrating perceptions that the modern mind, benumbed by urbanism, has achieved. The quality and scope and grandeur of the achievement are above question. It is the work of an ageing and always untidy and increasingly subjective genius who had nevertheless attained a strange vision of the timeless in race-history, of the occult reality in earth-

[1] Letter to Louis Wilkinson, 9 January, 1952.

initiation. No writer has ever gone further towards reconciling human life with the animate life of 'inanimate' nature and relating them in a creative unity. *Porius* comes very near to obliterating the distinction between conscious and unconscious life altogether. However fantastically, a sense of immanent divinity sanctifies both for John Cowper.

Like *Owen Glendower, Porius* is a work of enormous, loving, precise (sometimes pedantic) erudition. In *Owen Glendower* the dramatic sense had been vividly awake in many memorable scenes, though the tale lacked dramatic grip as a whole. In *Porius* drama is merged in dream. A nightmare unreality blankets the whole of the action, though it heightens rather than otherwise the poetic impressiveness, the supercharged atmosphere and the vague menace.

John Cowper in fact was now placating the tutelary spirits of Edeyrnion rather than devotees of the neo-Georgian novel. Porius, the slow-moving, quick-witted pocket Hercules is no Wolf Solent living and moving and having his being in a world of social and psychological contacts, though indeed he has a closely parallel way of escape, 'cavoseniargising', from the stresses of everyday experience. John Cowper found, in 495 A.D., a virtually blank page of history to fill and a mythology magnificently adaptable. So undeniable historic remains and ethically authentic Romans, Brythons, Saesons, Fifichtiaid and even aboriginal Cewri made an effective setting for superb while realistic embellishments of the Arthurian myths. The ritual of the Fisher King, the Feast of the Sowing, these were to prove splendid incitements to the mood. *Porius* is admirably free from sentimentality and the compelling nostalgia is kept in suspension. The mystery and eternal remotenesses of Wales, more dominant here even than in *Owen Glendower*, never shed an unreal glamour on the men and women of the story as happens in the literature of the Celtic Renaissance where the Irish are so often falsely stylised.

Portrayed with exceptional sympathy and vision, the battle of the races and creeds for the soul of Wales does still generate for the reader something of an intellectual mist just as the actual battles are fought in a physical mist. Liberty of mind and body and the challenge of Christianity emerge as the urgent issues. But in the end as Porius releases Merlin from his rocky prison the triumph of the occult, of the spirits of earth is decisive. This does not mean, characteristically, that John Cowper repudiates Christianity; on the contrary, the temper of the whole novel compels one to feel as never before that the author is no Pagan. He may wear his Pelagianism with a difference; but he wears it. Still protesting in the recesses of his deeply religious soul against his father's religion, John Cowper comes nearer than ever before or after, in *Porius*, to substituting the darker forces of magic. Yet it is a magic that still subserves a Christian ethos.

But intuitiveness about magic or the Pelagian heresy does not, unfortunately, ensure a fine, rounded novel. Nor do (banal and inadequate phrase) descriptive passages. Despite its wealth *Porius* remains, beyond all special pleading, labyrinthine and unassured. The level shifts bewilderingly, the military operations would make even Balaklava seem a sensible affair; and the characters wander about as if they belonged to *A Midsummer Night's Dream*, a very different sort of 'romance' where nobody is supposed to be bothering about Mithras or Pelagianism or the soul of a country. In fact *Porius* is a self-fulfilment for one who is weary or impatient of looking at real life as the novelist looks at real life, of one who now inclines irresistibly to represent emotions and imaginings at random rather than in the behaviour of human characters interacting. One reviewer owned to 'a pleasant sensation of controlled nightmare'; and the reaction is surely authentic.

The trouble is, artistically, that John Cowper's transition from the novel to the fantasy is not deliberate and controlled: the machinery still suggests a purposive re-creation of a past age, and so demands a realist mood and assent which can only be given at intervals in reading *Porius*. It is a little as if in place of his *Julius Caesar* Shakespeare had written a sort of *Midsummer Night's Dream* round its plot and called that *Julius Caesar*. The poetry, the enchantment would survive the ruin of a play; and similarly John Cowper's occult vision and the restrained, sombre, lyrical beauty of his description survive the dramatic failure. Sometimes the strength of his uniqueness seems actually intensified in this senescence, 'the old age of Homer in Longinus's phrase.

Brochvael stretched out his arms, as he leant against that

L

worm-eaten post, stretched them as wide and as far back-
ward as he could, so as to touch with the tips of his fingers
the tails of both the tethered creatures. There was no perceptible wind; but two or three dead leaves came drifting
in at the open door, and with them, from a strip of the old,
damp, mossy woodland that no human axe whether of flint
or bronze or iron had yet touched, came a strong lechery
sweet smell of funguses. And with those things there rose
upon him the feeling of all the weight of all the accumu-
lated masses of dead leaves, falling and fallen, moving and
still, that the deep forest about him had shaken from its
swaying and dripping branches to the wet ground. Miles
and miles of things that are feverish and sick, or lying in
piled-up heaps, corpse-cold and motionless, entering, it
might seem, with some huge, dark dumb mysterious process, reeking with sepulchre-sweet rot, and fetid with lust-
satisfying decay, of the enormous vegetable dissolution, out
of which autumn by recurrent autumn, the organic life of
the earth is renewed. And with this sense of the piling-up
of mountainous vast earth-ridges of dead leaves, from whose
decomposition emanated a deadly sweet sexual longing
that seemed to be diffused through the whole approach
of this unnatural mist from the precipices of Cader Idris, he
was now sure he detected the faint but unique odour,
more sex-drugged than any piling up of dead leaves, of
fungus-growths upon the air.

Even if we do not rank *Owen Glendower* and *Porius* among
John Cowper's most urgent challenges to our times, we must
recognise that they have something the novels of his prime
haven't: a little more of his passionate animism, his occultism,
his power of evoking the spirit of place and the miraculous
ecstasy of *sensing the unknowable*. Now more and more, as he
grows old, John Cowper's liquid mind flows like water, seeking
all the while its own level, unchannelled.

Like all John Cowper's novels in this *Porius* had a mixed
reception. Enthusiasm contrasted with indifference. Printing
House Square was on the whole supercilious and most of the
more conventional or modish journals ignored it. But in other
quarters—sometimes unexpected—its 'scope', 'magic' and
'wisdom' were acclaimed in responsible terms. *The Scotsman*,
James Hanley, Julian Symons were among the champions of
Porius. Not long after *Dock Leaves* (now the *Anglo-Welsh
Review*), dedicating and largely devoting a special issue to
John Cowper, acknowledged its seriousness and importance at

length and with a salutary stringency. G. D. Painter the Proustian and Roland Mathias were specially convincing. Mr. Painter saw *Porius* as an untidy, unartistic embodiment of John Cowper's 'contemplation and magic', while recognising acutely the 'multiverse without any primal unity' bound up with 'the First Cause itself as partly good and partly evil'. The creative calibre of John Cowper was seen as something altogether outside the range of his English contemporaries.

In the third[1] and last of the trio of histories *The Brazen Head* (1956) there is no mist or labyrinthine groping; the atmosphere is clear and sunshiny and the gait almost tripping. In this semi-serious work of what he well called his 'second boyhood'—he was eighty-two—John Cowper returned to the Middle Ages (1272, to be exact) and Wessex. Appropriately, for Roger Bacon the fabricator of the brazen head had been born just outside Montacute. So in his last work of fiction that makes any claim to realistic mood John Cowper returned to the background of his first. His intimations from nature had become far more spontaneous and vivid with the years.

Though in the nature of a personal diversion and a *tour de force, The Brazen Head* is, to him who runs, among John Cowper's most readily *enjoyable* books. His concentration was undeniably waning and the structure can hardly be called compact or shapely, but the narrative is free of *longueurs* and refreshingly easy to read. The metaphysical projections—and there are still plenty of them—are carried lightly. Bacon's legendary robot with the endowment of prophetic speech is not in fact a dominant theme, and the action revolves loosely around the ideas of a quartet of conflicting schoolmen and the personality of a bizarre baronial introvert significantly entitled Sir Mort—a Crusader and huntsman half-whimsical but wholly Powysian. In the lovingly reconstructed world of the thinkers there circulates a lively galaxy of romantics and grotesques, dubiously thirteenth century but never wanting in animation. Non-human life is, as usual, as active and participant as the men and women. The magic properties of nature are, to be frank, more convincing than those of Bacon's robot or its rival, Peter Peregrinus' lodestone.

Once again we are faced with great inherent anachronism

[1] *Atlantis* (1954), a reconstruction from Greek legend, is really too purely a fantasy to be ranked with the historical novels.

in conflict with great mastery of period, and it is impossible not to regret once more that the humour, delightful of its kind, is of a type perilous to the illusion of historical fidelity. Dialogue persists in being up-to-date and too often shatteringly so. 'It's a terrific secret, of course,' a character will say, or 'he's the top boy, so to speak, of the whole Schola mundi'. In a work of less serious evocations this does not jar as much as does King Arthur's chatty style in *Porius;* but the falsity of tempo is still disconcerting. It is ultimately attributable of course to the fatal Powys lack of social ear, the deafness to the real tones of conversation outside the family cave.

The Brazen Head is a John Cowper historical novel with the grandeur left out but not the scholarship or the zest. In Sir Mort unabashed Powys is still writ large—Sir Mort, in whom the sensationism of enjoy-defy-forget is once more exemplified and who fears nothing but Death. To Sir Mort, in the most serious passage of the story, John Cowper does indeed give a great deal of his own old-age conclusions on the meaning of the soul and what manner of life it enjoys.

> When we thus speak of the projected thoughts and feelings and emotions of all things, it must be remembered that we are not suggesting the existence of actual souls that can survive the death of their bodily presence. When we are dead, Sir Mort maintained, we are absolutely dead. But while we live we are all, including the myriads of sub-human lives in air, on land, and in water, from whales to earth-worms and the tiniest gnats, in constant contact with an invisible overshadowing atmospheric mist, crowded with feelings and dreams and emotions and what might be called sense-emanations and thought-eidola issuing from all that exists, whether super-human, human, or sub-human, whether organic or inorganic. This atmosphere dimension does not, Sir Mort argued, contain the sort of entities we are in the habit of thinking of as souls; for these perish when we perish, but it contains the thoughts and feelings and intimations and sensations which, though they grow fainter with time, do not cease to exist when the body and soul which projected them have both come to an end.

The quartet of schoolmen who provide the true *motif* of *The Brazen Head* are conceived in a vein of intellectual comedy. They recall, if less subtly, the dialectic of the bland casuistic ecclesiastics in *Owen Glendower*. The mediaeval science theme of *The Brazen Head* develops into a sort of

rubber of clerical whist, Roger Bacon being partnered with
the great Albert of Cologne (his master in Aristotelian science)
against the forces of evil personified, whimsically perhaps
rather than seriously, in a vivid St. Bonaventura and the
sinister Petrus Peregrinus of the lodestone. There is more than
a touch of Rabelais in the handling of the scheming, lecherous
Peter, the anti-Christ. Bonaventura is drawn with some
elaboration and a lively irony. *Corruptio optimi pessima* indeed we reflect of this portentous Franciscan, this 'page-boy of
omnipotence'. He is an ambitious Pharisee and self-deceiver
and yet one in whom John Cowper can indulge an occasional
hit at himself.

> St. Francis had regarded it as a perpetual miracle of
> grace the way in which his young friend resisted tempta-
> tion; when all the while his young friend was enjoying the
> process of temptation itself more than he could possibly
> have enjoyed any fruition of desire.

It would be making too heavy weather of this historical fantasia to read into the wrangles of its churchmen a studied
commentary on the many-sidedness of truth: even more so to
detect gropings in John Cowper towards a tardy theological
commitment. It is doubtful if he now sought for theological
solutions any longer. Probably Uryen in *Maiden Castle* comes
nearer to John Cowper's religion than all the Fathers. But if
in his later years the faith of his forbears no longer came near
to the bone with John Cowper, *The Brazen Head* does testify
to his inexhaustible curiosity and skill in dissecting Doctor
and Saint and indeed to his consistency in 'coming out by the
same door...'

CHAPTER XII

Rabelais, Dostoievsky and the Critic

THE over-catholic-critic tends to cancel out. It would be diffi-cult to envisage the essential John Cowper through his copious literary criticism, because of his extreme *esprit hospitalier*. His cult of humility and his excessively fluid make-up did much to disqualify him in this field. Yet, although he contributed no original theory, no key idea to criticism, he was undoubtedly a success here—far more successful on the whole than he was as a lyric poet or empirical philosopher. His criticism is of a type far from fashionable today. He has sought to prove nothing, to establish no canons, no theories of 'maturity' or perfect expres-sion, to erect no philosophical criterion. Nor were exegesis and elaborated comparison his chosen tools. He was a late-come but inevitable devotee of the interpretative or appreciatory school, to which Lemaître, Anatole France, Gosse, Arthur Symons, Virginia Woolf in their slightly differing ways be-long. Patently he travelled more happily than he arrived, but amassed much treasure and many observations on the way. He cut indeed, very often, deeper than earlier exponents of the interpretative method. His conspicuous effervescence was often a strength, though it was a recurrent source of weakness as well, for though his essays are far more finished and deliberate than his heady lectures can possibly have been, they do show the platform and revivalist influence. He does not *talk* on the paper; but he does seek to engage readers by almost un-relieved enthusiasm. His scope and sympathy and humorous penetration fortunately provide a ponderable alternative to austerity and philosophic sinew, and over-diffuse as his manner often is, he does achieve a weight and a gravity in his most deliberated judgements.

John Cowper displays the common merit of the best expository critics in projecting himself creatively into his subjects; but also the defect of projecting himself too far. What is most astonishing in him, seeing his subjective temperament, is that so little should be outside his appreciation. Seneca cannot be too heavy nor Plautus too light. Writers with whom he has no common touchstone (even early Max Beerhohm) are as likely to have unsuspected—possibly non-existent—subtleties and overtones revealed as are the most Cowperian objects of veneration. It is a sign that he positively gains by detachment that he—the least Gallic of mortals—should be better on French writers than on English, especially when one finds hardly a Frenchman in his surveys except Rabelais with whom he shares obvious earth-roots. He is notably excellent on Proust, on Remy de Gourmont, on Verlaine, on Anatole France (although satire and aloofness are repugnant to him) and so Protean is he that it is often as difficult to detect the idiosyncratic John Cowper in his responses as it is impossible to mistake his style in their expression. One cannot but smile when in appositely deploring the fashionable neglect of Anatole France a generation ago, he was so self-forgetful as to complain that 'the Rousseau type with its enthusiastic, neurotic mania for self-revelation, dominates the entire literary field'. There may have been some truth here, but a better instance of the Rousseau type with its enthusiastic, neurotic mania for self-revelation than John Cowper himself it would be difficult to find!

Guy de Maupassant ranks almost as ignobly high as Browning and Swinburne among John Cowper's aversions, because of his supposed cynicism and constructional slickness, and also because what the critic sees as concentration on things in lieu of words and bodies in lieu of souls—the surface approach, may we say—is despised as artistically contemptible. Yet the exposition of Maupassant's fiction is extraordinarily penetrating and conscientious: it is difficult to think of any other critic of 1916 who isolated thus distinctly the Frenchman's immediacy of perception, his hard actuality, his quality at best of a miniature crystallised Balzac. After this feat of sympathy one is not surprised that in his riper age John Cowper should have gone out of his way to interpret Flaubert,[1] his own antithesis with the 'unshaking artist's hand', with whose virus he could never inoculate himself. The whole appreciation, with its emphasis on Flaubert's 'vast disgust with ordinary human life' is as original as it is wide-seeing. How good, incidentally, how apt, the reference to 'those occasional hollow lapses, like a great bassoon gone cracked!'

John Cowper's usual questings and preoccupations are not discernible at all in his brilliant proclamation of Remy de Gourmont, as unpredictable as his enthusiasm for Peter and Verlaine. In an essay as remarkable as any he has left he chose this super-Gallic touchstone to find the cultured world of 1916 sadly wanting. The Frenchman is most convincingly acclaimed for a μηδὲν ἄγαν mind, a classicist objectivity, an innate sense of form that might well have been supposed to lie outside John Cowper's wide but very different understanding. Gourmont is seen as a classical spirit in several carefully differentiated senses, and at the same time almost topical with a curious, many-sided mind. His words admit the reader to 'that psychological borderland existing half-way between the moving waters of sensibility and the human shores of mental appreciation'. He is characterised as the seeker of Truth for the sake of the quest only; the journey being everything.

John Cowper was impelled to attack the puritanical, Philistine new bourgeoisie of the first war, and Gourmont—brilliantly pressed into service—was no doubt as much the pretext as the motive of it. (John Cowper was usually too courteous to assail his fellow-men directly.) An almost willed irresponsibility, said the John Cowper of the period, is essential to a true civilisation. Puritanism must be rejected and in a lesser degree politics and social leftism. Mere abstractions must be shunned —and here indeed he concurs with Gourmont who as a classicist made war first and always on the abstract. Only by the concrete, John Cowper summarises, can we make the abstract live. Moreover 'only by the senses do we understand the soul, and only by the soul do we understand the senses'. Remy de Gourmont, making the abstract concrete and the concrete abstract, in practise as well as in theory, achieved more nearly than anybody else an ideal corrective for 1916 deliquescence;

[1] Introduction to *November*, translated by Frank Jellineck (Bodley Head, 1934).

none the less for being so much of a hedonist, for the hedonism was itself a product of the search for truth. Now this striking interpretation of Gourmont, though it may not be based on a coherent philosophy, is not only persuasively apposite but casts a rare light on John Cowper himself and on his capacity to approach an alien genius without prejudices. Nor does his preoccupation with the artist's philosophy distract in the least his alert perception of the art: nothing could be more apt or vivid than for example his appreciation of Gourmont's poem to the rose 'with its melancholy and sinister refrain which troubles the memory like a swift wicked look from a beautiful countenance that ought to be pure and cold in death'.

It is of course an obstacle to accepting a critic that he is multiform, that the values and convictions affirmed through his experience of one writer are apparently forgotten in his appraisal of another; that there is, so to speak, no religious residue. The great critic has a moral core by which all his responses to art (and life) are to a great extent conditioned. It is sometimes better for a critic to be too rigid at heart than too accommodating, too adaptable. A certain dogmatism, a set mind in issues outside the aesthetic, can be a valuable basis for one's Poetic. John Cowper, with all his brilliant insight and all his impressive power of entering into alien sensibilities, suggests (except perhaps with Homer and Rabelais) a sublime advocate making a case. So occasionally, as when in expounding Milton he roundly says *Paradise Lost* is worth many of Shakespeare's tragedies, he not only fails to be credible but is all the more incredible because his affirmation of the values of *Lear* is eloquent of the heart and his heart is palpably not in any Miltonic view of life. Elsewhere,[1] lauding Shakespearians with extreme moral fervour, and plainly identifying himself with them, he makes it clear that Milton could only be a supreme poet to one whose *Weltanschauung* is outside even John Cowper's wide-ranging sympathies altogether. More convincing than 'Milton' are his writings on his apparent antithesis, the urban Henry James, with whom he did in spite of all seem to have something piquantly in common in a passion for intimate psychological exploration. Indeed but for piling Pelion upon Ossa in literary comment one could well write a volume on John Cowper on Henry James. This intellectual

[1] *The Pleasures of Literature*, pp. 299 ff.

dalliance had a disconcerting upshot in later years. In John Cowper's extreme old-age his sister-in-law Alyse Gregory had been discoursing to him with her usual eloquent enthusiasm on the old master when the veteran unexpectedly rose on his couch, struggled to his feet and, shaking his fist passionately in the air, exclaimed 'I *hate* Henry James'.

The revolution in literary criticism in the 1920's virtually passed John Cowper by. There is some development in responsibility and control, though little in thought, between the critical essays of 1915-16 and those in *The Pleasures of Literature* collected in 1938, the *Obstinate Cymric* volume of 1947, the books on Dostoievsky and Rabelais and the very finished Prefaces to Sterne of 1948-49. He did, certainly, arrive at an understanding of wider social potentialities for the novel through immersion in James and Proust and it is rare in the later criticism to meet with such banalities as his early sweeping aside of Dryden's poetry, or such shocks as the comments on comedy[1] where he had characterised Congreve's wit as 'faded and old-fashioned' and in the next sentence Wilde's style as 'hammered and beaten out of eternal bronze'—judgements which would be as true, or rather untrue, if transposed.

The John Cowper who surrendered himself, during the second war, to the urgent craving to sort out his relations to his great masters Rabelais and Dostoievsky had long proved himself a stimulating critic of the highest abilities indeed, but not of the highest order. There is no strain of the blood royal, no reminder of Longinus or Dryden or Lessing or of the Arnold he so loved and showed himself able at need to pronounce on so judicially.[2] In view of his extraordinary equipment, sensibility, perception, and power of communication, one must seek a reason. In addition to his incapacity for *true* detachment and for the balance of the thinker by vocation, he was, by a sort of paradox, too aesthetic. He could easily become an Aeolian harp. What lay—however deeply hidden—under his wide, teeming life of culture was not a true philosophy, a philosophy regulating and fortifying the mind; but something quite different, a longing, an unsatiable desire underlying all the dissembled *malaise* to revert to satisfactions far more elemental, more simple and instinctive, than those of the

[1] *Visions and Revisions.* 'Oscar Wilde.'
[2] *The Pleasures of Literature* 'Matthew Arnold'.

'thinker'. His enthusiasm for most literature was fine and genuine, but in the last analysis rootless. His mind was ever active among ideas; but his soul could find a home only in the soil.

John Cowper brought to his study of his 'greatest of all novelists', Dostoievsky, unwonted care and patience which does not imply—nor does he claim it—that he comprehended all of his subject. He was of course to some extent self-conscious, championing as he was a fellow conservative and fellow masochist whose introversive method was to dominate very obviously his own creative technique. He was in some degree writing an *Apologia* for the modern novel itself, the form of art which he had himself striven to deepen, or to revive at a deeper level. 'A great modern novel' he boldly pronounced, 'consists of and ought to include just everything.' Dostoievsky is seen as the true heritor of Homer's fullness of life, but a fullness realised in psychological terms rather than in physical, with values Christian (or one might more justly say Pauline). The novel with Dostoievsky became the supreme art: the novel after him had a new dimension previously unguessed at. Further, Dostoievsky is seen as the only creative moralist adequate to the modern world with its problems at all. His work is 'the fifth Gospel'. This is a highly persuasive and inspiring point of view, though we should bear in mind that John Cowper is a man for whom moral liberation is at least as clamant as truth itself and a more urgent need than spiritual exploration.

Though ineradically coloured by sentimentalism and written in what Hugh Fausset delightfully calls 'his old rascally style', *Dostoievsky* must be ranked as John Cowper's most substantial contribution to criticism. It is, admittedly, a good book that opens badly, for he has difficulty in shaking off political velleities conditioned by the experience of the Second War and far less valuable than the alert sentiments that make vivid his concurrent letters to Louis Wilkinson. His incongruous cult of the common man and his transient unconvincing 'Communism' are in relaxed moments half-communicated to Dostoievsky; but these are minor lapses. Indeed John Cowper's psychological thrust is seen at its most uncompromising in this book in his realistic dissection of 'romantic' love (a non-Russian ideal) and in his argument that the 'nerves' have their reasons that the heart does not recognise. 'Dostoievsky's novels are the subtlest in the world,' he boldly declares, 'not merely because he has soaked religion with sex and drenched sex with religion, but because he has explored sex to the wild beat of the tom-tom of nerves and *not* to the gentler strings of the heart's harp.' The great Slav, the alien with his unfamiliar Christianity, 'dipped his pen in his own nerves' and undermined the assumptions of the old conventionalised novel and relegated them for ever.

John Cowper's 'Dionysian and Euripidean' interpretation of Dostoievsky is of course yet another interpretation of himself: as always he finds what he seeks. Still he convinces us that he is seeing his subject pretty clearly, for Dostoievsky is *his own man*: there is no need for idealisation. When he acclaims 'this greatest of all psychologists and the closest interpreter of the 'elemental' we recognise—not forgetting that he has recently said the same thing of St. Paul—that it is almost an acknowledgement of discipleship. Nevertheless, neither as psychologists nor as initiates of nature have Fyodor Mihailovitch and John Cowper the same endowment or the same objective: the critic is in fact now bringing his sympathetic discrimination to bear with particular enthusiasm upon a tantalising remoteness-in-nearness. The study of the Russian deepens the younger novelist's awareness: it does not lend it direction. It is the very strength of Dostoievsky's people that they have objective reality free from self-projection or other-worldliness, as John Cowper does acknowledge, though he may arguably be right in saying that 'we can only be a *medium* for the kind of good and the kind of evil we have the potentiality for in ourselves'. (Is this why Hardy and John Cowper, though they are well aware of the evil in life, have no villains or only very tentative ones?) Both Dostoievsky's whole instinct rejected the capriciously subjective or the idiosyncratic, and one can only shudder to think of his probable response to *Jobber Skald*.

What Dostoievsky showed John Cowper was the way of psychological deepening, by which the pupil came to achieve his magical effects of nature initiation counterpoised by what we have called super-psychology. But of course John Cowper's discernment of the essential Dostoievsky involves something far more complex than recognising a great Christian psychologist.

It is as an outsider that John Cowper evaluates Dostoievsky's Christian ethic: his own novels are not penetrated by it. His humility has no spiritual quality. All through his study he is deeply aware of Middleton Murry's early book on the Russian; and to compare the two approaches sheds a considerable light on John Cowper. Both books are remarkable; both partial. These highly gifted men achieve one and only one thing in common: they create a significant figure though all the while re-creating Dostoievsky to their own preconceptions, and this without ceasing to be literary critics in consequence. (Murry could never abdicate as master critic, indeed, however hard he might try.) But the difference between the two books is immeasurable. Murry had one quality John Cowper could never encompass: he was a transcendentalist. John Cowper had, and groped to find in Dostoievsky, what Murry never grounded himself in: the knowledge that man cannot be fully himself apart from the earth and the rhythm of the elements. For man cannot live by man alone. John Cowper was compelled, in consistency, to claim that Dostoievsky is the most elemental of all writers, but the claim reveals his own urgencies rather than the Russian's. For Dostoievsky was not really an elementalist in terms, so to speak, of Powysian elementalism: to him human relations were the absolute rather than was identification with 'nature'. His sense of social problems and human interdependence was immeasurably more compulsive than John Cowper's. The Murry Dostoievsky and the Powys Dostoievsky do however between them approximate to the complete man. To Murry the creative prophet stands out: in him and in Tolstoy 'mankind stood on the brink of a great revelation'. (John Cowper himself has surprisingly little use for Tolstoy.) To John Cowper Dostoievsky is above everything else the supreme creative psychologist, both by virtue of his power and by virtue of his unique saturation with the Pauline *ethos*, the Christ *within* us. This compassion, never evinced before—or indeed since—reveals men and women at an unprecedented depth.

Dostoievsky is, to put it very broadly, a claim for the paramountcy of the conscience in sophisticated art. But the book is not just exhaustingly devoted to expounding a central conception of a super-novelist. Besides many suggestive and brilliant phrases ('Nature's over-novel') there are floods of illumination which seem to penetrate the very depths. 'His relations with life are like those of a formidable man with a dangerous woman'—insights such as this atone generously for occasional ramblings and repetitions; and it often happens that after rather exacting spells of groping we are suddenly galvanised by the touch of a stylist.

> While making life a much more complicated gladiatorial show, Christianity has also made it a much more horrible Dance of Damnation.

But by far the most important of John Cowper's claims for Dostoievsky—indeed a fundamental one—is that alone among *novelists* he transcends the 'stupid being'[1] in creator and characters: the encasing shell, the conventional assumption of one's own values. Even the greatest fiction writers, albeit far from superficial themselves, have left unchallenged some life-illusion or protective attitude in their protagonists. The heroes of Balzac or Thackeray or Tolstoy or even later of Proust are not psychologically all-questioning. They are not sensitive to *all* human experience. Somewhere there is an unconscious complacency about accepting what life gives them: they limit life to their own terms.

> In regard to the characters invented by naturalistic novelists, such as Thackeray and Trollope and Turgeniev, their 'secret', or the essential quality of their existence consists in the presence within than of a vigorious 'life-illusion' confronted by a considerable quality of *stupid being*. Now this latter substance, in the make-up of their characters, is, in the case of the naturalistic writers to whom I have just referred, a conventional, racial, social and class-conscious sort of 'stupid being'. The deepest life-illusion in the breast of a gallant youth like Pendennis or of a grave and honourable gentleman like Henry Esmond, assumes and takes for granted and is quite complacent about the presence within him of this social 'stupid being', in the midst of which his personal soul preens its proud feathers as if in the safe folds of a warm home-knitted vest.

Whereas Dostoievsky and his characters have, except in a racial sense, no *protective* individuality, no sheltering or transmuting cover at all. In this honourable succession John Cowper seeks always to give his own characters—at least the elaborated ones—this naked awareness; stripping them,

---

[1] The phrase is Gertrude Stein's.

especially, of the protection of a solid material background.

But it is in the *Memoirs from the Underground,* even more completely than in the four great novels, that John Cowper finds the quintessence of Dostoievsky's contribution and inevitably in his study of this book he reveals the most of himself.

> *Memoirs from the Underground* is a revelation of the power of the lonely, self-existent, unpropitiated human mind. The hero of the story, who speaks all the way through the book in his own person, defies everything and in this very defiance he possesses and enjoys everything. He enjoys humiliating himself. He enjoys lacerating himself. Above all he enjoys breaking-up by some wild, unexpected, crazy gesture the superficial coating of the propriety of life. Stavrogin in *The Possessed* has the same diabolical life-zest and the same love of spitting in the face of common decency by doing something totally ridiculous like *biting the ear* of the leading official of the town.
>
> Very rarely has a novelist been able through the hounding of his characters to reveal to the world a completely new and very revolutionary psychology. But this is what Dostoievsky does in *Memoirs from the Underground.* He reveals the fact that what the soul of a man wants above everything is absolute freedom of the will. He wants to choose, to decide, to govern, to dominate, to determine. And he wants to do this purely for the sake of doing it—that is to say for the sake of showing to himself that he can do it! He wants to abolish all motivation for his actions. Arbitrary irresponsible will-power exerted by himself in a complete void is what every man wants. We all want to do certain things just for the sake of the delicious sensation of wilful arbitrary power that the doing of them brings with it.

A brilliantly penetrating examination of the great novels—of *The Possessed* especially—leads to the conclusion that, broadly speaking, Dostoievsky is the supreme modern because he comes nearest at once to the heart of Christ and the heart of nature. The estimate gains in detachment, probably, from the fact that neither in Christianity nor in 'nature' do author and critic gravitate towards the same centre and also John Cowper's anarchism—very lively in the 1940's!—was in total conflict with Dostoievsky's political complaisance. It may have conduced also to a juster perspective that unlike John Cowper or his other literary demi-gods such as Homer Dostoievsky's genius could flourish in the busy haunts of men and did not depend on Nature in the popular sense for the breath of life. *Dostoievsky*, anyhow, is John Cowper's first major critical effort. With Dostoievsky, alone of all the modern except perhaps Walt Whitman, we have the feeling that John Cowper is accepting him whole-heartedly and not with courteous reserve. The only disappointment is that though he appreciated liberally Proust, the two great Russians' one superior in scope if not in depth, he derived no great impetus from the Frenchman either in creation or in thought. But as we know, for all his *flair* for French writing, he was fundamentally anti-Gallic: it was his father and not his grandmother who loomed dominant in his make-up.

The question of Gallic or anti-Gallic sentiment did not seem to arise when John Cowper at last confronted his idol Rabelais, perhaps the one great French writer who has transcended nationality altogether. *Rabelais,* the complement of and complete contrast to *Dostoievsky* and John Cowper's only other full-scale critical study, was commissioned by the Bodley Head at the end of 1942. It was to be called *Introducing Rabelais* and to contain—as indeed it does—substantial specimen passages of translation. Most of the writing must have been done while *Dostoievsky* and *Porius* were still on the stocks. The biographical and critical matter grew—as might be expected of John Cowper—far beyond the original intention and between delays in writing and the difficulties of post-war publishing the volume did not finally appear until 1948. By that time it had swollen monstrously—from the projected 30,000 words in fact to over 200,000!

Of all writers except Homer Rabelais appealed the most to John Cowper's primitive and earth-loving instincts—and of all his demi-gods left the least trace in his own imaginative writing. The great Frenchman's freedom from inhibition, his almost universal acceptance of things, made a great appeal to what was hesitant and inhibited in John Cowper himself. However they were really contrasts yet with a sort of blood-kinship. It was sympathy with all life as life that Rabelais quickened and strengthened in John Cowper, and not occult intimate nature poetry or psychological delvings, for neither of these characterised the great sensationist. For Rabelais *was* of course superlatively a sensationist, in fact the supreme artist of sensationism: though his sensationism was something immensely deeper and more instinctive and more integral than the rather restricted attitude expounded in John Cowper's essay books.

Rabelais is a good book. The author himself had no doubt of this from the beginning. He wrote to Louis Wilkinson[1] 'You wait—you'll like this work of brother John's best of all he's done'. If the study lacks the deeper insights of *Dostoievsky* it contains his most vigorous criticism, that in which he is most positively inspired by a desire to isolate and exalt his subject's individuality. One has no suspicion here of the over-appreciative lecturer, the literary taster who at the end of an hour might vanish like Alice's Cheshire cat leaving only a smile behind. He wears his enthusiasm more convincingly than of yore. In *Rabelais* he glories in acclaiming an all-embracing life-lover: a need even more clamant in him than that of the 'Christ within us' he had identified with Dostoievsky. So, beginning by rescuing Rabelais from both Urquhart and the Rabelaisians, he goes on to interpret the great medieval-modern as the master of all who accept life generously. He finds in the world of the greatest of humourists a hugely-imagined world wherein is made possible the transference of reverence from religion to 'the mystery of life'.

Long since John Cowper's standard-bearer against dogma, science and urban values, Rabelais is now seen as one who fortifies a humanised Christianity with Pauline, Pelagian and counter-medievalist convictions. This Christianity is not one which any traditionalist of faith would have acknowledged as such: Rabelais is in fact the Christian pagan and the pagan Christian. Ultimately we arrive at Rabelais' true 'Christ' who is the creative mystery. John Cowper does not of course fail to recognise that all this is inextricably bound-up with the intense vitality of a great imaginative artist.

> I think that like Walt Whitman he thought with his intellect, with his senses, with his soul, with his spirit, with his skin, blood and bone, and with all his most imponderable instincts, inhibitions, urges, feelings, sensations, intimations at the same time!

There is a criterion here which could be illuminatingly

[1] *Letters.* p. 121 (18 January 1943).

M

applied to all the great—and nearly great—writers of the world. There is a vital difference between those who think in this all-feeling way and those who think arbitrarily.

John Cowper's image of Rabelais—which was formative to a great extent of the translations as well as of the criticism and biography—is that of one who rejects no experience, who is wholeness, who takes life with a smile as young children and simpletons take it, and who is supreme humour and tolerance devoid of all satire. The old Powys resistance to satire and to destructiveness—evinced long before in *Rodmoor*—is constantly evident in *Rabelais*. It is the image of a scholar, as self-indulgently erudite about the remote past as Robert Burton, of one who is equally open to the Renaissance and the Reformation, in which the 'human religion' he never quite embraced or repudiated enters upon 'a new Zodiacal epoch'. The image of a monk without sense of order or austerity (*fay ce que vouldras*) and of a blaspheming pantomime innocent of negativeness and contempt altogether. The image of one whose unabashedly earthy humour is yet one of the supreme assertions of Charity or *Agape*.

This vivid conception of Rabelais does serve to illuminate him far more than most critics have done. Of course it tells us even more about John Cowper (if we do not know it already). And it could be confidently inferred from the inspired quality of the study that Rabelais is a central and vital part of John Cowper's constitution. Of all writers *with true moral vision* Homer, Rabelais, Whitman and Hardy are most deeply rooted in the earth; and they are those to whom John Cowper reveals the strongest affinity. Common to all these masters is the instinctive feeling that human life fails of real richness and ultimate significance when it seeks to be independent of, to soar apart from, the simple, the physical, the primitive, the elemental. This underlies Rabelais' refusal to seek satisfaction except through the physical life, his preference of earth-bound adventure to more rarefied topics to engage his teeming comic imagination.

So long and deeply has John Cowper been reconciled to Rabelais' dissembled poetry that the supreme humorist (as he sees him) is now in his eyes the Christianised incarnation of the Homeric *Aganophrosune*. It is because John Cowper's sympathies so chime in harmony with this great forerunner that *Rabelais* is a valuable clue to his nature. With that *positiveness* especially, which goes to make John Cowper so much larger than his gifted contemporaries. 'Where Rabelais and Walt Whitman,' he reveals himself in declaring, 'differ from Materialists, Atheists and Rationalists is that they are *always positive.*' In Rabelais the truly comic, elemental and positive and centred in our animal nature, not only dispenses with but outsoars the satirical. So far would John Cowper carry us along these lines that we see Pantagruelism, in the new Zodiacal epoch, as the authentic vehicle of *Agape*. It is not a simple claim; but it is the claim by which John Cowper ultimately triumphs or fails.

It would be a pity to give the impression that *Rabelais* is purely a moral treatise. On the contrary it is entertaining and a positive stimulus to enjoyment; unlike so many ingenious interpretations (or apologies) that have been devoted to the great son of Touraine. It is hardly necessary to tell those who know John Cowper that the study illuminates its author as much as its subject. It would be too much to pretend that the critic furnishes, even in this exhaustive and elaborated essay, complete chapter and verse for the comprehensive Rabelaisian ethic he expounds. Or that it is not diluted or supplemented with some contribution of his own. John Cowper's own complete incapacity for contempt leads him to deny the least trace of such a sentiment in anybody he respects; and he does blind himself to the definite satirical element—since prevailing burlesque must imply some adverse judgement—in the great book. The distinction is that Rabelais creates life far more memorably than he belittles living. His challenge, his creativeness in positive art and therefore positive morality, is indeed gigantic. The horseplay, the childish exuberance, what John Cowper calls the 'reckless bubblings over' are all part and parcel of a humanism that is possibly unsurpassed. He does indeed put a case, often brilliantly and always sincerely, for Rabelais as one of the great religious forces, achieving the divine through the luxuriantly, impenitently gross.

John Cowper took the opportunity of his translation to repudiate Urquhart and to propound a theory of his own of translation—though a theory dubious in itself and curiously little formative of his own successful enterprise of bringing the great *Tourangeau* nearer to our own shores. His protest against the Scot's being accepted as the equivalent of his original, though overdue, is not so thoroughgoing as one might have expected. The sesquipedalian and bawdry-relishing Cavalier naturalised Rabelais in Britain and made him popular, yet in the end created a false image of him. An image tinged with his own less attractive disposition. In addition to being nearly a genius himself he had a pretty clear field, for Rabelais' French is not the French most Englishmen can read as they run. John Cowper's censure of him is almost entirely for over-elaboration and 'comic hyperbole'; in particular for imperilling *humour of character* by *humour of comical extravagance*. While, beyond all stylistic incompatibilities, the deeper trouble is surely that Sir Thomas cannot measure up to Rabelais' stature but perches on his shoulder, guffawing and cocking snooks.

John Cowper envisages only two methods of translation. The first is, broadly, creative paraphrase, to produce a real contribution to the literature of one's own country; and here the better the original has been 'metampsychosised' into 'the mental atmosphere of the translator's tongue' the greater the achievement. This distinguished category of paraphrases embraces the Authorised Version, Cotton's Montaigne, Fitzgerald's *Rubaiyat*, Rossetti's Italian poets—and, as is demonstrated, Urquhart's Rabelais. But the really valuable version, to John Cowper, is that which supplies the experience a reader needs outside his own native culture: 'the delicious shock of the foreign ways, the foreign characters, the foreign adventures, and the sense of feeling familiar sensation in a foreign land'. It is the more difficult task and the more laborious and self-effacing. The very *look of the words* is vital if we are to land, so to speak, at a foreign port. Constance Garnett with her Russians achieves, for John Cowper, this ideal as well as anybody.

With Rabelais John Cowper did, on the whole, what he set out to do. We have no sense of distortion and we sniff faintly the Gallic tang. It is almost the only prolonged translation of Rabelais one can go on reading without discomfort or any uneasy feeling of disloyalty to the original in spirit or letter. There is relish without bravura.

How near a translation comes to Rabelais, how much nearer than others, seems to be largely a question of *tempo*. The

veiled deliberateness of Rabelais' sentence-structure is of the
very essence of his style: he had to move nimbly enough to
hold the reader's attention without gliding into a mere narrative pace, for like most of his contemporaries he has little skill
in narrative technique and relies on the reader's pausing to
look for meanings. A carefully-modulated, middle *tempo* is
essential. Now in Urquhart for instance we habitually find not
only extravagance of words but deficiency of movement: the
structure of the sentence is comparatively flaccid.

> When Pantagruel had withdrawn himself, he, by a little
> sloping window in one of the galleries, perceived Panurge
> in a lobby not far from thence, walking alone, with the
> gesture, carriage and garb of a fond dotard, raving, wagging
> and shaking his hands, dandling, lolling, and nodding with
> his head, like a cow bellowing for her calf, and, having
> called him nearer, spoke to him thus:
> 'You are at present, I think, not unlike to a mouse,
> entangled in a snare, who the more that she goeth about
> to rid and unwind herself out of the gin wherein she
> is caught by endeavouring to claw and deliver her feet
> from the pitch whereto they stick, the fonder is she be-
> wrayed with it, and the more strongly pestered within. Even
> so is it with you. For the more that you labour, strive,
> and inforce yourself to disencumber and extricate your
> thoughts out of the implicating involutions and fetterings
> of the grievous and lamentable gins and springs of anguish
> and perplexity, the greater difficulty there is in the
> relieving of you; and you remain faster bound than ever.
> Nor do I know for the removal of this inconveniency any
> remedy but one. Take heed, I have often heard it said
> in a vulgar proverb: The wise may be instructed by a fool.'

This is a leisured but not whimsical example of Sir Thomas's
style, a style formed in a Jacobean and Caroline environment
and showing the influence of Robert Burton and even re-
motely of Lyly. John Cowper was in revolt against both the
rambling and the whimsy: he knew it was a formidable distortion of Rabelais he had to supplant. Here is the original of
the passage just quoted:

> 'Pantagruel, soy retirant, apperceut par la guallerie
> Panurge en maintien d'un resveur ravassant et dodenilant
> de la teste, et lui dist: 'Vous me semblez à une souriz
> empegée: tant plus elle s' efforce soy depestrer de la poix,
> plus elle s'embrene. Vous, semblablement, efforçant issir
> hors les lacs de perplexité, plus que devant y demourez

empestré, et n'y scay remede fors un. Entendez! J'ai souvent ouy en proverbe voulgaire qu'un fol enseigne bien un saige.'[1]

Now here is Mr. J. M. Cohen's Everyman rendering, where, whatever the merits of scholarly fidelity, the pace is too fast and there is no suggestion of John Cowper's desiderated alien tang.

> Pantagruel persuades Panurge to take
> counsel of a Fool.
>
> As Pantagruel was retiring, he saw Panurge from the gallery in a state of deep reverie, mumbling and nodding his head.
>
> 'You look like a mouse caught in a trap,' he said, 'the harder it tries to free itself from the pitch the faster it gets stuck. It is the same with you. All your efforts to escape from the noise of your perplexity only leaves you more firmly caught than before. I know of only one remedy. Listen. You've often heard the vulgar proverb quoted, that a fool may well give lessons to a wise man.'

Less bold and obviously out of period is the late Victorian version of W. F. Smith of Cambridge, which John Cowper rejects with typical courteous appreciation, as too Addisonian. But it also lacks flavour and the enticing *timing* of Rabelais.

> *How Pantagruel persuadeth Panurge to take*
> *Counsel of some Fool.*
>
> As Pantagruel was retiring, he perceived from the gallery Panurge with the appearance of one in a Dream, mumbling and nodding his Head; so he said to him:
>
> 'You seem to me like a Mouse taken in Pitch, the more she goeth about to clear herself of the Pitch, the more she is bewrayed thereby. In like manner, by your Efforts to get out of the Nooses of Perplexity, You remain there faster bound than you were before; and for this I know of no Remedy save one. Now listen. I have often heard it said in a vulgar Proverb, that *a Fool may well teach a Wise man.*

John Cowper is alert to avoid the enticing pitfalls of such modernisers as Putnam, whose version he hails with excitement while seeing the danger of treating Rabelais as 'international' and 'adaptable'. He recognises too that the idioms of Jacobean courtliness do not mirror the individuality of Rabelais. He avoids both the archaic and the modern, effect-

[1] *Tiers Livre.* Ch. 37.

ing a working compromise. He deliberately arrests the pace of the Smiths and the Cohens, so conducive to superficial reading, while eschewing the artificial self-expansion of an Urquhart.

How Pantagruel advised Panurge
to Consult a Fool.

As he traversed the galleries towards his private quarters he suddenly caught sight of Panurge behaving like a person in some kind of crazy fit, jubbering all sorts of gibberish and wagging his head from side to side.

'What's this,' he cried, contemplating him with concern. 'You're like a mouse caught in pitch. The more she tries to extricate herself the more she gets entoiled. And you too, struggling so desperately to get out of your slough of despond, are only sinking into it the deeper. Now I assure you there's no remedy for your evil case except one. Mark me well, my friend. There's an old proverb, known to us all, which says: 'A fool can teach the wisest.'

As would be expected in one of his erratic temperament, John Cowper has a few bad lapses in his translation. He can make Pantagruel refer to 'a man who has become a medium for the spirit of psychic divination'. He can anachronise Panurge's idiom into 'By God, lad, you've said it! Everything comes to the man who can wait. So far this business of seeing Popes has done us no good. But now by all the Devils we're really going to get something out of it!' But far more often his sympathy and toleration and genius for character and informality bring him nearer than anybody else to that very elusive phenomenon, a translator of Rabelais:

Panurge estoit de stature moyenne, ny trop grand, ny trop petit, et avait le nez un peu aquilin, faict à manche de rasouer; et pour lors estoit de l'eage de trente et cinqs ans ou environ, fin à dorer comme une dague de plomb, bien galant homme de sa personne, sinon quil estoit quelque peu paillart, et subjeit de nature a une malodie qu'on appelait en ce temps la. 'Faulte d'argent c'est douleur non pareille.' Toutesfoys il avait soixante et troys manieres d'en traver toujours a son besoing, dont la plus honorable et la plus commune estoit par facon larrecin furtivement faict; malfaisant, pipeur, beuvoir, baleur de pavez, ribleur, s'il en estoit en Paris, au demourant, le meilleur filz du monde. . . .

Here is John Cowper's version, and it is particularly interesting to notice how he eschews not only the obvious alien digressiveness of Urquhart but the disenchanting terseness and cursoriness of a Smith or a Cohen:

> Panurge was of middle stature, neither too tall nor too short; he had a somewhat aquiline nose, made like the handle of a razor; and he was at that time about thirty-five years old, good for gilding like a leaden dagger, a fine fellow in his person, only a bit addicted to lechery; and subject to a malady they used to call in those days 'Lack of money, the painfullest disease in the world!' All the same he had sixty-three ways of getting hold of what he lacked, the most honourable of which, and the commonest too, was by petty larceny perpetrated furtively and featly. As shameless a scamp he was, card-sharper and tippler, swash-buckler and thief, as you could meet in the streets of Paris; and for the rest as tidy a lad as the world could want.

We have the feel of Rabelais: we are back in his world. When we read him in John Cowper he is a living fellow-being to us, as Shakespeare when we read *him*. One is not, as with other translators, conscious of an attempt to adapt him or suspicious that he is being 'sold' in a possibly unreal guise that is a projection of the translator. Nor does one feel with John Cowper that he is impelled by duty. And the prose of his rendering is creatively enterprising in itself; it is disciplined by loyalty to his author; and the 'old rascally style' is for the first time (except in letters) overcome, Rabelais' mood is faithfully and subtly recaptured. In truth John Cowper seems perfectly happy: nothing so stimulates the best in him as a liberal dose of the good herb Pantagruelion.

But *Rabelais* is of course virtually two books, though the translation and the criticism are in some degree interdependent. As a whole *Rabelais* is the least wantonly written of John Cowper's works. But the critical study does invite a few minor reservations. Towards the end concentration relaxes. The claims for Rabelais as a sort of universal moralist become rather overwhelming and his champion begins to *load* him with transcendent qualities, sometimes illustrated by unconvincing passages. Amid much admirable comment, sentimentality creeps in, often keyed incongruously to John Cowper's left-wing exuberance from the war years. The common man of

his fantasy,[1] the tramp, even the anti-social degenerate, became a sort of Rabelaisian ideal. John Cowper's eternal reaction against the powerful was again in evidence—it was
possibly animated by a twinge of unconscious guilt about his
father's serene privileges. And Rabelais—Rabelais was his
heaven-sent ally against 'the Power-Prelates of the Cosmos'.
John Cowper never quite ceased to think rhetorically.

John Cowper hated the eighteenth century, and its people
'all wigs and wiggles'. It held too little of the sustaining and
healing elemental. He had no real relish of Pope or Swift or
Johnson and little even of Fielding. But the two Prefaces for
reprints of Sterne which he wrote in 1948 for his new publishers Macdonalds—who generously paid him a badly needed
hundred pounds for each of them—are so excellent a pendant
to his major critical works that they must be specially mentioned. It is the more to be regretted that they were his last
essays in literary criticism: they are polished and shapely and
almost objective. His zest for Yorick is at first blush surprising.
It is an achievement to have done justice to so anti-Powysian a
writer. John Cowper did, perhaps inevitably, over-persuade
himself that Sterne was a miniature Rabelais. In truth it is
only in *Tristram Shandy* and rarely there that any filiation at
all can be detected. But the essays, especially the more detached of the two, that on *The Sentimental Journey*, evince as
memorably as anything the versatility of John Cowper's mind,
as flexible as ever despite three-quarters of a century of
overuse. As examples *in parvo* of his very real significance as a
critic they could not be bettered. At last the responsible writer
had forgotten the platform.

[1] Louis Wilkinson once told him his cringing before the common man
was a symptom of fear. He cheerfully conceded this.

CHAPTER XIII

Wales, Homer and Sunset Fantasies

'We Aboriginal Welsh People.'—*Obstinate Cymric.*

Words, the magic of words, is a deep and occult part of the
mystery of life. Gibberish—the inventing of nonsense—
is an irresponsible tendency of mine, and to me it is
never comic or facetious or amusing.—*Autobiography.*

THE last twenty-eight years of his life John Cowper, a good
deal of a defiant invalid, resorting nervously to his eternal
cigarette and often subsisting on such detestable fare as milk
and raw duck-eggs, lived in almost uninterrupted retirement
in Wales. He strove with what stubbornness there was in his
fluid make-up to persuade himself he was Welsh. Since the
second year of the century he had fallen deeper and deeper
under the spell of a race-illusion more harmless than Hitler's
but quite as irrational. Characteristically he delighted in
identifying himself with a conquered race. In reality, as we
have noted, his ancestry for many generations had been predominantly English; and the traces of the Celt in his character
and disposition are extremely slight. His long seclusion among
the mountains and his intensive study of Cymric cultures
resulted in little or no change in his real outlook: in fact with
all his ever-widening curiosity and interests there is small
evidence that his *ideas* matured after early manhood. At the
level where we may call him a seer he advanced in self-knowledge only: he attained no new understanding or insights in
philosophy or living, no real adjustments. In his deeper

creative being he became more and more exclusively avid of the past. Modern science—apart from modern psychology—he ignored; anything mechanical he detested. He loved life with uncommon intensity, but it was always life humanised by tradition verging on archaism. He took his contemporaries to his heart almost too readily, yet ignored the revolution of which they were a part. His anarchistic and 'communist' politics were innocent of any active purpose. Alert and sympathetic and unaging, he remained unshakably rooted in the primitive: if the 'Chinese culture' of Wales held now more of wisdom for him than did his boyhood culture it was chiefly because it was associated even more with nature and even less with urban or communal sophistications. While alert to advances in social knowledge he distrusted them: he not only preferred the magical but declared that 'we have too much knowledge' and turned his back on an age growing more self-conscious and on any background impervious to magical suggestion. As an enthusiastic supporter, Mr. James Hanley, put it:

> The bloodiest battle being fought today is that in which the imagination of man is being slowly murdered by knowledge. Mr. Powys from his own recluded corner in the mountains knows this, and from time to time strikes great blows in defence of it:[1] 'The greatest obstacle to any real and mellow wisdom' John Cowper wrote in *Obstinate Cymric* 'is the superstition of modernity.'

It is necessary to point out his impenetrability by the wind of change; but this criticism is not of course any disparagement of his imaginative power. If we get down to bedrock, he is probably more right than most of his contemporaries: he is certainly deeper, if only because instinct is deeper than acquired knowledge. His 'mania' (in his own words) 'for the *organic* as contrasted with the aesthetic' is no mania but an assertion that our being is larger than our self-awareness. In his old age he is still referring, with his familiar forced humility, to 'an old Pantaloon of the Elements like me'; but he is declaring himself the novelist to whom perceptions of the primitive, merging into a divination—if you will—of the occult, come far before artistic considerations. He is perhaps

[1] *Dock Leaves*. Spring, 1956.

asking to be read for something to which topicality, experimental awareness, even social realism, are completely irrelevant. He is drifting out of the world of Proust and Joyce and Virginia Woolf altogether.

The Berwyn mountains and the untenanted primordial spaces were a background and a sedative—even an inspiration —for him. He trod the hills in the freshness of morning and sniffed the bracing air and savoured the primal timelessness with a relish even he had rarely experienced in a long three-score of years and over. His first Welsh home, at Corwen in Merionethshire, was found for him by James Hanley in 1935 and he stayed there twenty years. He described himself in *Obstinate Cymric* as 'established in one of the model workmen's cottages only just built by a retired British Admiral on the southern slopes of the Berwyn range, overlooking the spacious valley of the Dee'. He added rather gleefully 'I live within Owen Glendower's patrimony'. He derived enormous satisfaction from going around in the parts where Glendower was still a live memory, as he did from living within the borders of Powys (at its entrance north) where he was actually crowned as Bard at the Powys Eisteddfod—a proof, incidentally, that his Welsh was not so weak as he was given to pretending. After the publication of *Owen Glendower* (not over-well received in wartime England) the Welsh were to take him to their hearts; and the writer who had revivified Wessex became, ironically enough, the local hero of another race. A radio programme on the Welsh region was on two occasions devoted to him, as well as a special number of the *Anglo-Welsh Review*[1] in 1956; and in 1962 the University of Wales, recognising his genius rather belatedly when he had reached eighty-nine, conferred on him a doctorate. In 1955 he migrated, for various domestic reasons, to Blaenau Festiniog, nearer to the sea. His equally modest retreat here was a quarryman's cottage in which he lived contentedly till the year of his death. In a local solicitor's office they still cherish a delighted recollection of him. He called in to enquire after a dwelling; and on being asked for specifications he declared with feeling: 'I make only one condition, I *must* have a flushing lavatory.' His letters over the whole Welsh period give a vivid picture of his blissful contentment within these unpretending fastnesses.

[1] Then *Dock Leaves*.

In the vast temple of nature he found daily consolation from those prayers which, on his own showing, were polytheistic rather than pantheistic in their direction. 'I *worship* Pallas Athene,' he told Mrs. Harry Coombes not long before his mind began to fail in 1961. But it was on the earth, not on any altar steps, that he loved to tap humbly his forehead.

Owing to his slowly increasing recognition it was John Cowper's fate—a not unprecedented one—to be warmed by a stronger blaze of publicity from his sunset than from his high noon. Poor work was sometimes acclaimed where real achievement had never been recognised. Among the more seriously-minded in Britain, anyhow, acceptance is very slow. His writings of the long Welsh years, excepting of course the historical novels and the private letters, are of relatively minor import: several books he indefatigably produced in old age add nothing to his stature. *Morwyn*, 'my anti-vivisection romance', which was turned down by Simon and Schuster in New York and received with 'contempt' by the English Press on publication over here in 1937, was not in the succession of the novels down to *Maiden Castle*. The trouble was partly that he allowed himself to be carried away by his obsession and partly that his oddities were here wanton, unmoral oddities in the vein deplored by Llewelyn in his letters of 1935. Now, in a late fling, the old sadic guilt had taken control. *Morwyn* features Torquemada, de Sade, Socrates and Rabelais in an allegorical novel of the otherworld that smacks strongly of the fifth form. (It is perhaps not necessary to say that the Marquis comes off far better than the Inquisitor, and Rabelais very well indeed!)

Mortal Strife, an essay-book and the first product of the Hitler cataclysm, embodies—though far less happily than the letters written *pari passu* to Louis Wilkinson—John Cowper's reaction to total conflict. His judgements of current events were remarkably sane and penetrating by any standards: it is the turgidity and irrelevances in the presentation of them which mar *Mortal Strife*. The diffuseness and the laborious failure to reproduce the plain man's thoughts take away a good deal from persuasiveness. John Cowper himself saw this as a 'very *fierce* book', but it is only fierce in a Powysian or Pickwickian sense. The author was as well aware as anybody of its distracting digressiveness and its descent into the old

familiar sensationism.[1] The *Times Literary Supplement* put
the demerit well:

> he spreads a darkness of his own, a darkness of inchoate
> thought and undisciplined words; too often the light of his
> less communicable visitations is promptly put out by a
> cloud of phrases—or, if that is too hard a criticism, of half-
> formed and esoteric ideas. It is a pity, for the emotion that
> informs the book is obviously true emotion.

Mortal Strife, which strove all through to indicate the catho-
licity and essential decency in the average English attitude to
the struggle, had a considerable wartime success. *The Art of
Growing Old*, which followed it two years later, was a rather
undistinguished sequel to *The Art of Happiness*—the more
uninspiring because so repetitive of its predecessor. It is
notable that now for the first time in ratiocinative writing
John Cowper accepts superstition as natural and inevitable. It
would be uncharitable rather than inaccurate to say that the
book is in substance an essay on how (or how not!) to leave
Religion out of Old Age. The assumptions are sometimes
superficial and the conclusions vague, as in 'when God is taken
from us there is only one sensible thing to do—to become god
ourselves'.

Obstinate Cymric, published from Carnarvon in 1947 and
embodying the class of essays (written over some twelve years)
roughly indicated by the title, merits far closer attention. Here
he is not haranguing his quaintly unconvincing image of the
man-in-the-street and certainly not outlining a popular code
for living. Almost the whole of the book is fascinating and
redolent of John Cowper in a mood nearly as frank as in the
intimate *Letters* of the same period. Eloquent from the first of
his enthusiasm for Wales and for a retreat into its semi-
legendary remotenesses—and we must recognise that John
Cowper always clutches at his joys rather than allows himself
to be possessed by them—it reminds us that the author in age
is further than ever from believing in any form of quietism or
from resigning himself to a negative happiness. His description of this often brilliantly penetrating book is startlingly
deprecatory, even for him. He called it:

> that rather Academic-Mandarin-cum-Powysian-tribalism-
> cum-Shilly-Shally-Chaoticism-cum-Scim-scam-sewn-together-

---

[1] Letters to Louis Wilkinson, 12 December 1940.

Auntie-Jane's-patchwork-quilt sort of Collection of the scum of porpoise spoutings. . . .[1]

Six of the nine essays in the book, which contains some of his liveliest hitting-out, are chiefly devoted to a sort of eloquent *apologia* for Wales and for himself as a restored Welsh spirit. They are in a sense an explanation of the *Porius* world (or underworld): fifth-century Wales and the Wales of today and yesterday are very much one to John Cowper. *Obstinate Cymric* indeed reveals one who has absorbed intensively the lore and the emotional aura of the land. Yet his ageless sympathies are always pointed and tempered by modern awareness. And his exposition of the Welshness of the Welsh is implicitly a criticism of our modern world where very different cultures prevail. Oddly it is where he is most subjective that his perceptions are most illuminating.

Welsh culture deserted—save for a few notable exceptions —by the Welsh aristocracy, restored itself, like the Titan Antaeus, by touching the earth. The most noticeable aspect of Welsh scenery are [*sic*] the numerous little white-washed 'bythynnod,' or small homesteads, grouped about the slopes of the mountains; and it is from these and from the gwerin or common folk who inhabit them that Welsh Culture springs. From these small farms come the scholars and the bards and the preachers; and indeed the present writer might boldly compose a *Triad* himself and say: The Three Peculiarities of a Welsh farm is [*sic*] the power to produce preachers who praise God, poets who criticize the preachers who praise God, and scholars who criticize the poets who criticize the preachers who praise God. The Welsh, in fact, for all their preference for preachers, who work themselves up into an ecstasy of musical chanting which is called the *hwyl* are not stern, moralistic Puritans like the Scotch. Their ecstatic musical religion is in many curious ways beyond the level of ordinary morality; and in this they resemble the ideal taught in the writings of Kwange-Tze.

Of the three other essays 'Pair Dadeni', (obviously inspired by Spengler) deals with the rather forlorn hope of a better future for the world. 'The Simple Vision' is an introduction to the Welsh poet Huw Menai containing John Cowper's own poetical *credo* as modified by modernity; while 'Finnegan's

---

[1] *Letters.* p. 276.

Wake' is a thrusting dissection of his chief concurrent rival, Joyce. *'Pair Dadeni'* (the cauldron of rebirth) argues that the aeon of *Pisces* is ended and the aeon of *Aquarius* is at hand. Eloquent in its religious enthusiasm and its historical persuasion, *'Pair Dadeni'* becomes wishfully speculative in its prophecies; and most readers will finish it stimulated rather than convinced.

In his generous tribute to Mr. Huw Menai (and to Wales) John Cowper lets us into his hitherto private mind touching the poetry that most reflects our contemporary world. Hailing in 1946—with too ready optimism—a return to directness and stronger feeling, qualities he finds pre-eminently in the prolific bard of the Welsh collieries, John Cowper 'who knows the wasteland [sic] by heart and who regards it as the greatest poem of my generation',[1] reveals indeed his own craving for the past but also his alertness to the values of his own day.

> Dull would he be of soul (he continues) who turned an adder's ear to a whole epoch. . . . But the relief of escaping from the complicated terraces of those misty gardens of Gothic impressionism, 'ridiculous and charming' as they are, is indescribable. These poets of the 'twenties' and 'thirties' deepen their mole runs of mystical lust by studying Donne, sharpen their talent for satire and wit by reading Dryden, and their response to the horrible and morbid by dipping into Coleridge. Their dominant note is a sardonic contempt for what they regard as the popular 'cliché' in emotional reaction. Their desire to be original is feverish and frantic; and taking the short cut to their fulfilment they become obscure. They set themselves to deal out pain instead of pleasure, and riddles in place of revelation. They make mock at idealism with the puritanical zest of religious zealots. They force themselves to face up to their awareness of their lack of real imagination by an awareness of this awareness as a higher poetic dimension. In their loathing for the obvious they become idiotic. In their contempt for the common-place they nourish abortions. In their hatred for daylight they veer between the kaleidoscopical and the pyrotechnical. Under the spell of their weakness and their melancholy the poor captive Muse is forced to dance on a wire in bangles and spangles, while she exchanges conundrums not only with the weary

---

[1] There is an astute reference to our chief poet, unusually candid for John Cowper even in private, in his Letter to Louis Wilkinson of August 2nd, 1945, where he admires T. S. Eliot's free verse despite his 'exclusive fussy anxious white soul.'

clown in the arena, but with excited clergymen in the audience. With their assumption of satirical pessimism these experts have to be exhaustingly 'quick in the uptake.'

John Cowper professed himself incapable of writing *vers libre* and never attempted any sort of 'modern verse'—though he certainly did not boast of this abstention. But the essay on Huw Menai is (when the writer does not turn aside to enlarge upon the superiority of the Welsh or of manual labour) a more deliberated piece of work than most of his late writings and worthy of attention as almost the last in which he succeeded in truly concentrating upon a definite aim. This was, to prove to the post-war world the potential validity of a poet —albeit not a major one—who is a man not primarily introversive or political or a scholar aesthete after John Cowper's own fashion. That a directness such as Huw Menai's could be vital at that day was an important reminder.

The coming-to-grips with Joyce is exciting in quite a different way. Compeers, contemporaries, contrast, and arguably competitors, the two represent, obviously, complementary achievements. John Cowper is very much in the English tradition; Joyce is definitely outside it. The whole drive of Joyce is to make more conscious our sensory experience, to make us aware of our intimate life-experience on a more realistic plane. While John Cowper was struggling to revivify psychological contacts at a new depth, and to relate men and women more richly to the elemental things without succumbing to generalisation or becoming detached from homely detail. It cannot really be claimed that his forerunners, Emily Brontë say or Hardy, work poetically towards the elemental by way of a precise and loving dwelling on *everything*. They approach the poetic novel as poets: they do not attain some new poetic significance through deepened awareness of the prosaic. They do not make something creative, as John Cowper does, out of the eternal child in us. They do not start from the favourite iron kettle or the loved wooden doll.

In paying a much qualified homage to Joyce, John Cowper is deeply aware of the immeasurable gulf between every presupposition of the defiant Dublinist and every presupposition of his own background and tradition. He recognises too that Joyce originates a new technique, challenges with a readjusted

N

perspective. while his own insights are not reinforced by any remarkable originality in the *presentation*. John Cowper is really far more a respecter of Joyce's writing than of Joyce. So far as Joyce is satirical or brutal ('like all Puritans he loves to cause pain') he is found wanting; while so far—not very far— as he is Rabelaisian, and in his broad acceptance of humanity in the rough, he is generously acclaimed. It is characteristic that John Cowper greatly prefers *Finnegan's Wake*, vastly inferior as a novel, to *Ulysses* because of the comparative generosity and human tolerance he finds in the later work. He realises at moments a deeper compatibility, discerning in Shem the Penman affinities with St. Paul and Dostoievsky.

In Joyce John Cowper discerns, beside the essential alien, a fellow-champion of *life* in a decadent age; and in this revolutionary reveller in ugliness something akin to his own evolved idealism—that idealism rooted in the earth yet earthy in so different a way from the Irishman's actualism.

As if out of a chrysalis of horny and husky erudition scrawled over a palimpsest of indecency, the New Age breaks forth in *Finnegan's Wake*; and though in its own word-juggling it does have something of that stylistic filigree in which those fifth century pontifical magnates catch the twitterings of the departing swallows of their perishing time, yet in its inherent nature there is something so robust, so brutal, so vigorous in its aesthetic violence, that it suggests on every page if not exactly the wholesome farmyard-disgustingness of birth—for Joyce seems scarcely one for farmyards—at any rate, something more inspiring than the leprous phosphorescence of death ... instead of giving up the ghost with a super-sophisticated grace, Joyce's Phoenix Park would leap forth out of its beer-sprinkled ashes, and swallowing its own horrible afterbirth, renews its life before our very eyes! In fact, 'so bristling' with raw life, as Henry James would say, is Joyce's 'Wake' in comparison with the Fifth Century 'Wake', that you often can hardly disentangle the wings of the new-born Creature from the clammy and scrummy shards of its cindery cradle!

Yes. Joyce's work does indeed contain all the erudite sophistication natural to the end of a vast Aeon of spiral evolution; but it can hardly be called degenerate, for it also reeks of the harshly-obscure, jarringly-obscure, jeeringly-blasphemous, filthily agglutinate birth-pangs of life being born afresh.

The essay on 'Finnegan's Wake' is undeniably a brilliant one: a triumph of difficult sympathy never losing critical balance. At the core is John Cowper's half-welcoming, half-reluctant awareness that British culture has widened beyond the horizons of his own inherited world. Here, he recognises without undue resentment, is a *'pit of the stomach loathing* for the whole British conception of life', an 'abysmal loathing for everything an English gentleman represents'.

> The result was a seething, surging, mounting, over brim-ming inflation of every aspect of human life that could con-ceivably be labelled with the words that best describe what our good gentleman, in *his* turn, loathes with *his* pit-of-the-stomach emotion, namely 'caddish vulgarity'. I am pretty sure I am not drawing too long a bow when I say that whenever the very nicest kind of Englishman reads Joyce, he is brought face-to-face with what to him is the accursed double concept vulgarity-caddishness; and whenever Joyce calls up in his imagination an English gentleman he is brought face-to-face with what to him is the accursed double concept *snobbishness-hypocrisy*.

After the *Obstinate Cymric* volume John Cowper published no literary criticism and almost nothing—except the two his-torical romances—which adds seriously to his reputation. (His private *Letters* are of course another matter; and in his in-defatigable way he was keeping a copious Diary which one must devoutly hope will be released.)

The Inmates, which appeared in 1952, belongs definitely to the private world of John Cowper. It is compounded of whimsy and propaganda, and contains in the hero John Hush one of the most undisguised of the many projections of his author. The underlying fondness for childishness and 'gib-berish' are now conspicuous. The scene is Glint Hall, a private (and very odd) mental hospital, where experiments in the prac-tice of vivisection have a prominent place. What strength there is in the novel or fantasy lies in John Cowper's intimate psycho-logy, and conspicuously at the heart of its weakness is the vagueness of his conception of mental sickness. He can hardly have read his beloved Jung from a doctor's standpoint. The action of the tale is curiously unreal; the insight often start-ling. John Hush is a failure as a psychopath and a revelation as a lover.

Though *Maiden Castle* showed John Cowper in search of a way of being that should be outside the actualities of modern life, *The Inmates* is perhaps the first of his books where the desire for a closed world, for asylum from the pressures of ordinary existence, predominates entirely. All the same the issue is not, as we have observed, wholly disastrous. Whatever we may think of the eccentrics and the vivisectionists, the study of Antenna Sheer ('Tenna'), strange mixture of sensitive lovingness and deranged violence, is peculiarly convincing and indeed brilliant. The presentation of her feelings for John Hush recalls as an echo some of the most intuitive passages in *A Glastonbury Romance*.

The next year, 1953, John Cowper published *In Spite Of*, the last and weakest of his essay-books: one of which he himself thought little and which was seemingly written largely under external pressures. Not surprisingly in one always inclined to ramble, his rambling had now, at eighty, become very pronounced. The inclination to clutch at experience, rather than absorb it inevitably, had now become almost caricatured. So had the characteristic of projecting the author's own consciousness into other people. The book really falls to the ground, despite some delightful interludes and touches of endearing shrewdness, between an essay in living and an essay in thought. The prevailing hedonism and over-facile acceptances are really not true to John Cowper's inner experience. A 'Pantagruelian quest for a pleasanter life', as he calls it could never express or liberate his complex sensitivity and conscience. From religion, he insists even more unconsciously than in *The Art of Growing Old*, we must run away: we must not think about it—it is too dangerous. In fact the book is constructed without real imaginative conviction; and, as always, where conviction wavers style wavers too. In essence perfunctory, *In Spite Of* is the amiable deviation of a man in his decline, a man intent as ever on showing others an easy way to a happiness he had only achieved himself after long years of suffering and endurance.

John Cowper now focussed his attention on 'the old indomitable indefatigable Homer of my heart', earliest and most instinctive of his great literary loves. To him Homer was always the supremely alive, and especially the most *physically* alive, of all creators. Homer was verily one with nature, for

him. Such a poet therefore held the essential key to the elemental life. 'No one has a right to say he enjoys Homer,' John
Cowper declared, 'until his actual reaction to sun and moon
and earth and sea, and to the significant groupings of people
and things, has been liberated by the Homeric open secret.'
Homer, he insists in his *Rabelais*, made the great French sensationist possible; Rabelais is a Homer with the finer poetry
wanting but Christianity superposed. A smiling scepticism
is common to both. Homer gloried in and glorified the life of
the senses that Rabelais was to make conscious and deliberate.
John Cowper was always disposed to exalt Homer above
Sophocles and those other great tragic poets whose greatness
depends after all upon a philosophy. To John Cowper
Homer's instinctiveness was larger than any intellectual consciousness. It may be that in his later years John Cowper tired
a little of morality, of his inheritance, of the exactions of his
own conscience; that he grew a little more sceptical and more
disposed to abandon himself to the primitive things. Certainly
in the well-written Preface to *Homer and the Aether* (composed when he had reached four-score and six) he stressed
little except Homer's 'deeper humanity'. Oddly, he found this
most refreshingly evidenced in the Pagan scepticism (not to
say insouciance) of the men and women of the epic: their
being unsicklied by the pale cast of later religious refinements.
Polytheism, horror of a single implacable First Cause, most
probably lay behind this feeling.

John Cowper had now ceased to be in any considerable
sense a 'thinker': he had nothing to set against a Sartre or a
Camus. His books did not present considered problems: there
was no relation to behaviour. The author's personality was
now the motive, not adjustment to reality. Despite the lively
interest he showed—in his letters especially—in everything
about him, the old man had ceased to worry about the advanc-
ing frontiers of art or psychology. He was just being himself as
fully as he knew. His pleasure in telling a tale, once scarcely to
be suspected in his fiction, could now be fully indulged. If the
old uneasy conscience ceased to trouble him, the old sense of
intellectual urgency had faded also. Wolf Solent would no
longer have recognised his creator.

The lengthy *Atlantis*, which appeared in 1954, was intended
to be named after Odysseus; but the title was changed in

courteous consideration of his rival's *Ulysses*. It is, unlike
Joyce's book, a reconstruction of the prehistoric world, if that
can be called a reconstruction which is almost wholly whimsy
—not the less whimsy for being supported by much learning
familiarly wielded. Animism, consciousness without personality, characteristics unrelated to a character, separate
Atlantis widely from any recognisable novel. It is something in
the nature of an allegorical fantasy, with an extensive *dramatis personae* (human and subhuman) centring in fabled
Ithaca, but one where the fantasy runs away with allegorical
coherence altogether. An anonymous critic perhaps put it best
when he said that *Atlantis* 'may have an allegorical significance, to do with the advantage of the spontaneous life and
the deadliness of law. In fact, it must have an allegorical
significance, for otherwise it would signify nothing at all,'
which is not, of course, to gainsay the fact that some devotees of
John Cowper have found enjoyment, satisfaction and significance in the fanciful pages. In the author himself, certainly,
the sense of wonder[1] was more alive than ever. He cared little
now for his reputation as an artist. When Louis Wilkinson
charged him with writing long dull novels he was in no way
indignant, abashed, or penitent, and declared gaily that he
loved long dull novels.

Homer and the Aether, the delayed culmination of his
passion for the first poet, appeared in 1959, when he was
eighty-six. For several years he had been engaged on the *Iliad*
daily, 'with almost barbaric devotion'. The book is a sort of
Lamb's Tales from Homer. 'A pretty poem, Sir,' said Bentley
to another free translator, 'but you must not call it Homer.'
John Cowper would not in fact call his own effort so. His
professed aim, characteristically, was to help the uninitiated to
enjoy the *Iliad*, ignoring—also characteristically—that it
would be more difficult to make the tyro understand John
Cowper's conception of the Aether than to make him under-
stand Homer. This $\alpha i \theta \acute{\eta} \rho$, a sort of upper air, is conceived, on
rather thin classical authority, as the all-seeing and nearly
omnipresent divinity, independent of Olympus and in a sense
more absolute. John Cowper's wish was, evidently, to engage
Homer as a fellow polytheist rather than a theist and as one

[1] This revealing phrase was contemporaneously applied by Mr. Clifford
Tolchard.

who did not really accept the survival of the soul as implicit in the mythology of Hades and Persephone. In fact the most memorable thing in *Homer and the Aether* is the englimpsing at the close of a reconciliation between Pagan survival and the human *mortality* of which John Cowper was now so firmly convinced. For the book in the main is far from being a success. His intelligence, great and adaptable as it was, never of course had anything of the clear-cut Greek directness. He proved as bad a translator of Homer as he had proved a good one of Rabelais. Not only is the language diffuse and over-colloquial and over-fluid but the whole impression is unconvincing. The narrative interpolations are arbitrary in tone, and sentiments and motives which are quite anachronistic are imposed upon the characters.[1] It is fatally easy to destroy the reader's mood, as when Pallas Athene says 'I am off now'. The trouble is that John Cowper had no sense of a grand style and little of period, however Homeric his response to the earth and the fullness of human life.

This is, no doubt, making unconscionably heavy weather of what can be best relished as another *divertissement* of an aged man who had earned all too richly the right to relax. But unfortunately, owing to the growth of a perceptible Cowperian cult, immoderate claims were made for *Homer and the Aether*, such claims as a generation before had scarcely been made for *Wolf Solent* or *A Glastonbury Romance*. It is difficult not to conclude that the enthusiasts for *Homer and the Aether* were inspired by unreflecting loyalty to their unique and long undervalued Titan. The conception of the Aether proves little more than narrative machinery: the element of Cowperian philosophy involved is very meagre. Comparison with the Lambs' Shakespeare is really too flattering: for while in Lamb the tales are speeded irresistibly along by the Shakespearian language, cleverly adapted, in *Homer and the Aether* only a raconteur's English prose bears one on, instead of the 'rushing wind'—the phrase is John Cowper's own—of the greatest bard.

To be realistic, what *Homer and the Aether* conveys—evergreen charm apart—is enthusiasm for the *Iliad* (sometimes infectious) and an honest desire to put it over intelligently,

[1] An extreme instance of this is to be found in the incident of Menelaus and Adrastus (see p. 116).

reinforced by a rather glib rendering of the *Iliad*, unfaithful to Homer in spirit and pace and idiom, often indistinguishable from the style of his concurrent juvenile fantasies in fairy tale and space fiction. *Homer and the Aether* is attractive only where it sparkles with John Cowper's keenly felt and highly individual appreciation of the *Iliad*; the passages of paraphrase usually prove merely disillusioning: they are too relaxed. The author's old wilful indulgence of his idiosyncrasies is caricatured in his extreme age. Let us, in ultimate fairness to the author's fame, accept the enterprise as one of the Curiosities of Literature.

The occultist (or Paracelsus) belief, much in evidence in *Porius*, that intensive thought can engender physical happenings, never deserted John Cowper for long and is to be felt almost everywhere in his last two books of fantasy. Likewise we meet constantly his belief in omnipresent sensation, and his dramatisation of the souls of stones and slugs. Strangely, the most anti-scientific and anti-modernist of men succumbed to the juvenile enticements of science-fiction; even if a very Powysian science-fiction. He is now found indulging a love for irresponsible story-telling, recalling his nursery and dormitory feats, and a release of the defiant love of childishness foreshadowed so strongly in his greater novels, especially *Jobber Skald*. As undeniably we find that his desire to be free of social pressures leads to hyperbole and an unattractive petulance.

In *Up and Out* imagination has almost entirely handed over to fancy. Writing to a sceptical Louis Wilkinson in February 1956 he remarks

> I love to hear that Malcolm Elwin [Messrs Macdonalds' editor] prefers 'The Brazen Head' to 'Atlantis'. I can't imagine what he or Harvey or anybody else will think of this 'Up and Out' which might be called a sort of Mythical Skit on the Space-adventure Tales of today's fashion. But I think I'd better write another skit of the same sort and of the same length so that together the two of them would make a proper book.[1]

Really this is science-fiction with so great a difference as to be science-fiction in form rather than nature; for science-fiction is

---

[1] *Letters* Pp. 348-349.

in purpose and in practice inhuman while John Cowper's fantasies are not only human but extend sensitive human feeling to the lower creation and to inanimate objects. John Cowper's space fancies are as untypical of the genre in their lack of robotism as in their unblushing lack of science. The miracles are really contrived in order to repudiate the human race in the cause of a better humanity. Time, involving the wrong sort of progress and conscious evolution, has betrayed the Ideal: so let us abolish time and the evolution of consciousness. Eternity, misappropriated by priests and falsely involving a spurious immortality, is similarly suspect: if we are to tolerate eternity, eternity must be divorced from our present experience of time.

The machinery of the story is simple enough. It opens by introducing us to a typical late Powysian world centred in Gor and Rhitha, a pair of boy-and-girl lovers now married, full of Cowperian ideas and in fact scarcely distinguishable from the young *inamorati* of *The Inmates* and *The Brazen Head*. The earth is destroyed by a hydrogen bomb and the pair are transported out of recognisable space on a sort of flying lawn or magic carpet. Thereafter the story becomes a very riot of ideas: a dance of animism and drunken physics. The author abandons himself to 'sardonic gibberish', now reinforced with alliteration and echolalia. Ultimately only space remains real. God and the Devil commit suicide: *abyssus invocat abyssum*. Not, of course, that John Cowper in his radiant-sunset mood is in any way depressed by all this. Lack of a heaven in the widest sense, purposelessness, the death of the individual consciousness, have long been accepted and fairy tales can flow on happily all the same. There is a great deal of humour as well as absurdity in these fantasies.

The companion story to *Up and Out, The Mountains of the Moon*, cheerfully conceived in the realm of Pantagruel and Prester John's daughter, is appreciably the better of the two. Described as 'a lunar love story', it shows more shape and coherence, the cerebral whimsies are rather less distracting and —to appease a little those who pardonably dazzle at John Cowper's literary gymnastics—the human or astral beings are more sympathetic. The love of all things balances the testiness towards all thought. There is an eleventh hour glow, reminiscent of Arctic summer, to light the bizarre logic and the more bizarre allocation of opinions and comments. The anthropomorphism does indeed take strange forms: this loquacity of the inanimate is one of Theodore's unexpected devices, elaborated. Presumably in order to suggest continuity while defying time, anthropomorphic objects, fragments of history or legend, furnish much of the dialogue and indeed of the happenings. The strange and anachronous *Dramatis personae* include Nero's fiddle string, the rock from Sinai, the spearhead of Boadicea, Alfred's charred cake, the apple core (of that forbidden tree), the heel of Achilles and a feather of Noah's white dove. Dramatic differentiation has, understandably, proved difficult.

All or Nothing, superficially a children's story about giants and eccentrics in Wales and elsewhere, is in much the same vein as the *Up and Out* volume: it is gay and tripping and rambling and individual. But beneath the sprightliness there is a certain purpose, tinged with the natural impatience of extreme age. The pervading derision of human limitations or incomprehensions may be rational and justifiable enough, but it achieves little persuasiveness in such a story as this. The reader's attention is kept veering, rather dizzyingly, between a plan of universal destruction and schemes, no doubt prompted by the old belief that Nature abhors a vacuum, to satiate the whole universe with a thronging fullness of life that never will be on land or sea. The positive qualities of *All or Nothing* could hardly be better put than by the anonymous critic who said that the book transcends the world of appearances and offers a key to other space-time continuums with their different qualities and experiences. It can be regarded as a metaphysical discourse, a mockery of rationalism, meta-fiction, or space poetry.

Undeniably John Cowper's last novels are full of ideas, however fanciful and disconnected. They add little to his stature since, of course, the interplay of ideas without aesthetic integration, without living embodiment, does not amount to positive creation. There is no communication in terms of reality. His enthusiasts have fallen into the error, which would have horrified Coleridge, of writing as if ideas by themselves, not imaginatively vitalised, can constitute imaginative achievement. A significant, convincing 'imitation of life' the late fiction is not and was probably not intended to be. There are well-written passages, as for instance in the close of *The Mountains of the Moon*: but that is another matter.

John Cowper in the evening of his life was as memorable a figure as Samuel Johnson. Happily he is his own Boswell, the letters amounting to a sequel (from a subtly different angle) to his unsurpassed autobiography, if a little more difficult for a reader who has not gained some familiarity with the writer's background and idiom. The 'little language', the gently mischievous humour, the grotesque drawings, have their own irresistible charm to a reader who has once found the wavelength. There is a bubbling, gnome-like quality in the unflagging self-revelation; yet the letters are as judicious in comment for the most part as if they had been laboriously pondered. The observations, on almost everything—or so it seems—that is going on, however superficially he may have been involved, are never negligible. Reading, to invoke Bacon, has made a full, writing an exact man. The instinct to seek truth that was always part of the Powys in him remained uppermost in his approach. Not that he ever ceased to be unaware of its uncommonness: to him all *confrères* were truth-seekers first and entertainers afterwards, the optimism a Powys inheritance. The Powys belief that others are as themselves is as inescapable as it is ill-founded.

That unhoped serene that men call age, in Rupert Brooke's happy phrase, was doubly unhoped in him. The uneasy childhood and youth, though ineradicable from his being, might have been unsuspected by those who knew him in age. Completely resigned to simple living—rather boasting of it—he enjoyed exceptional domestic happiness under the devoted care of Miss Phyllis Playter, who also entered with rare understanding into his intellectual moods. His many financial and family worries he bore uncomplainingly. Blind in one eye from cataract, his medical history including fits, constantly a victim of gastric torment, he remained as buoyantly sociable— not to say loquacious—as ever; and he could dissent vigorously from Louis Wilkinson, who, through a long life, a thousand times more smoothly adjusted to existence than his friend, was unwilling to survive into the third World War which threatened around 1950.

John Cowper suffered bereavements and depressing changes

in his world that might well have shattered his *bonhomie*. His only child, Littleton Alfred, a redoubtable parish priest in his Anglican days, died in 1954, having not very long achieved his half-century. His mother pre-deceased him in the cold early spring of 1947. Littleton had latterly been received into the Catholic Church and taken Orders. He was over fond of adventurous motoring and met with an accident which proved fatal after a protracted illness. Accounts make it clear that he brought to the pulpit much of his father's *verve* and eloquence.

Hospitality, the entertainment (unflaggingly verbal!) of visitors, was John Cowper's great delight in his old age. He loved a congenial early caller who would share his sturdy mountainous walks. One companion of those early morning delights was Gilbert Turner, the genial librarian of Richmond, who had complicated the rigours of fire-watching in 1940 by striving to typewrite the difficult MS. of *Dostoievsky*. Nowadays, some MSS., contrary to the writer's usual practice, had been bewilderingly revised by interlining. John Cowper habitually rambled about the page with a magnificent disregard of alignment, but fortunately his hand was clear and shapely—his one manual dexterity.

It is to Mr. Turner that we owe an inimitable account of John Cowper's slow triumph over the perilous task of boiling a kettle and making tea for his visitor (*not* himself). Every step in the process involved enormous, studied deliberation. His pride and delight in the feat had to be seen to be believed. His dress in those days had not become less individual or his appearance less formidable, and he was once hailed by some bibulous soldiers as 'the Old Man of the Mountains'—which, needless to say, delighted him. It was not only from afar that his eccentricities were cherished in Wales: he would talk to anybody he imagined to be individual. To down-and-outs—or apparent down-and-outs—he was now more recklessly open-handed than ever, giving away more and more half-crowns that he could less and less afford. His tolerance and indulgence were unbounded, excepting always a few literary or political dislikes often as apparently capricious as they were honest-to-God. All the time, let us gratefully bear in mind, he had not the slightest desire to be venerated or venerable. He was humorously aware that there was an unregenerate side of him; as he had foretold years before he must inevitably become 'an old man for whom the mere fact that Providence had endowed girls with legs at all, instead of making them "all of a piece" like leeches, or with fishes' tails like mermaids, was the most blessed miracle in the world'.[1]

It is difficult to convey the quality and scope of the letters by description and without inordinate quotation: it can only be said—and that is much—that they can stand beside and only just below the great *Autobiography*. If a reader does not at first blush class him with our foremost correspondents, Dorothy Osborne or Chesterfield or Cowper or Keats, it is only because he takes more knowing. In personal approach volatile yet considerate, in digression fanciful yet shrewd, he never ceases to endear himself to us by his quaint self-dramatisation. Humility and perkiness are inextricably blended in his conception of himself. His signatures are as revealing as his primitive drawings: 'old brother John' he will call himself, or 'your old Jow-Cow-Pow' or 'Jack-not-yet-in-the-box'. His delight, half-sly and half-affectionate, in outrageous flattery, in laying it on with a trowel, had not abated since the long ago when a young Louis Wilkinson, recently received by the aged Meredith, was put to the blush by a reference to 'the Heir-Apparent'.

It needed only a meeting with one of the eminent and esteemed—however unlike himself—a Bennett or a John, to bring to the surface all the child and the worshipper and the hyperaesthete in this unwithered old man.

Augustus John thrilled one simply because he looked so exactly like a statue I've seen of Zeus! When he rose to depart I leapt at him exactly as a devoted Dog of considerable size leaps up at a person he likes, and kissed his jovian forehead which is certainly the most noble forehead I have ever seen. I kissed it again and again as if it had been marble, holding the godlike old gent so violently in my arms that he couldn't move till the monumental and mermoreal granite of that forehead cooled my feverish devotion. His final drawing was simply of my very soul—I can only say it just *awed* me. This old Diviner had caught some inner secret in the heart or in the midriff of Ἡαινομενοιο Διωννσοιο, of your crazy Dionysus that the mad sad myself never knew—though I had *felt* it once and again—that I possessed.

[1] *Autobiography*, p. 624.

But, more than ever with age, the outer man contrasted piquantly with the humble lover of all life. With a sculptor's eye Jonah Jones recorded him memorably:

> John, now full of years, rests his long limbs on a sofa across the upper window of his tiny quarryman's cottage. His head lies back on the cushion, the silver locks still curling in Powysian splendour over the vast cranium. The brow is Socratic, deeply furrowed, but untroubled. The eyes, deep set are piercing and benign. It is with the nose, hawk-like, the nostrils wide-winged, that the Powysian spirit begins. Then comes the great upper lip, cruel, ready to boom. This is John. The mouth is built for rhetoric, his greatest love.... The whole effect of the head is of the falcon, of Horus the hawk-god, belying the underlying tenderness of the John who prays daily for the delivery of animals from the agony of vivisection.[1]

George D. Paynter the Proustian encountered him by chance walking on Brighton front, and was both impressed and startled by the odd, formidable apparition.

> Benevolence and menace, humility, cunning and violence were inextricably mingled in the expression of his face. His mouth was simultaneously sensual and as straight as a rat-trap—the lips of a Powys always contrive to appear at the same time unnaturally thick and unnaturally thin. He had a low forehead, and above his eyes were the primitive, long projections that an anthropologist would call supra-orbital ridges. An impulse, which I resisted in time, to go down on my knees before him, came before rather than after my realisation that this must be John Cowper Powys.[2]

In 1955 he had a serious relapse, but floated cheerfully back to the surface. His rather rugged walks were resumed, and he read and wrote more unflaggingly, if possible, than ever, though spending most of the day on his couch. He delighted in children and would not suffer Harry Coombes (who was finishing his elegant book on Theodore) to visit him without taking the entire family. He refused to broadcast or be televised in his home and indeed showed a certain aversion from being considered as a 'personality' or written about apart from his writings. It is strange that one who so challenged attention by his outer oddities should have recoiled from the imputation of being a 'character', yet, looked into more deeply, perhaps

---

[1] B.B.C. broadcast.   [2] 'Dock Leaves.'

not so strange since his natural humility was at least as strong as his wilfulness. He had a wistful longing all his life to conform, to be merged in his fellow men, though he knew it to be impossible. But his desire, so far as we can judge, was to be remembered as an intellectual and a poet rooted in the elemental—perhaps he felt himself to be the one earth-rooted poet now?

Though his relish for living was as great as ever, personal survival of death he no longer expected or even desired. In a Preface to a new edition of *Wolf Solent* published in 1960 he declared 'I am now satisfied that when I lie dying I shall be feeling a perfect contentment in the sure and certain knowledge that no consciousness of mine will continue after my last breath.' (Is that 'sure and certain knowledge' a murmur of defiance towards childhood paternal dogma?) 'Continuation of consciousness' by no means covers what most believers today envisage survival to be, but from a man of eighty-seven it must be taken in a rough-and-ready sense. Though always possessed by religious awareness John Cowper was not a spiritual man, and any transcendental conception of a soul as something beyond the mind was outside his experience. So the contentment in extinction may well have been unclouded—let us hope so. His lifelong flirtation with Roman Catholicism—not unrelated to his avowed fetichism—was sustained to the last: the large photo of John XXIII duly replaced the large photo of Pius XII in the place of honour on his little table. One recalls ironically Theodore's unexpectedly impercipient 'of course, we know you only do it to annoy your father', of sixty years before. But whatever his readers might well imagine, those who knew him best never seriously expected the priest to be summoned to administer Extreme Unction. And they were right.

As he approached four-score-and-ten his long over-taxed body at last declined service—which perturbed him little— and his memory began to fail. But his intelligence and discrimination lived on while he complained that his mind was being 'killed'. He loved to be read to and enjoyed and appreciated the radio tribute paid to him in honour of his nineteenth birthday. There were no signs of special organic illness and it seemed he might go on for years yet; but on the 17 June 1963 he died, quite suddenly and peacefully. It must be confessed that the passing of one of England's three or four really major writers caused far less stir this side of the Atlantic than believers in our civilisation could have expected. The death of any one of a dozen successful playwrights would have attracted as much attention. There were a good many, certainly, who felt that the last genius of the depths as against the surface, and the last writer of the quality of Hardy, was now gone; but they were, after all, only a small minority. His day was not yet.

CHAPTER XIV

The Essential John Cowper

ONE cannot attempt an all-over summary of John Cowper or of his contribution and achievement without some consideration of his verse, although this may well seem the least essential part of him. His failure fully to become what he earliest desired is an indication of his nature: in effect it emphasises the dangers of his fluid and chameleonish make-up. He had virtually abandoned verse composition before he found himself as a creative writer and there is little intellectual *progress* —less even than in his literary criticism—to lend any significance to the chronology of the poems. Of the enriched and deepening intimacy with nature that gave a greatness to the novels of his maturity there is hardly any foreshadowing in his verse: the verse comes out of books. *Lucifer,* sumptuously produced in 1956, being thus John Cowper's last serious challenge as a writer of verse, was in fact written just over half-a-century earlier. By the 1950's he had seemingly long ceased to compose metrically—free verse he never wrote—except for some interpolations in his novels, such as the lyrics given to the bard Taliessin in *Porius,* which like the poems of Jason Otter in *Wolf Solent* are much fresher and more individualised than the general run of John Cowper's collected verses.

The Edwardian *Lucifer,* a short epic-style poem in the grand manner, combines a strong ninetyish aura with awakening political sense. Its sociological and semi-Marxian awareness is so strong as to make one suspect that it has been retouched here and there by an author sensitive to a more

o

revolutionary atmosphere. But of sustaining philosophy, of really facing up to the implications of the original title 'The Death of God' there is little trace.

Except for a few traditionalists of genius, Hardy, Doughty, Masefield, the Edwardian decade was a lean one for English poetry: there was accomplishment but it was derivative accomplishment. In *Lucifer* the protesting message is not really fused with the pastiche. So the reader's enjoyment— which can be lively—is too consciously literary. John Cowper is writing the super prize-poem, being a marvellous copy-cat— to use a favourite pejorative of his. Here, even more than in Milton, 'Satan is the hero'. The revolt of a philosophic Lucifer against the accepted gods is not wholly realised, but the hero in his apotheosis touches momentarily a certain exaltation, and the Buddha notably is made a living and memorable figure.[1] But this class of achievement does not really add to the creative John Cowper, however much it evinces the subtlety of the aesthetic John Cowper. The extent to which in youth his mind had become a sound-box is astonishing. The impressive First Book of *Lucifer*, Miltonic in its deliberate aural effects and its elaborate similies, is followed by a Second Book where echoes of Keats and Tennyson vary the Milton-isms to give the victim the sensation of luxuriating in a sort of Aladdin's cave. But all the while the ensorcerised one can smell the lamp; and doubt and amusement mingle with his euphoria.

> Fluttering the perfumed eyelids of the dusk. . . .
> Sprinkled cirque-spotted fretwork on their scales. . . .

Yet through the aestheticism of Lucifer there did emerge, probably for the first time, John Cowper's deep abiding pas-sion to defy the First Cause, to burst the bonds of the narrow theology of his upbringing, and to build some sort of *credo* upon a more creative kinship with the principle of life. It was spontaneous concord with nature, the acceptance of simplici-ties, which in his tentative poet days he could not achieve.

Of the three collections of lyrics written between the ages of twenty-seven and forty-five *Wolf's Bane* 1916), *Mandragora* (1917) and *Samphire* (1923), *Mandragora* is, broadly, the best. We find the lyrics of 1900 improved, the cleverness polished,

---

[1] *Lucifer.* p. 103.

the handling more lissom, the feeling a shade more sensitive.
But one is conscious of a Yellow Book man only half at home
in the Georgian heyday. There is something almost perverse in
John Cowper's weather-vane responsiveness to the lightest
breath of so many exemplars and indeed in the facility which
here weakens rather than aids. Yet as far as the feeling, the
prevailing mood, of *Mandragora* and its predecessor *Wolf's
Bane*, is concerned the dominant influence is palpably
Thomas Hardy. 'The Shoes', or 'Love' in the earlier volume,[1]
may be instanced as an extreme example of this, but the influence is everywhere. John Cowper was strangely emulous
even as late as his forties of finding vicarious satisfaction in the
Hardyesque experience, and at times in *Ducdame* a few years
later the younger novelist almost *was* Hardy. Such a mood is
not so much conservative as static; and stasis usually engenders
pastiche.

John Cowper's verses are as easy to read as his major fiction
is exacting. There is no need to take *them* in small doses for
mental digestion—a method many find essential in order to
absorb the novels. But the verses, even when they stimulate,
for the most part evaporate very quickly.

There is no question of just bad poetry. It is precisely because *Lucifer* and *Mandragora* are minor successes that they
are major failures. The lyrics are not, as are recognisably
Lawrence's and even Joyce's, *griffes de lion*. It really seems
simply that the necessity for brevity, for an economy of presentation, imposed a demand foreign to John Cowper's nature
and mental habits. Of all men he could least 'burn with a
hard gem-like flame'. With so insistent an urge to be writing
and writing he did not *concentrate* enough in his lyrics. He
had a Swinburnian fluency and exuberance without a Swinburnian exultation in sparkling surfaces.

John Cowper has often been called of late a Titan of letters,
mainly by those who have his novels in view and especially by
those who wish to vindicate him in comparison with the more
artistically effective Theodore. Certainly what strikes most
formidably anyone who makes a survey of John Cowper in all
his variety of effort must be his vast scope and capacity. His
power of absorbing and reproducing any sort of literature (in

[1] *Wolf's Bane: Rhymes.* p. 47.

several languages) was enormous, and a novel like *Owen Glendower* shows a knowledge of its period so varied and intimate that one could suppose he had spent an academic lifetime in mastering it. His observations of the world, his sympathies, his interests have a range surely unsurpassed among English novelists, and might have brought a respectful salute from a Balzac or a Tolstoy—deeply as such masters must have been puzzled by John Cowper's failure to reproduce any *social* world. To say that John Cowper is the opposite of Proust is in a manner to define him; yet his psychological penetration—in his very different kind—is equally deep and creative. While his persistent amateurishness of manner seems to defy current 'sophistication', his intellectual resourcefulness, his readiness in allusion, his flair for precedents and parallels, are almost breathtaking. In his vitality there is something un-fashionable: this vitality slightly disguised by his over-leisurely and sprawled writing, puts him beside Dickens, the giant even more inartistic than himself. In sustained vigour John Cowper is really comparable—large as the claim may naturally seem—though the vitality of the one is drawn from the earth and of the other is the upsurge of a sort of sur-charged common humanity, a fascinated humorous fellowship with human beings as human beings that is Dickens's alone.

Since Hardy John Cowper is almost alone among writers on the grand scale in his wholeness, his integrity, his devotion to his own truth. In England Doughty—his complement, all solid where he is all fluid—is perhaps alone of his company. Since D. H. Lawrence certainly there has been no achievement of such a largeness. John Cowper is not of course so brilliant or so lyrical as Lawrence: he is very far from being in the same class as a prose artist or a genius in human *behaviour*. The fire in the belly burns less intensely. But John Cowper's roots are deeper and his sympathies far more lively. He is positive to-wards human nature where Lawrence and other contem-poraries have been often contemptuous and he is of the ideal where they are 'sick'.

As modern in his psychological awareness as any of his younger rivals, John Cowper at the same time differs from all prominent novelists since Hardy in realising that our place in nature and our responses to the elemental background that conditions our life are older than our social experience and

equally significant. Before urban, industrial, mechanical civilisation grew overripe the greater writers knew this—with
Shakespeare, or Scott, or George Eliot, or Hardy, man's soul
resided as much in the elemental world of 'nature' as in the
world of casuistry and sex and social contact and religious
psychology. We need not revive the crudities of Rousseau. But
we should recognise that the novel, drained of the healthy sap
of primary things, is losing much of its potentiality, greatly
though it may have gained in the last few decades in awareness and intensity of focus and pruning-off of the conventional
sentimental. But however great John Cowper's shortcomings as
a novelist of society and its problems, it is just to say that he
has never as a man failed to respond to Proust or Joyce or
Miriam's historian or the modern Americans.

It does not add to John Cowper's status at the moment that
he is so much closer to the older *roman* than almost all his
contemporaries. Yet, a story-teller by nature as he is a psychologist by nature, he has never sacrificed the enquiry to the tale.
The two are often awkwardly balanced, but they are balanced.
His amateurish manner in fiction is patent and has perhaps
already been stressed more than enough. But it is part of him.
Away from books he was essentially a countryman—the man
who could write down his beloved Hardy as a townsman! In
his fiction he was reluctant to assume the urban or urbane
tone, and indeed his father's distrust of the artistic never quite
left him.

It is, inevitably, the greater novels that reveal most of the
essential John Cowper, even more than the writings where his
purpose was—honestly perhaps rather than quite ingenuously
—to portray himself in his life. As autobiographer he reveals—
who better?—all of himself except the initiate of the elemental world, the votary of Merlin, the exile from realms
lying below and beneath the realms of social and cultural life.
And the John Cowper of the great autobiography is not the
less valid and unique and satisfying because partial: however
inharmonious and unintegrated, however incurably an uneasy
snatcher at life, he stands revealed to us as clearly as Montaigne or Rousseau. He is the more piquant for seeming odd—
it is really his emphases rather than his ideas that are odd—
and indeed it is the common experience that the more closely
we get to know people the more unusual they seem, and we

know nobody better than we know John Cowper. His strange guilt, his half-innocent lusts, his benevolence, his endearing awkwardness, his patrician courtesy, his garrulity, his humorous quizzing, his quasi-masochism so unusually free of self-pity, his egoism untainted with egotism, his excessive aestheticism, his contempt for his body and his writing, his courage in cowardice and cowardice in courage, his erudition—all these characteristics, in a man with a colossal brain, make up the most memorable English introvert of the modern, the conscious age. The John Cowper he himself deliberately if formlessly portrays—talking always rather than composing a book —is essential John Cowper. And from beginning to end of the *Autobiography*, covering his first three score years, he remains unchangeably himself: the man sensitive to all the winds of change is yet sensitive to none.

The author of the poems, the essay-books, the articles is not the essential man. He is the Powys adapting himself to modernity, to other men, trying to accept a commonality he never could accept, an impossibility. The world of his own day his intellectual honesty and his goodwill forced him to recognise, but his deeper being recoiled and—how clearly in *Maiden Castle* for example—he declined to accept it. In novels increasingly unlike anybody else's he came to portray men and women conceived in almost entirely fundamental terms. His fictional world had always lacked authentic social structure or social values, and one grows increasingly aware of the dominance of—for want of more precise words—the inanimate, the unseen, the occult. In *Jobber Skald*, and still more in *Maiden Castle*, the characters dwell apart from the rest of mankind, and their relationships are all passional to the exclusion of social realism. To feel the true achievement of his greater novels it is essential to recognise that he was— probably 'on instinct'—intensifying psychological reality in indifference to the sacrifice of social verisimilitude. It is probably incidental to his ever-increasing social improbabilites that while he honestly recognised the passing of rurality he could never bring himself, when depicting modern life, to face that same passing. His Wessex remained an Arcadia, albeit a rugged one over which the Cerne Giant in all his animality towered. In fact John Cowper desired to escape, whether by magic or fantasy, a mechanical world unillumined by faith;

yet not wholly, not cravenly, to escape it. So, while he strove to make consciousness more conscious, he staged his largest action in a Glastonbury that is not merely literally and geographically an island but—implicitly untouched by any administrative or economic relations with the rest of the world—emerges as an island outside space and time.

John Cowper's feeling for the immemorial and primeval nature of earth and sky and sea, held much of the transcendental, much of the occult which colours richly, for example, all his broad and masterly handling of the Glastonbury mythology and of the Cymrian remotenesses and fastnesses. But while we recognise the rather vociferous claim of the devotees that the mysterious, the magical, the 'occult' are what imparts greatness to the major novels, we must be wary of inferring that he was himself predominantly mysterious, magical or occult in essence. He told his sister-in-law Alyse Gregory (one of the most ardent, as the most balanced, of his *personal* admirers) that he had 'nothing mystical or metaphysical in his vision of life, it was a combination of magic and common-sense'.[1] In truth, however visionary he shows no appreciation of mysticism, let alone shows possession by mysticism, in a spiritual sense. What we must call his occultism—a dangerous word—was a retreat into nature by one whose faith in God had weakened and who was always *au fond* an exile from communal life, incapable of its apparent satisfactions. Magic is the opium of the *dévot* bereft of his belief.

Those who apply the word magic to John Cowper's novels are commonly using it loosely or as a metaphor. His was, as we have constantly seen in his writings, one of those vigorous imaginations in which the frontier between the conscious and the unconscious, the animate and the inanimate, is blurred. Of psychic radiation he was certainly convinced: the phenomenon contributes vitally to the ensorcerising otherworldliness of *A Glastonbury Romance* and *Porius*. A belief in radiation he explicitly attributed to his most considerable character, Geard of Glastonbury; and in him we are very close to his creator on the elemental if not on the introversive and sceptical side. Crudely masculine, uneducated, unaesthetic, the Mayor of Glastonbury is by no means just another projection of John Cowper but the embodiment in forceful form of his

[1] *London Magazine:* March 1958.

author's half-religious, half-terrestrial faith and awe of primitive power: he is the vulgarian Messiah, the coarse-grained Merlin ('Are you dipped in the blood of Christ?') who can heal the sick, and give his life to preserve the spirit of the Arthurian heritage. He is not John Cowper as sensitive and suffering anti-hero, as Wolf, but John Cowper rampant, John Cowper as he would rather like to be externally. Geard is no poet but he has always 'believed that there was a borderland of the miraculous round everything and that everything that lived was holy'. (This was surely a most vital belief of John Cowper's, coy though he might be of avowing it directly.) Nevertheless the Mayor, a great creation and invaluable for the knowledge he affords us of the essential John Cowper, is no true mystic or exemplar of the supernatural: his religion is *voulu* and he remains one of the unforgettable figures of fiction not for his possession by newly-sensed and unseen power but for the intensity of the earthy humanity with which he is conceived. His powerful imagination is bounded by the life-experience of a man close to Mother Earth: one might almost say it is practical.

Geard's dominant and almost pantheistic faith in the principle of life (not to be, one must repeat, exactly identified with John Cowper's), is not of course unconnected with John Cowper's gnosticism. Whatever either of them worships, it is not the single and all-suffusing Power that commands unquestioning reverence, a reverence that is the mainspring of life: the unquestioning single faith that moves mountains. Between faith—even the most poetic faith—in the heavenly and identification with the elemental there lies a whole heaven and earth. This is by no means to imply a moral judgement: but the reminder is most apposite to any estimate of modern literature, a literature which in supporting or rejecting religion almost always conceives of religion in terms of submission or of ecstasy deriving from submission. The 'religion', the quasi-occultism of Geard—and of John Cowper— may be (and probably is) a form of wish-fulfilment; but it is truly a religion in being a worshipping: a freshened communion with the elemental.

But if John Cowper never so far outgrew the faith of his fathers as to come to believe that dark gods of the earth controlled the human race and its destinies, he was from the day of his vision at Trumpington Mill, increasingly persuaded that hidden forces in nature swayed men and women—especially his 'intuitive' men and women—literally as well as imaginatively, and so directed their behaviour. Owen Glendower is an obvious instance of this control. It is illuminating to observe how little revelation comes to the saintly evangelical parson's son Sam Dekker in *A Glastonbury Romance,* for all his vision of the Grail, in comparison with the more earthly Geard. Sam remains unconvinced and unconvincing in his conversion, however understandable as an individualist and a lover he was before. In *Porius* John Cowper largely went outside, as never before, the Christian world, wandering in a misty half-civilised hinterland of the imagination that is almost—but not quite—a Wonderland. Here, with Merlin, with Brochvael, with Taliessin, the magical and the occult go well beyond the experience of a Geard. Merlin finds magic as well as performs it:

> instead of inscribing things on the air now that he had found a hollow place dark enough for his purpose, he was *tracing out things,* that had already been written upon it.

The John Cowper of *The Art of Growing Old* accepted superstitions, but the dividing line in his 'occultism' between the beliefs of a Geard and the beliefs of a Merlin, between the ultra-natural and the super-natural, is not easily fixed. But on a broad survey of the beliefs that sustained rather than distracted from his true *achievement* in creative art, we must conclude that his novels belong to the world of Geard rather than of Merlin: they assume the ultra-natural rather than the miraculous. The man who could not credit any life after death was not truly persuaded, either, that the miraculous has a spontaneous life. Nor, however fruitfully he held to the 'borderland of the miraculous' did he believe that the divinity of his polytheistic pantheism manifested its power in reversals of the laws of nature.

Compelling as is his animism, his relish of the *unlimitedness* of life, John Cowper remains in the final analysis a realist—a realist at least in being as much a man of this world's values as the creator of a world of fantasy. He is neither a fabulist, an allegorist (as his brother Theodore) nor in the fashion common today a counter-realist using unrepresentational forms.

Though most psychological novelists have inclined to social sophistications and urban backgrounds, John Cowper was always most at home in a primitive environment; indeed he was at his ease however 'occult' the atmosphere, however terrifying the mysteries, for he was one who feared the world and the flesh but not the devil. His Hamlets were all First Gravediggers as well. His Elsinore was peopled by ghosts and gravediggers but no courtiers. He was more in his element with a ghost than with 'an attendant lord'.

There remains of course that puzzling unresolved hiatus between the author of the great earth fantasies and the author of the most revealing of autobiographies and the liveliest of letters, essential John Cowper as both obviously are. Perhaps the only bridge between them he gives us is afforded by the vision of Trumpington Mill and the rare references to his instinctive Hertha-worship, the reverent kneeling on the ground and tapping the head on the bare earth as he prays. But in the later self-revelations—the letters especially—he does play down his inwardness. It is possible that in his later letters, since they are written for Louis Wilkinson's eyes, he adapts himself too obligingly—it is after all his nature—to his genial friend, his antithesis and one curiously unresponsive to the depth and significance of his novels. The problem may indeed call for a more complex clue: as there was something of the sceptic as well as something of the pantheist in him there is a certain dichotomy between his mind's world and his imagination's world.

John Cowper is surely the most *amiable* man of genius since Hardy, the most benevolent and least resentful among all the *genus irritable vatum*. Vanity and jealousy are the weaknesses that commonly touch the highest order of minds, and of vanity and jealousy John Cowper in all his candour shows barely a trace. In all his involutions and complexities he never quite ceases to be endearingly the child that survives in every one of us. In the long run his greatest enemy, despite some successful showmanship in his younger days, is, probably, the buffoon and field-preacher in him. It speaks the oddness of human nature that the man longing for protective colouring should have so persisted in displaying his difference—though his hatred of dignity is of course in itself honourable. Being no little of the patrician himself, he was obsessed by the 'great deal of the tramp in one' and cherished a—purely theoretical—prejudice against the aristocracy of birth or mind. In reality he had a pronounced relish of every kind of distinction. But he had a constant urge to escape from the mellownesses of culture, seeing in them complacency. 'Surrounded by historic buildings I invariably sneaked off to find the nearest lane or towpath, or cattle-drive, where I could be alone with the elements.'[1]

Though he loved to see himself as a sort of super-tramp, it would miss the whole point of the *Autobiography* to class it with W. H. Davies's, perhaps the most distinguished book in the same field by a contemporary. It is a cardinal fact about John Cowper that he could not be external or fix his attention on action, while the *Autobiography of a Super-Tramp* owes its whole savour to its movement and its responses to outer experience. The more popular self-record is the work of an extrovert and an instinctive artist: John Cowper's that of an introvert with no care for *shape* in presentation. By no possibility could an extrovert and a man preoccupied with his art write a masterpiece of the order of John Cowper's memoirs: if it were a masterpiece it would be a different and minor masterpiece. In John Cowper scope seems to involve spontaneity and lack of art. He was like De Quincey in never ceasing to be introspective. They could not escape their inwardness or truly parallel the experience of the plain man: nothing either of them ever did was innocent of implications.

Absorbed, perhaps, in John Cowper's vivid personality, we must beware of overlooking, even for a moment, the aesthete, the intellectual, and the poetic kinsmen of Wordsworth and Emily Brontë. His reckless plunging into life sometimes obscures his vital difference from the great majority, for whom the visible world not only exists but provides the main theatre of experience, the inspiration of art and fancy. While with John Cowper it is always the invisible world that predominates. Beneath the adaptable, accommodating portrayer of the human round, common or uncommon, trivial or significant, there lurks the John Cowper ever in communion with elemental influences. After all a Davies, or even a De Quincey, is not carrying inside him a *Glastonbury Romance*.

John Cowper remains beyond question one of the most

[1] *Autobiography*, p. 170.

complicated and richest personalities of our time; if not the richest. He had a puckish desire to irritate, not by any means always conscious; yet at the same time a strong untiring ambition to understand common humanity, his fellows, all the men and women he encountered, better than did anybody else. He emerges predominantly lovable in all his obliqueness. He survives the most ruthless self-revelation; and there is no gulf between the unsurpassed autobiographer and the *alter ego* drawn: no half-conscious editing of the authentic Adam for self-enjoyment. He laboured to underwrite himself as most men to magnify themselves; and Alyse Gregory's tribute—the tribute of one who knew him well—may fairly stand. In the *London Magazine* of March 1958, she wrote:

> Of all the people I have known intimately over a long lifetime, it is he, with all his malice dances and his buff-ooneries, his phobias and obsessions, his proclaimed sadism and his invisible perversities, that most nearly approaches my idea of a great and good man. Faithful in friendship, magnanimous at all times, courageous in adversity, compassionate to the point of self-destruction, it is enough to have him in the room for life to lose its ordinary aspects, for the most apathetic mind to be suddenly wide awake, the most obdurately melancholy heart to yield up its burden.

CHAPTER XV

The Earth Man and the Novel

If there is one gift more essential to a novelist than another it is the power of combination—the single vision—*Virginia Woolf*

A great modern novel consists of and ought to include just *everything*—J. C. Powys: *Dostoievsky*

IN the last thirty years or so the novel, most important of all art forms for more than a century, has become sundered as never before from life's background, from nature, from all that elemental vitality and fullness of being which is supreme in a Hardy or a Melville and implicit in most of their compeers. In their successors of today there is some poetry of conception, certainly, but a minor poetry. Few of us can help feeling now that the prolonged reign of the great novelists is over. It is not necessary to go so far as to murmur after La Bruyère that *tout est dit* or agree with Sartre that literature has become impossible. But the shrinkage may well have come about because there is little obvious experience obviously still waiting to be explored, because man is over-conscious, choked with his own subtleties, and morally inhibited from taking life naturally before scrutinising it. Analytic psychology, the post-Freudian mind, enormously valuable in intensifying awareness and enriching variety and indeed in stimulating close and serious attention by the reader, has probably diluted and diffused the sheer untrammelled creativeness of a Homer, a Fielding, a Tolstoy, a Dickens. Until comparatively recently novelists—as apart from poets—were given an unpretentious, indeed too unpretentious and naive, conception of their aim as writers. They were to be story-spinners, entertainers. The twentieth-century novelist, on the other hand, is all too tensely aware of a social and educational role. Yet as lately as with Hardy we have seen a *poetic* grandeur and a realisation of the elemental going together with melodrama; while the greatest of all novelists, Dostoievsky and Proust, achieved a perfect balance and a triumphant harmony between re-creating life and probing the character and impulsions of those who live. In their creation, urbanised social values are never transmuted into art without awareness of the wide frontiers of common humanity or without the consciousness of underlying destiny. But there is hardly a figure of stature since Lawrence or Mauriac in whom wholeness and integrity of experience has really vitalised and shaped the ubiquitous curious or satirical attitude to human nature and society. Religion—to use the word broadly —and the elements have almost gone from the novel; and in our amused or sceptical or disgusted moderns there is inevitably a triviality as well as the spirit of analysis and enquiry.

The novel can hardly progress without modern psychology, but so long as it fails to get closer to the 'inanimate', the extra-human, it is doomed to relative superficiality, comment on individual man as a mere variety of the communal man. It is perhaps because of this tendency that the novel attracts more and more exclusively writers without real belief in life. On the other hand, because we are so sophisticated as to character, because we are so conscious, a simple experience, however rich in imagination (as Dickens') cannot satisfy. An 'intellectual' is needed to revive an art a Henry James and a Proust have mellowed and polished and matured. The minor rural novelists and the lyrical fantasists have, really, lacked intellectual seriousness—have usually, indeed, lacked intellect altogether. Whereas the more considerable novelists of the last few decades have generally been far from unintellectual—quite the contrary indeed—but their experience is of a life without natural roots or background. Their characters are self-consuming.[1]

---

[1] These remarks are less true of certain of the more serious figures in the American revival; but these figures like John Cowper, are not by any means generally accepted.

These writers are clearly to a great extent the heritors of symbolism, of the flux philosophies of a Bergson or a William James, of a quasi-scientific psychology absorbed in a pragmatic rather than a poetic spirit. In their hands criticism of life, in a sense narrower than Arnold's, precedes the imagination, precedes vitality, humanity, creative love. This is not of course to suggest that they are without talent—there is a positive glut of talent; or that there is not remarkable achievement of a sort among them. It is greatness that is wanting. We are living in a day distinguished at best by the Greens and Camus and Montherlant and Compton-Burnett and a few other of their peers in talent; but mainly by slighter brilliancies. It might almost seem as if the notion fashionable a couple of decades ago, that Proust had been ordained as a sort of novelist to end novels, was not altogether unfounded! Whether any real development is possible after Proust that does not imply a progress virtually negative, a hopeless narrowing of purpose and loss of depth, is the serious question for criticism. Do we, more conscious, criticise life rather than create it?

John Cowper Powys, whatever his artistic laxity, is obviously too large to be fitted into the narrowing art that fiction has become in the last quarter century. His very existence is a criticism of the current English novel and for that matter of the French equally. Out of his abundance he has been restoring some seriousness to a fictional world conditioned by those who ignore that man is a part of all life and 'nature' the essential background of man. He reminds us that life is not merely what moves in the soul of man but what might and should so move: we are what we may become. To depict human existence without its primal contacts, to disregard the poetry that is founded on elemental things, has been to lack seriousness. To be satisfied with such limitation is really a form of immaturity, however mature or intelligent one's understanding of community inter-actions, or urbanised men and their motives and relationships.

This is not of course to reason that the 'rural' novel is the only true novel, or even that the only major novelists are those whose *oeuvre* is constantly related to elemental things. Not every novel can be so near to poetry, so little conditioned by society, as *Wuthering Heights* or *Moby Dick* or *The Return of the Native*. Richardson, Stendhal, Jane Austen, Henry James,

Flaubert, even Dostoievsky, have been mainly concerned to
depict man in an urban or communal setting. But these
writers were not in *our* civilisation, not faced with the particular problem of today, which is the disappearance of the
simple and the natural from most people's lives altogether; the
rapid mechanisation, organisation, levelling-out and levelling-
down of existence. the elimination of distance, grandeur; the
loss of contact with those mysterious processes which are outside and before and after human society. The great writers of
the past simply did not conceive of a wholly artificial civilisation: a state of being in which nature could only be found
by deliberate aesthetic or 'religious' searching, and in which
your only spontaneous man is your super-educated man. Nor
did they disregard the religious *sense* even when they questioned it. For them something more than a visible world
always existed. For most of the talented novelists of the last
quarter-century there is only a *monde visible*. For John
Cowper, when he rises to the creative level, the invisible
dominates all imagination, all emotion, all action. His
cardinal figures, his intuitive men and women, are in the
thrall of forces greater than themselves, forces they do not
understand. Geard, Uryen, Owen Glendower are only outstanding examples of this. Whether or no artistically perfect,
they could not exist within the good novels of our times.
They would burst their confines.

One need scarcely stress that John Cowper entertained no
cult of 'Nature': not only implicitly but explicitly did he
deprecate the touch of preciosity in Borrow, Stevenson, Jefferies.
With him there is no Back to Nature: it is essentially Forward to Nature, a nature realised with fuller and keener
awareness, more urgently identified with the human condition, transfigured and given fresh power of evocation by
modern psychology. It is really not too fanciful to say that
John Cowper is the vanguard of prose fiction—because he is
the rearguard. Because he has not forgotten old poet in new
sociologist, he is not, unlike his contemporaries or immediate
successors, to be caught wanting in the rear: he has not left
the richest part of experience to the poets.

In his forward drive he has driven over—and this is a personal contribution made possible by his individual vision—

certain frontiers between what is commonly regarded as the conscious and the unconscious. In him animism has become, so to speak, creative. However imperfectly John Cowper may seem to have fused imagination and realistic art, no English writer before him, not even those who deliberately made nature their overriding theme—he himself actually did not— has felt so keenly and instinctively that man achieves his full stature and destiny only when he ignores the distinction between conscious life and 'inanimate' life. Such a distinction seems to John Cowper intellectual, not vital. This is a contribution quite different from Wordsworth's. With the poet nature-worship remained consciously moral and indeed anthropocentric: 'we receive but what we give' and John Cowper, though professedly a disciple, is not at his best as a Wordsworthian. In his critical essays he does not enter into the heart of the poet as he can that of some others; he attributes to him an *identification* with nature that is rather his own. It is the difference between the transcendentalist and the occultist: the man who understands from above and the man who listens from within.

But although his oneness with nature may distinguish John Cowper's creative writing more strikingly than does anything else, his own most deliberate effort was towards a freshly intensified psychology, a super-psychology. He was strengthened in this by his unflagging interest in every minute working of every mind and by his temperamental nearness to the child. He saw men and women with strange, intimate affection as grown-up children—a characteristic of the Powys in him. Very often it seems to be his chief aim, as if inspired by a sort of oblique Freudianism—he rather disliked Freud, actually—to show us as conditioned by simplicities and the child in us: his relish of the childlike could indeed be indulged to the verge of perversity. He could never assume or accept, as Henry James or Proust would, that men and women are plain adult; in truth in his more intense, creative mood he could not have liked a stark uncompromising adult. But this seeing of adults always as grown-up children, this assumption of an ubiquitous spontaneity and simplicity, is a crucial element in his originality. Those critics who stress prominently his 'bi-sexuality' go probably too far—nearly all important art is bi-sexual. What John Cowper has done in drawing his un-exampled women is to balance their socially formed personality by the eternal child in them which is not socially formed at all. He remembers their dolls; and so do they. It is of the essence of his novels that their characters never for a moment wear, *for the author,* a social mask. Virtually all other writers have allowed themselves to slide into the assumption, part or all of the time, that in growing up a character has become completely adult, that the child no longer lives in him. They have accepted half consciously the pose and the poise of social maturity as a valid and complete facet of the personality. What a Diana Warwick or a Hedda Gabler we should have had if their authors had recognised all the time, as John Cowper does, how the child *unceasingly* lives on in the woman, and how the two are inextricably one!

John Cowper's inclusion of 'just everything' does of course emphasise by contrast the selectiveness of the modern novel. The symbolist novel, the *roman à thèse,* the stylised and the allegorical, all leave out much of experience. John Cowper's capacity for being always interested is akin to a child's interest; and in his concentration on the minute he is willing to forgo intellectual selection in what he describes. In some curious way this almost childlike (and very Powysian) interest in the child element, the socially innocent element in living, lies near the heart of his contribution to imaginative psychology. He moves towards fuller experience in repudiating, on behalf of his characters, self-conscious maturity. Less aware of social pressures they are more sensitive to nature and better attuned to life's deeper music. Certainly John Cowper's rejection of the normal adult aloofness from little things, from very homely things, has much to do with the compelling sense of *closeness* to life which he always conveys. To take him at his best in such a justly celebrated episode as that where Geard passes a night in the haunted chamber of King Mark. The whole thing is as extravagant, as sprawling and as over leisurely as it is surely unforgettable. On close examination we find that the writer does not deliberately choose his details to impose a coherent picture, or to crystallise a mood or some arresting aspect of a sensibility. In fact he seeks less dramatic satisfaction than complete expression of experience. So his unfashionable exploratory manner, his leisured tempo, his obliviousness of form make him seem at the same time conventional and remote in the modern world of a Joyce and a Woolf, and make a different sort of demand upon the practised reader of today *who has grown aesthetically purposive.* Too original and not 'modern' enough, for John Cowper the hour has not yet struck.

The novels do not of course achieve their depth of poetic and psychological truth without constantly falling far below the best modern standards in dramatic realism and convincing action. From no measurable contemporary would it be so difficult to extract a scene to turn into a play (a mercy in one sense!) or a dialogue that would be convincing outside its author's own particular world. Nor can it be pretended that John Cowper is always really aware of the gulf between inward truth and outward verisimilitude in his fiction. He indulges just that implausibility of social behaviour that the modern psychological novel has worked to minimise.

It may fairly be claimed that John Cowper has gone back and refounded the novel of today at a deeper level, building on a more vital sense of all life, importing more of the poet's imagination, greater reverence, and more mysterious awareness of the ultra-natural. For however large the earth-poet may loom in John Cowper's emotional make-up, he never becomes dominantly a writer of 'poetic prose' and never falters in the psychological approach. Contrasting with Dickens or Hardy, for example, who are dramatic in impulse, he is one who primarily builds up his characters from within and elaborates their inwardness: they are not conditioned by the atmosphere or the action—and indeed with John Cowper it is questionable if things do not seem, too often, to be happening in the minds of the characters rather than happening.

His is a rival to the fashionable psychological novel, an alternative. Though he derives in his own fashion from William James and Proust, he parts company almost defiantly from the forms of the novel they have inspired. He has really the maximum to communicate of experience newly and more deeply realised, but seemingly no desire for any new method of communication, no very urgent feeling about the significance of the intensified focus, no apparent dissatisfaction with the Dear Reader approach. He wishes the reader to be involved, to participate, more seriously but not more tensely.

He differs from the significant contemporary novelists (not only the 'psychological' ones) more than they can differ from one another: he is definitely apart. He is nearer to Samuel Richardson than to Dorothy Richardson; and remote as Lawrence and E. M. Forster, for instance, may seem from each other in every impulse of their being, remote in everything except being contemporaries, one can still feel that they are contemporaries: a link of which one is never conscious with John Cowper as a novelist, so much is he of another dimension.

The novel today has on the whole ceased to be expansive and its more serious practitioners tend to eschew not merely the panoramic (in Percy Lubbock's phrase)[1] but—as does, differently, John Cowper himself—narrative tension, in order to achieve direct grip on readers. The house is smaller, it has been aptly said, and the inmates seen from closer: there is less background and more concentration on the individual in himself than—for all our social conscience—on the structure and manner of society. Not only since, say, *Vanity Fair* but since *A la Recherche du Temps Perdu* the artist has become less and less interested in the way of the world and more and more in the mystery of the mind. The psychological novel *de pur sang*, moving towards the 'stream of consciousness', naturally reflects this inclination in the extreme degree and has been largely instrumental in stabilising it. Even the historical novel, the most traditional type in its emphasis, has of late become largely dominated by the individual in his inwardness; though we must admit that this has often aroused in readers an uneasy feeling of anachronism which was not provoked by, say, the brilliant study of Louis XI in *Quentin Durward* or the ineffaceable vignette of Napoleon in *War and Peace*.

For the last two or three decades the more fashionable criticism has been over-obsessed, with symbolism always and ultimately with an exaggeratedly analytical approach to life. So it has inclined to impose a conception or ideal of the novel which goes far to exclude the expansive, the loosely constructive writer, especially if he be such an individualist as John Cowper or Theodore Powys. This enticing criticism, persuasive in its very narrowness, has usually concentrated on a handful of individuals (related always in some degree to

[1] *The Craft of Fiction*: 1922.

Henry James and Proust), a majority of whom are primarily committed to exploration and experiment on 'inner monologue' lines, and far more remarkable for their technical advances and self-awareness than for creative scope or afflatus or grandeur of imagination. Joyce, remarkable most for making sensory experience more conscious, is the outstanding novelist for specialists, however indigestible he may remain for most readers of fiction. He did indeed effect a revolution, or at least bring it to a head, and the image of the novelist has ever since had Joycean features.

Critics do imply that novelists have a homogeneous objective, or should have; and this objective is an art closely bound up with Joycean realism. Two novelists whose achievement is really free of the symbolist influence are now usually admitted to the small circle that is allowed to matter: D. H. Lawrence and E. M. Forster. But even they are far more concerned in man's relations with his neighbour than man's relations with 'the armies of unalterable law'. John Cowper, the only figure of comparable size to mature since their heyday, is equally outside the symbolist influence and is very much more deeply involved in man as part of all nature. Also, or hence, he is much less fashionable. But it is none the less significant that it is a genius of psychology who now stands most challengingly outside 'the psychological novel'.[1]

It would be a little sweeping but not inaccurate to say that John Cowper's preoccupation with another dimension has left him lax in art and method, whilst the post-Proustians' preoccupation with art and method has left them indifferent to other dimensions. The core of their efforts to develop the novel since Proust has been the *intensification* of it by readjusting the reader's participation, and thence in another sense the author's involvement is to be made closer and more subtle. Concentrating upon focus, angle, perspective, standpoint, has induced a more precise and calculated handling of language. The 'interior' or 'stream' technique has tended, however, to become exclusive as well as inclusive. Whereas Proust's great if untidy art had excluded nothing. With the 'interior' method the writer is almost bound to shrink himself

---

[1] I am very conscious of being indebted to the acute criticisms of Mr. Leon Edel and Mr. Walter Allen in understanding (more or less) the real achievements of this predominant and all-influencing *genre*.

into his central character—and Hamlets, we know, are lesser than Shakespeares. Further, the experience presented tends to be secondary to the presentation—a dangerous development of the axiom that it is the handling alone that can make an artist's experience vital. ('It is the intensity at which the fusion takes place...' wrote T. S. Eliot in 1920.) Indeed, aiming at the most intimate experiencing, the 'interior' narrative, which has been traced back to Edouard Dujardin's *Les Lauriers sont Coupés* and is most characteristic of Dorothy Richardson, Joyce Faulkner, Virginia Woolf, aims to capture, to crystal-lise the moment, the uniqueness, the individual mood: to pin down, perhaps, the evanescent. The unique mood is cherished as a microcosm of mankind's experience. So the character's consciousness tends to overshadow the author's. Action and ideas and central tendency are minimised and life seems to exist for the sake of sensibility. (This is clearly perceptible in Dorothy Richardson's Miriam.)

Such a brief characterisation is not, of course, the whole case for the psychological novel nor does the psychological novel completely fill the scene today. But it may at least help to indicate the remoteness of John Cowper and that there is a need for him, a *desiderium*. His eye is instinctively on the eternal truth and not on the evanescent significance. He does not care—except as a critic—about experiment or refinements of method. Conscious, again, of Proust, he is indifferent to all the master could teach him of time, of how life is heightened by awareness of the inevitable relentless force of change. He is the psychologist rather of the universal than the individual— and indeed it should be remembered that psychology illumin-ates both. In one of his novels, *Wolf Solent*, John Cowper did work through the mind of a single character (to great struc-tural advantage); but though Wolf may be the most rounded character in recent English fiction and the most prophetic of deeper understanding of ourselves, it is not purely as a tensely focussed sensibility he lives, as does a Mrs. Bloom or a Septimus Smith.[1] (Nor indeed does he gain convincingness by behaviour, as Swann who walks unquestionable in a com-

---

[1] It is a little difficult to make this clear enough. Mrs. Bloom is a proto-type of many characters in modern fiction in being designed only to reveal more and more fully herself. Wolf, as much as Don Quixote or Becky Sharp or Tess Durbeyfield, has moral dimensions and implications.

pletely solid social world, making it more solid as he walks.) Wolf is as much a moral problem as Hamlet and his significance is always the significance of his author—as the reader indeed cannot ever help feeling—and he has no life independent of his author. But what a receptive and sensitive experience, how vibrant with the fullness of variety of nature, his earthly pilgrimage is!—his is an existence, socially implausible certainly, but unprecedented in sheer introspection. In him thought and feeling are shown in a new way. John Cowper does not inwardly conform; so his 'intuitive' characters are free of all presupposition. They are men and women not defiant of what everyday people think and feel but incapable of understanding it. We hardly know, as John Cowper scarcely seems to care, whether Dud No-man is being Everyman or Wolf Solent is being no man at all. What matters is that indeed the King has no clothes on. We see ourselves anew because we are brought nearer to childhood in its complex simplicity and the primitive in its eloquent silence.

Though it is difficult to avoid concluding that nobody else has *significantly* extended the novel in the last thirty years or so, John Cowper with his fresh-eyed approach and his astonishing intellectual equipment has deepened, so to speak, its roots. That is not to say that he is a great artist or that he is wholly understood. It is misleading to imply, as the enthusiasts do, that he is already 'with' Tolstoy or 'with' James. Patently he is not: they are accepted because they are in addition to anything else, master artists. John Cowper's wilful artlessness may be regarded as one of the tragedies of modern literature, but on the other hand it may be felt that if he were not abandoned to being wholly himself he would be nothing.

His qualities and limitations are so different from those of his rivals that he cannot be measured (such measurement is probably fruitless anyhow). It is difficult to imagine them writing either so badly or so largely. John Cowper is far out of the current of our day. He is as unfashionable as Barbusse—and as overwhelming. The mood of this generation will have to change before he can be seen in his true proportions and conceded his true place as a novelist. (His pre-eminence as an autobiographer should be very much more evident.) The most obvious weakness of his fiction is in verisimilitude and its most obvious strength in its underlying universality. His manner may not help him at the present moment. In an age of sharpened technique he uses language (in his fiction) as a blunt instrument with magnificent insouciance, save in deliberated descriptive passages, where he can unfold a prose that has a sort of greatness.

He will often write nobly about places while writing oddly about people, which is certainly an oblique way of liberating his essential, poet's, conviction that man is incomplete except when bound up with 'inanimate' nature. As we have seen he will almost ostentatiously exhibit places—Weymouth, Dorchester, Cader Idris—as the 'heroes' of his story while all the time he is an unremitting as a beaver in his rather quizzical psychologising. In a letter of his old age to Louis Wilkinson he expressed a distaste for having his prose anthologised; but we may suspect, as with Hardy, that he found a certain relish in unfolding the measured period. He may well have helped incidentally towards restoring some day the love of locality to English fiction, which has become both rootless and subtopian.

It would be affectation to close this hopeful estimate without mentioning one or two homely and minor blemishes which go unduly far to hamper John Cowper's reception. The titles of his novels are appallingly dull—for duller ones it would be necessary to go back to Elizabeth Gaskell. *Jobber Skald* with its suggestion of Icelandic saga is a classic of ineptitude and *Porius* is conspicuously misleading. The half-serious historical fantasy *The Brazen Head* almost alone has a live title. Again a minor but persistent irritation to any possible reader of John Cowper is caused by his frequent and meaningless exclamation marks (a trace of primitive Powys *naïveté*) and his profuse Victorian—in a double sense—italics. He has also a curious uncertainty of touch: for instance *A Glastonbury Romance* has probably the most portentously bad opening in the whole history of the novel, and abrupt deflations of style have distressed everybody but the parodists. But of course these are small considerations beside the real question for criticism today: can the novel go on developing as our experience grows more conscious and our adjustments necessarily more hurried and more complex? Or must it become sterile—as it shows signs of becoming—through excess of specialisation and conscious experiment? Art cannot fill the spiritual vacuum of modern man by describing or discussing or even intensifying his patterns of living. And the novelist, since he works necessarily within a communal framework and is busied with social relationships is the most tempted of all artists to make the visible world an end in itself, to forget that man does not live by man alone. Psychology can only irradiate and enhance human life by merging the visible world in the invisible world. We may put it otherwise by saying that there must always be a poet behind the social realist: psychology only has *creative* power if reinforced by some deeper impulsion.

It is difficult to claim in summing up John Cowper's contribution to the novel as unique and highly significant—as one surely must—without appearing to be dogmatic and to slur over his impracticabilities. The enthusiasts write as if his novels were all-satisfying works of art, while other critics find what they term his absurdities destructive of all seriousness. It is maybe, if sweeping, simplest to say that if Proust has written the novel to end all novels (to reduce successors to seeking relatively minor and partial novelties), John Cowper has perhaps alone achieved an added dimension—even at a considerable sacrifice of outer verisimilitude. In a prose—not prosaic—world of man as a social animal, Proust has veritably achieved a culmination that is a sort of perfection. To surpass him in breadth of understanding or flexibility of intelligence would seem rather a forlorn ambition. Nobody has shown such a scope or such a freedom from one-sidedness. Proust has in effect contained a poet in a supreme student of human nature; and the merging, the absolute balance, involves a new completeness, the poetic imagination disciplined unswervingly to the realities of prose fiction. It is difficult to see, *within a social and anthropocentric framework* of life, any really valuable advance on Proust. But if we go on struggling—as we have so far—to keep moving forward by narrowing and intensifying social awareness, human reciprocities, we come up against the law of diminishing returns. The more closely we peer the more we restrict our vision.

It is within this confined social framework that the novel is really struggling, if at all, to develop now. We have had since

Proust a prophet like Lawrence or a religious seer like Mauriac or an intensifier of the past like Faulkner, but their vein seems in every case exhausted. (They have left, in a way Proust has not, a sense of something wanting; they have not had the same staggering range and infallibility of *understanding*.) John Cowper, large and careless of art, seems the one great original who can yet advance the frontiers. He is unique and outstanding not merely in having enriched creative psychology by reviving man's feeling for the 'inanimate', but in having positively released some elemental force into a world becoming man-bounded and intellectually introversive. It is—one must insist—nature and not any human cult of nature that has brought this fresh life into the imaginative world and offered a tired art vitality. Can it be denied that without what John Cowper stands for, without the primal and ever self-renewing things, the world reflected in today's literature is sterile and empty and desiccated and old? With John Cowper at least one does not feel that the novel, emitting however brilliant sparks, is coming to a dead end, grinding to a halt. It is not just that the rural ('strange she is and secret') is richer and nearer to reality than the urban, though the issue is likely to be over-simplified into these terms. It is that John Cowper has instinctively realised that if we cut ourselves off from extra-human nature we shall not learn much more about human nature. This understanding some may call occult, but it is not *essentially* occult, and though John Cowper's imagination may often seem to have an animist leaning it is bound to no animist dogma. There is certainly no formula for the deepening of human experience through the extra-human: it is John Cowper's genius that has balanced creatively nature and psychological discovery. There should be richer novels because of him; there will be no new sort of novel.

The literary climate of the moment, heavily charged with the symbolic and the non-representational, does of course little to incubate John Cowper's renown. As we have seen, he can be, at best, no ready charmer of even the most intelligent novel-readers. The fairy godmother was not all-bountiful at his christening. Not his the style, the language, which transmutes as it records. His imagination has to do the work the hard way: his words have no infallible alchemy. Rarely do power and magic leap out of some inspired phrase. His fluency can obscure: his ease in writing is often the critic's difficulty. His genius was patient of research and inquiry, but with John Cowper the infinite capacity for taking pains never had application to the act of composition. He was, by and large, faithful to his conception of the novel of the future as 'just everything' and the infinite reward of reading him is a slow reward. His characters, conspicuously full and subtle as they are, need some disentangling from their author, of whom in truth they are never wholly independent. They do not leap into spontaneous life: their vitality, though it springs from an enormous human interest and curiosity, is a *described* vitality. Again, John Cowper has not, especially not in fiction, the gift of being simply convincing. Whether from his positive genius for hiding from himself, or from his wilful over-indulgence in idiosyncrasy, some readers are hard to persuade that he has felt deeply, that he writes out of the genuine passion without which there is hardly major literature at all. Though this feeling of doubt is strange to those who accept the man as a whole, through all his writings and all his inner adventures, it is a doubt that readily invades many readers of good faith who have persevered in him with only ordinary enterprise. So we must not be ingenuously surprised if there remains a certain resistance to John Cowper, a resistance not necessarily to be attributed to mere superficiality. But it is something more than surprising, it is deeply incongruous, that some really respectable critics can be found treating him as just an interesting and unusual writer, one of the Hundred Best Novelists as it were. The conception of John Cowper as a minor, quaint, attractive novelist would be grotesque and almost amusing if it did not lead inquirers to read one or other of his lighter stories and then put the idea of him aside.

In the absorbing history of the English novel he is bound to find his place as one of the greater figures: how far his achievement may be felt to fall short of his essential integrity and imaginative power is more of a problem. But taken in the round, he must emerge as one of the most challenging and formidable—as he is certainly one of the strangest—figures of our age, and it is as a novelist he must emerge most powerfully. It is by his novels, where he has explored the forgotten riches of the Earth our Mother and given freely from his intimate communion with her, that he will enrich, more and more, generations for whom most of the art of our day will diminish as the experience out of which it springs is seen to be restricted. John Cowper Powys is the founder of no school, but the fertiliser of all possible futures.